BLIND PONY

As True a Story as I Can Tell

A MEMOIR BY SAMANTHA HART

ISBN 978-1-64871-010-0 (paperback)
ISBN 978-1-64970-093-3 (hardcover)

Copyright © 2021 by Wild Bill Publications

All rights reserved. No part of this publication may be reproduced, stored or transmitted in any form or by any means, electronic, mechanical, photocopying, recording, scanning, or otherwise without written permission from the publisher. It is illegal to copy this book, post it to a website, or distribute it by any other means without permission.

Cover art and design by Nick Egan
Book design by Asya Blue

First edition

This book is dedicated to my daughter, Vignette Noelle. Seeing the joyous woman and wonderful mother you have become fills my life with gratitude that can't be measured.

Thank you to my soulmate, James, for inspiring me to tell my story and helping me on every step of this journey.

To my sons, Davis James and Denham Charles, a mother could not ask for two finer young men. You are the change the world needs.

To my granddaughters Andromeda Emmeline and Ondine Evergreen, I wrote this book for you and every other little girl in the world to empower you to have the courage to stand up for yourself, believe in yourself, and follow your dreams.

CONTENTS

Preface i
1 A Farewell To The Farm 1
2 An Accidental Meeting 8
3 The Road to Shangri-La 21
4 Princess 29
5 Return to Sender 41
6 Old Coins 51
7 Pink Platform Shoes 60
8 Rumi Told Me 71
9 Get Me Pam Butter 82
10 A Seismic Shift 97
11 In Cold Blood 124
12 Crossroads of the World 139
13 London Calling 152
14 Traa Dy Llooar 164
15 Hatching a Plan 178
16 European Tour 187
17 A Strange Affair 199
18 Mais Oui! 212
19 Meeting a Devil 225
20 A Girl Named Sam 237
21 Waking Up In Woodstock 246
22 Coming Clean 256
23 Samantha Song 265
24 The Mystic Bums 273
25 Purpose, Priorities and Perfume 290
26 Vignette Noelle 305
27 The Hart Family 317
28 Judgment Day 327
About the Author 341

The author at seventeen.

PREFACE

Rummaging through some old boxes in the attic, I came upon a journal I wrote when I was twelve years old. It was the beginning of a book I felt compelled to write.

It's hard to believe how much time has passed since I penned the first line, "This is a story about me, nobody special."

I realized it's time I fulfilled that twelve year old's dream.

The stories you will read in this memoir about my life are as they happened, as I documented in my journals over the years, and as I remember them.

My father and mother's stories were passed on to me over the years by relatives and friends. In some instances, I took poetic license to imagine how they might have happened. But, for the most part, I believe these stories are an accurate portrayal of what attracted them to each other and what ultimately drove my parents apart.

While my father was known to tell tall tales, he often laid bare his feelings when he had enough drink in him. My mother rarely shared her feelings, so I tried my best to portray her perspective accurately, and I hope she would approve.

Follow me down the dusty trail of my life and embark on the journey as a true a story as I can tell.

About me...nobody special.

1

A FAREWELL TO THE FARM

The towering seventy-foot billboard, a cutout cowboy smoking Marlboros, watched over me and bore witness to the woman I had become. Each time I drove past the Chateau Marmont, I gazed up into his eyes and wondered what he thought of the girl who'd arrived in Los Angeles in 1975 on the edge of seventeen with nothing to lose. It may sound crazy to say I hoped he approved, but that wish was no more insane than when I had once sought approval from another cowboy who'd also appeared larger than life, smoked Marlboros, and didn't say much or pass judgment.

I lived in the Hollywood Hills with my daughter, Vignette, and worked in the graphics department at a record company. As I drove Vignette to school each day, I told her the giant billboard was a picture of her grandfather, Wild Bill. Like my dad always said, "If you're going to tell a lie, it might as well be a big one."

Vignette loved hearing my stories about growing up on a farm in Western Pennsylvania with ponies and fields of wildflowers and fruit trees and forests inhabited by mystical wood sprites. It was a magical place of wide-open spaces where imagination could take flight. I left out the part about running away when I was fourteen-years-old.

When Vignette was five, I heard the farm changed hands again and was turning into a suburban enclave. I don't know whether I had a desire to see the old place one last time or if I felt a need to share it with my daughter to prove that all the stories I'd told her were true.

When our airplane touched down at the Pittsburgh Airport, I knew in my heart there was nothing magical about the farm, and my imagination was the only thing that allowed me to escape. Renting a car and trying my best to navigate with a map from Avis, I set off with Vignette to find the farm I left behind. Though much of the landscape had changed, I occasionally recognized a familiar landmark, and we found our way to 130 Clever Road.

What struck me as we drove onto the red-rock driveway was how decayed and desolate the once-majestic white clapboard farmhouse appeared atop the hill. As we walked up to the stone pathway, the house was barely visible behind the tall grass and weeds that had overtaken the once-manicured lawn. The morning glories in full bloom sprawled wildly up the front porch ignoring the yellow-tape warnings against entering the roped-off, condemned property. Seeing the farmhouse in this state made me want to throw caution to the wind and savagely yank down the yellow tape. But we ventured no closer than the edge of the forsythia bushes. I wanted to show Vignette the old swing hanging from the pignut tree but feared if I got that close, memories might overtake my better judgment, and the creaky old house would beckon me inside.

The springhouse bore the weight of too much sadness and was about to collapse. The old barn seemed unfazed by the secrets held within its thick wooden beams; the weathered structure stood in defiance of its impending fate.

My daughter clutched my hand as we crossed the fields of my childhood. Dandelion fluff on the breeze tickled our noses, and tall mustard plants tinted our skin yellow. Surveyor sticks mapped out how the property was to subdivide. I wanted to uproot every stick in the ground as if that would somehow stave off the inevitable.

We passed by an apple tree, and I hoisted Vignette up to reach the ripe fruit. On the first bite, her little cheeks puckered up before the sweetness lit up her taste buds. I remembered being five years old and climbing the same tree, reaching for that sweetness that became harder and harder to grasp until it eluded me completely.

Climbing a hill, at last, we hit the edge of the woods. The trees had grown taller, and the undergrowth had become much more entangled, so there was no longer a discernible trail, but I knew the way by memory. A beam of light dappled through the leaves upon an old, fallen tree trunk. It was my secret hiding place. Vignette intuitively sat down in the exact spot I used to sit. She looked so small and innocent, and I realized I was about the same age when I first met the wood sprites I named Copy and Kissy.

Vignette and I sat for some time on the tree trunk, listening to the sounds echoing through the forest. We spotted a mama deer and two baby deer and more bunnies than we could count as slivers of sunlight pierced the tree canopy, giving the woods a heavenly glow. The gentle breeze caressed us, quiet enough that any wood sprites—should they be around—would surely feel sufficiently safe to make themselves known.

After a while, Vignette gave up on seeing the wood sprites.

"Can we go see the barn? I want to see where Princess, your pony, lived."

So., we walked back through the thicket. When the barn came into view, it now seemed less ominous to me after our time in the woods. A loose board flapped against another in the breeze.

"Look," I said as we reached the entrance, "See here. It says 1685, carved right in the stone. That's when our ancestors built the original barn."

"You mean the Mexicans?" Vignette's little nose wrinkled.

"No, your father's heritage is Hispanic," I explained. "But my family arrived on ships from England and was among the first settlers in America. A man named William Penn, which is where the name of Pennsylvania comes from, signed the original deed to this farm."

"Pennsylvania sounds like Transylvania," she giggled as we walked. "We're not related to vampires, are we Mommy?"

"No, silly!"

I opened the door to the barn with a bit of trepidation.

The smells that once pervaded my senses—new-mown hay, leather, and living animals—had turned to a dank, musty odor. I held Vignette's hand as we stepped carefully past the empty stalls, ready for something sinister to jump out at any moment. We ventured toward a stable in the back, and above us was the plaque I carved with a wood burner, the name "Misty." Misty was born when I was eight years old and was the offspring of my beloved pony, Princess.

"Follow me." I darted up the narrow wooden stairs. Vignette stayed close on my heels as we headed to my grandfather's abandoned workshop to rummage around for something to pry off the sign. The remnants of a moonshine distillery sat cloaked in dust in an open cabinet, and as I breathed in the musky air, I could feel my grandfather's presence and hear the nasty whistling sound he made when he was coming for me.

"Mommy, are you crying?"

"No, honey, got some dust in my eyes. Let's get out of here."

I grabbed the crowbar, intent on rescuing Misty's sign. It was a relic from my childhood, and I was unwilling to leave it to the wrecking ball.

"So, Misty was your pony, Mommy?"

"No, but she was my pony Princess' baby, just like you are my baby. That's why I got to name her and made this sign for her. Look, I have a scar on my finger where I burned myself making that sign."

"That must have hurt. I love you, Mommy."

"I love you, too." Equal measures of joy and sorrow overwhelmed me, conjured by a place I thought I would never see again.

We traipsed outside so I could stow the plaque inside the car, and Vignette spotted an old tractor.

"Look at this cool tractor, Mommy! Can I climb on it?"

"Yes, but be careful," I said. My mind drifted. I could almost hear the chatter between my sisters and me as we saddled up at the corral to take our horses out for trail rides.

Princess was blind in one eye, so she kept a slower pace than the other horses as we galloped up past the oil rig with its rhythmic chugging and stench of old black oil. The sound of thundering hoofs would ring in my ears, and by the time we reached the top of Gobbler's Knob, the view would be invisible through the thick cloud of dust, and I'd be as blind as Princess.

The past was so vivid; I almost forgot I wanted to capture this moment with Vignette. As I went back to the car to retrieve my camera, the familiar sound of the gravel crunching beneath my feet unspooled memories of a story my mother had repeated to me throughout my childhood.

Late one night, Bill Butter pulled into the gravel driveway well past midnight. Dean Martin's just-released record "Volare," blared over the car radio. Bill continued his drunken crooning after turning off the ignition, though, in his stupor, he left the headlights on. My mother, Clara, peered out the upstairs window to see her husband silhouetted by the car's lights, stumbling up the stone path, cigarette dangling from his mouth, and a bottle of whiskey clutched in his hand. Annoyed and embarrassed by his returning from these late-night trysts with other women, which had become too frequent, she climbed back into bed, pretending to be asleep, and got tangled up in her oversized flannel nightgown.

A gust of frosty Pennsylvania wind followed Bill up the stairs to the bedroom. He pulled his pants down just far enough to expose his stiffened penis, then threw himself on top of his wife while endeavoring, with frustration, to unravel the nightgown.

Clara realized her best option for keeping their small children from waking was to make way for the inevitable drunken thrust between her naked thighs. When he found his way to an orgasm, he hollered out the name of his current mistress, Pammy Sue, and unceremoniously deposited the seed that would grow into a girl destined to be nothing but trouble. The first sign of said trouble began the very next morning with a dead car battery.

Nine months later, on the first day of fall, my mother gave birth to her fourth child. Dad thought I would be a boy, and he named me Sam. Maybe he hoped I would be a boy so he could stop hearing about Pammy Sue. As luck would have it, he pulled four aces; I was his fourth daughter.

My mother's frozen heart determined to immortalize her husband's infidelity and spelled it out on the birth certificate. But for as long as I knew my dad, he never called me by any other name but Sam. I always thought the name suited me. My mother prodded me so often with the reason my name was Pammy that my official name repulsed me.

Vignette tugged on my sleeve and snapped me back to reality. "Mommy, mommy, can we go now? I'm hungry," she moaned.

"Me too," I said, and we went back into the car. I threw my camera on the back seat along with the "Misty" sign, figuring I had enough memories of the place. Nothing could change what happened here.

As my daughter and I drove down Clever Road, I glanced back at the old farmhouse in the rearview mirror one last time. It would soon disappear forever, along with the lilac and forsythia bushes and delicate lilies of the valley that poked through the spring thaw each year. The springhouse and the old maple tree where I hugged my grandmother for the last time would be gone.

But they would live on in my memories, along with many things I wished I could forget.

2

AN ACCIDENTAL MEETING

Before being known as Wild Bill, he was Willard Francis Butter, the fourth of seven children born to Henry and Hermina Butter, immigrants from Germany and Austria.

The family settled in Pittsburgh, in a town called McKees Rocks, also known as "The Rocks"—a borough in Allegheny County, Pennsylvania, just along the south bank of the Ohio River.

Bill was a precocious boy who enjoyed taking risks, whether stealing chewing gum from the five and dime or shooting craps in the alley with kids twice his age. If his heart rate was pumping, he felt alive and in his element. While some may not have considered him handsome in a traditional sense, what he lacked in looks he more than made up for with his devil-may-care attitude and charismatic charm, which earned him the moniker that stuck with him for his entire life—Wild Bill.

At least to the extent that he had enough cash to throw down at the local bookie, he was a hard worker. By age fifteen, gambling was a part of his daily life.

His father, Henry, would tell him, "Go down to the bookie and keep your ear to the ground to find out who the guys like."

Bill obliged and became addicted to the adrenaline of winning, as well as the bragging rights. He didn't mind rolling up his sleeves to work, but much preferred the thrill of instant gratification he got from gambling.

Bill had a brother named Pinky, so-called for the redness of his skin, and Skinny, so-called because he was, well, skinny. His oldest brother was Dickey, which other than being short for Richard; it's anyone's guess how he got his nickname. Dickey loaned his car to the brothers from time to time so they could take house-painting jobs beyond the boundaries of the Rocks. One hot day in the summer of 1950, Bill, Pinky, and Skinny were driving down Clever Road when Bill spotted a dark-haired beauty mowing the expansive front lawn of a white clapboard farmhouse sitting atop a hill.

Bill wanted a better look at the young farm girl in the cutoff blue jean shorts. As the old beater pulled onto the curb, Bill rolled down the window and called out. The sound of the mower kept the girl from hearing him, so she paid no attention, disappearing behind a lilac bush. Bill hopped out of the car and sprinted up the lawn. When the girl emerged from the blind spot, a young man with a thin physique and slicked-back hair was standing in front of her, sporting a wide grin that made his sparkling eyes squint.

Startled, she switched off the motor.

Clara was seventeen at the time and unaware of her beauty. She wasn't the type to pay attention to boys, because boys didn't pay her much mind. Her clothes were simple, constructed from homemade patterns or hand-me-downs from her older sister and brothers. She wore her long hair in braids to keep it off her face in the sticky humidity of the Pennsylvania summers, and her gold, round, wire-rim glasses hid her beauty. She gave Bill a shy smile, revealing how handsome she thought he was before looking away.

Bill and Clara struck up a conversation as the brothers bided their time, aware they had no choice but to do so until Wild Bill ran out of small talk. It was anyone's guess how long that might take or how tall the tales might become. Bill had a unique way of making even the most mundane things sound exciting, and once on a roll with a captive audience, he could monologue for hours on end and still manage to hold your attention. Clara was so absorbed in Bill's stories that she didn't realize she still had over half the lawn to mow.

Having clung on every word, she finally removed her

wire-rim glasses to wipe a bit of sweat from her brow. With wide-eyed innocence and somewhat breathless, she said, "I can't believe you've met Frank Sinatra." Her blue eyes pierced right through Bill Butter's soul like arrows shot straight from Cupid's bow.

Realizing this conversation sounded a little too big even for him, Bill glanced away toward Pinky and Skinny, who signaled they'd run out of patience and might drive away without him. Wild Bill wasn't going to leave before he had sealed the deal; he would see her again. He was more self-assured when telling a tall tale than speaking the truth about his feelings.

"Well, we best be going... I would like to see you again. What did you say your name was, Miss?"

"I'm Clara. Do you like horses, Bill? If you'd like to come by next week, I am happy to show you around the stables."

Without hesitation, Bill hollered out, "You can bet on it!" as he left, bounding down the grassy lawn.

At supper that night, Pinky and Skinny taunted Wild Bill relentlessly about his latest infatuation. Their sister, Donna Lee, thought Clara sounded cute but couldn't quite picture her libidinous sibling with a farm girl. He already had every girl in McKees Rocks, throwing themselves at his feet.

The patriarch of the family, Henry, explained in no uncertain terms, "No good is gonna come from you sniffin' around some little farm girl. We're city folk; they ain't our kind. Those farm people aren't even Catholics."

Henry became more and more incoherent as the vodka and beer chasers took effect. Minnie cleared the table and remained quiet, made the sign of the cross, and mumbled a prayer. The quarrel escalated before concluding with the screen door slamming shut. The crisp smell of a fresh-lit Marlboro cigarette cut through the muggy air.

Bill Butter had been telling the truth when he told Clara

he liked horses. He reached into his pocket and pulled out some crumpled singles and two ten-dollar bills and headed to the bookie on the corner, putting it all down on a horse named Daisy Bell. She won, with 15-to-1 odds. Bill Butter knew his luck was about to change.

At the Deemer family dinner table the same night, quite a different conversation ensued. Clara's father, Jeremiah Davis Deemer, was known as JD. He was a brusque man with poor table habits, who never washed his hands, though they had been working the farm all day, leaving the beds of his nails black as coal. He hung his work jacket on a hook near the family dinner table, so the smell of manure could at times overtake the aroma of a pot roast in the oven.

"So, who was the young fella you were talking to all afternoon instead of doing your chores?" Two days old gray bristle and tobacco juice covered his chin, and his dentures clacked as he ate.

"It wasn't all afternoon, and I got the mowin' done. That nice boy's name is Bill. Said he wants to come by and look at the horses next week." Clara spoke without locking eyes with her father.

"You don't say? Maybe Bill wants to get them city-boy hands toughened up a bit doing some real work, Honey Girl."

He winked at Clara across the table, making her blush. He reserved the name "Honey Girl" for when he snuck up behind her to hug her, latching on to her ample bosom and squeezing her nipples with no more respect than if they were a cow's udders.

Days went by, and Clara had all but given up on ever laying eyes again on the young man who knew Frank Sinatra. Finally, the day came when Bill Butter, wearing a clean white t-shirt and jeans, appeared at the end of the long, red rock driveway. Clara showed Bill around the stables, then as they started up the hill to pick some apples, JD Deemer summoned them back to the barn.

"I could sure use a little help here, son. If you're up to it."

JD had a knack for being able to size up fresh prey, someone to get his hooks into, and get what he wanted or needed. The kid from the Rocks was an energetic boy with a lot of stamina, and what Wild Bill lacked in schooling, he made up for with grit and determination. JD never had much hope he'd marry Clara off to anyone of substance, so maybe this city kid, who he was sure he could manipulate, would do.

It was probably the most amount of work my father had ever done for the pleasure of being in a woman's company. But he was eager to learn what he could, and before long, he was returning to the farm almost daily for a small stipend of cash and Clara's companionship. Though he felt like a fish out of water on the farm, he swallowed his pride because he was beginning to enjoy breathing in the fresh country air while listening to JD Deemer's tales, some of which were taller than his own.

He also loved working with the horses. He was beginning to understand more about the animals than just the odds of their winning. He was learning what about their physique made them a potential winner or loser. He would take in tidbits of information from Joe, the blacksmith, when he came to the farm. Joe had put shoes on some of the most exceptional horses of all time, including a few Kentucky Derby winners.

"You look for a horse with a daylight win in a juvenile route. That's a winner," Joe would advise. "Sometimes it all comes down to when the damn horse was born. Foals born at the top of the year always have the best chance of winning. So, you have to do your homework. Look for the horse who comes from behind, not necessarily the one who comes first out of the gate. Those are the ones that'll win — every time. I see guys losin' their shirts puttin' money down on nothin' but a gut feeling. That's not handicappin'. That's just gambling. There's a difference, son."

JD overheard one of these conversations and got steaming mad at Joe for filling Bill's head with race talk.

"A man's gotta work for a livin'," he growled. "Gamblin' is like chasin' after fool's gold. This here's my barn, Joe. You best stop talkin' gamblin' with Bill, or I'll find myself another blacksmith."

"I'm the only good blacksmith willin' to put up with you, JD, you cantankerous old jackass."

JD chewed his tobacco hard, scratched his bald dome, and let out a sigh, "Well, you're right 'bout that, I guess. All the same, things are gettin' serious with Bill and Clara, and I won't be havin' no gamblin' man for a son-in-law, ain't that right, son?"

Wild Bill had grown up gambling. It was in his blood. He knew how to pick a horse just by instinct. Everything Joe shared would only make it so he couldn't lose. He considered it all before responding, "That's right, JD."

If there was one thing about dealing with Jeremiah Davis Deemer, it was always most comfortable to take the path of least resistance. Bill admired Joe the Blacksmith for standing up to JD, but it was something he couldn't bring himself to do. The man had gained control over Bill, which he didn't like but couldn't shake.

Before long, Bill and Clara got married and took up residence in the upstairs room above the kitchen. Bill enjoyed the home-cooked meals prepared by Clara's mother, Florence, and working the farm. But he soon discovered there was a price to pay for living under JD's roof, which was too steep. It was the way his father-in-law came up behind his wife to grab a full breast in each hand and squeeze them as he imprinted a kiss on her neck, calling her "Honey Girl."

Clara would say, "Stop it, Dad!" like it was no big deal. Bill didn't like it, and it chipped away at him, making him feel less of a man he could not stand up to his father-in-law. JD treated Clara like his property, and Bill wanted full ownership. Bill could tell she didn't enjoy it, but he couldn't figure out why she put up with her father's abusive behavior. There were times he was alone with Florence, and he thought to broach the subject with her for advice but couldn't quite form the words.

"Now, what's on your mind, Bill? I've raised three sons. I can tell when something's troubling a man."

"Oh, it ain't nothin'." Bill couldn't express to his mother-in-law the rage he felt inside each time he saw JD Deemer touch his wife.

When the eldest Deemer boy, Jim, returned to the farm from his missionary studies, he felt empathy for Bill seeing the way his father bossed him around. He was an intuitive soul who could sense the rage beginning to bubble under the surface. Bill confided in Jim how much it repulsed him to see his father-in-law kiss Clara on the mouth and fondle her breasts. Jim was, after all, a man of God. Wasn't his father's behavior un-Christian?

Jim listened but couldn't provide any answers, suggesting he pray to God about it.

It was a hot, muggy day in July when a stranger pulled his truck to the side of Clever Road and rolled to a stop right next to the big briar bush across from the Deemer farm. JD, Bill, and Jim strolled down the driveway, gravel crunching beneath their boots. JD hollered out, "Hey, what's the trouble here? You need some help?"

The driver, not much older than Bill, got out of his car and explained he must have run out of gas.

"Now that's a tough break," JD said, "because we ain't got enough gas to spare."

He paused, reaching into his Beechnut pouch, and pulled out a sizable chew of tobacco to stuff into his cheeks as he contemplated the stranger's dilemma.

"Lookie here. My son, Jim, is going that way, up past McGuire's gas station, ain't you, Jim? And he can drive you up there and go on his way, and you can walk back. It ain't far."

"What a lucky break. There isn't another place for miles back that way, and I had no idea what was ahead down the road."

"Oh, you ain't from around these parts?" JD asked.

"No. I'm from over in Johnstown. I got a contracting job up here in Moon Township. I can't be late for the job. It starts early in the morning."

JD made the familiar whistling sound between chews of tobacco, removed his cap to scratch his head. Tobacco juice drizzled from the corners of his mouth as he closed his eyes as though deep in thought.

Then he said to Jim, "Now go on, son, and get the truck and drive this here gentleman up there to McGuire's to fetch himself some gas."

Jim stared at his father. He wanted to believe his father was kind and noble, whose intentions of helping this man were real, but he knew there was plenty of gasoline stored in the springhouse to get the stranger to McGuire's gas station, if not to Moon Township.

"Now go on, Jim. Get the truck."

Jim dashed up the driveway and pulled the truck around, and the stranger hopped in. They weren't two minutes around the briar bush, just out of sight, before JD commanded Bill, "Strip it. Take every darn thing off this here truck, and don't let no one see ya."

Bill hesitated. But his father-in-law's orders were clear. "Go on now! Ain't nothin' here to talk about unless you and Clara don't want to live under my roof no more."

Bill loaded up a wheelbarrow with every tool on the truck, tires and all, and stowed the stolen goods away in the springhouse's upstairs behind some old wooden doors Lenny the Junk Man had in storage at the farm.

On the way to McGuire's, Jim Deemer took off his baseball cap and wiped the sweat from his brow. The stranger was breathing a sigh of relief, but Jim felt queasy. He attempted to smile at the man beside him but couldn't get the corners of his mouth to rise. He kept his eyes vigilant on the road ahead.

Just then, a male deer with large antlers darted out in front of the truck, and Jim swerved to miss it. The vehicle veered onto the shoulder of the road, grazing the briar bushes and startling a flock of black-winged birds that appeared from nowhere and flew across the horizon as though summoned by the Prince of Darkness himself. A foreshadowing of evil flashed through Jim's body as he regained control of the truck.

Jim dropped off the stranger at McGuire's as told to do and went on his way, cruising up Regina Drive and stopping to take in the expansive vista of farmland. There he slumped over the steering wheel and prayed for God to forgive him for his part in whatever scheme his father had in store.

When the stranger trekked a couple of miles back from McGuire's gas station to find his truck stripped down, he fell to his knees and let out a mournful moan and then shrieked at the top of his lungs, "What the hell happened to my truck? Somebody, help!"

The howl signaled it was "show-time" and brought JD out of the barn. He trotted down the red rock driveway, shoving a fresh wad of Beechnut chewing tobacco over his dry, wrinkled lips. When he reached the stranger, he looked straight into the man's tearful eyes and said, "I don't believe it. All of it, gone? Must have been those hoodlums driving up from McKees Rocks looking for trouble. Why don't you come up and have some supper with us, and we'll figure this thing out?"

The stranger cried on his shoulder as he escorted him up to the house.

Florence Deemer swung open the screen door, yelling, "What happened? You poor, dear. Let me get you a cup of tea."

Later, Jim Deemer drove past the stripped-down truck and rolled into the driveway around the loop parking out of view behind the springhouse. Jim calculated each footstep, careful to avoid attracting attention on his way to the barn as the gravel shifted beneath his feet. He climbed up the wooden ladder to the top of the hayloft, filled with enough bales to provide a vantage point of the house from a small vertical window. Jim could make out the image of the stranger through the screen door of the porch. He could also see Bill Butter out on the front porch, smoking a cigarette and could hear the muffled sound of dishes cleared after a meal.

Jim knew JD was evil, and it would take more than prayer to save his soul. He fell asleep, praying and hoping that he would be more capable of standing up to his father when he awoke. When the sun went down, the moon found its way through the tiny hayloft window, casting a bluish-white light across his body.

A tow truck arrived and put some spare tires on the stranger's vehicle's back two wheels. Florence loaded some homemade jam and biscuits in a small basket, and Bill and JD escorted the man down the driveway to meet the tow truck.

On the way back to the house, Bill said, "I'm never doing nothing like this for you again. How can you look in a man's face and lie after you took all his stuff?"

JD hocked a rocket of tobacco juice as though someone was keeping score of how far he could spit, and said, "I didn't take nothin'. You did. So, I ain't telling no lie. Some hoodlum from McKees Rocks did make off with that guy's stuff."

That night, Bill went to bed in the room above the kitchen and took out his rage against his father-in-law between the legs of Clara Butter. He pounded her as hard as he could, the small four-poster bed moving halfway across the room before Wild Bill collapsed on top of his wife as he sobbed, tears mixing with sweat. She cradled him in her arms until he rolled off her, pulled on his jeans, and went outside to smoke a Marlboro.

As the years passed, Bill Butter became determined to elude the grasp JD Deemer had on his life. He'd had enough of shoveling horse manure and bailing hay and walking into the room, seeing JD drunk on port and groping Clara, even when she was pregnant. Wild Bill had higher aspirations for his wife, and little girls than being a farmhand, and wanted to forge his way on his terms. Bill had a plan that involved enlisting the help of the only other person he knew who hated JD more than he did—his mother-in-law's sister, Martha Golling. Martha never understood what her sister saw in JD. It was clear from the day JD and Florence met; he had his eyes set on their land.

When Bill suggested to Martha and her husband, Chuck, that he and his family move into a small guest cottage on their property, they relished having the Butter girls nearby, given they had no children of their own. Chuck recognized Bill had an entrepreneurial spirit and encouraged him to start up an awning business. Bill was not only handy; he had what it took to make a sale and immediately adapted to his burgeoning business. The feeling of independence was a boon to his self-esteem.

Bill was now responsible for two children and a wife with a baby on the way, but he never outgrew the days as a carefree teen when he'd risk his entire paycheck at the corner bookie.

Some of his pals questioned his bets, but he proved them wrong by often winning at incredible odds. He would take the deposit from an awning job, throw it down on a horse, and often triple his earnings. Most thought he was just plain lucky.

He didn't dare tell Clara he risked their money on betting on the horses. Clara's upbringing taught her to believe gambling was sinful. He justified the habit by convincing himself it was beneficial to his family. Soon they could buy a home of their own if only he could keep his winning streak going.

Hanging out at the track became a regular ritual, and with it came temptations. The more Bill won, the more rounds of drinks he ordered, and the more women took notice of the kid who bore more than a slight resemblance to James Dean with his lean physique, slicked-back hair, and squinty brown eyes. Before long, Bill was living parallel lives: on the one hand, the racetrack and the women who loved him; on the other, the awning business and his wife and kids. He felt content. One balanced the other. Bill was a twenty-five-year-old man who felt like he had it all.

Unfortunately, little things began to annoy him. He resented Clara's insistence on loading up the family station wagon to make the hour-plus trip to the farm. She wanted to stay close to her mother and have her daughters learn to ride ponies. Clara often prodded Bill to spend the entire weekend with her and the girls in the spacious upstairs bedroom where there was plenty of room for them all to stretch out.

With an infant in the front seat and two little girls in the back, as they snaked their way along the rural road through a wooded area to get to the farm, sweat beaded up on Bill's forehead from the anxiety of being trapped in father mode. When one girl got car sick and threw up in the back seat, Bill pulled the wagon off to the side of the road, cigarette dangling from his mouth, to wipe up vomit with one of the baby's diapers. Overcome by the stench, Bill's temper was at a boiling point as he wondered how he got caught up in this mess of having four extra mouths to feed, wiping runny noses, and no one around him who understood what unique talents he possessed.

"If you love the goddamn farm so much, then why don't we move back there? I'm sure that would make old JD happy," Bill said, with an insinuating tone.

"I'm pregnant again, so maybe we have to move back to the farm," Clara announced with less fanfare than buying a ham at the grocer.

"What the hell? How can that be? We ain't even been doin' it cause you're always too tired. You sure you're pregnant?"

"I suppose you don't recall the night we spent at the farm a month back when you came home so drunk you left your car headlights on and drained the battery? The night you yelled out Pammy Sue. I guess we have your girlfriend, Pammy Sue, to thank, for another mouth to feed."

Bill kicked the tire, flung himself back in the car, and sped the family to the farm where he dropped everyone off, saying he had to take care of some business. Then he peeled away.

To blow off some steam, he went to see his bookie in the Rocks, and with reckless abandon, he put all he had down on a long shot to win. The horse came in last.

He went next door to have a beer to console himself and bumped into one of the bookie's buddies. Guzzling a beer, Bill began complaining about his pregnant wife, his lousy luck, and the fact he just lost the advance on his next job. The man told Bill he knew someone who could help and slid him a card with a phone number of a guy who could loan Bill some money. Bill took the card and nervously tapped it on the bar.

Over the next few years, Wild Bill got in deeper and deeper with the loan sharks in a fruitless attempt at a lucky streak that never came. The boy wonder, who once seemed invincible, was becoming a broken twenty-eight-year-old man with five girls under the age of nine.

One night the phone rang. It was the call he'd been dreading for some time. It was the thing that was keeping him up at night and making his stomach churn. Before he said goodbye, the phone went dead. Bill's mind was racing a million miles a minute.

"Who was that, Bill?" Clara asked.

Wild Bill stared off into space.

"Bill, is everything okay?"

"Wrong number," he said as he went outside for a smoke, wondering how on earth he would come up with $5,000 in two days.

3

THE ROAD TO SHANGRI-LA

Rocketing across the country in an old, beat-up Chevy station wagon in 1961, the Butter family was officially on the lam. They were running away from the past, the loan sharks, and as far away as possible from JD Deemer. It's hard to say who my father feared more—the loan sharks or his father-in-law since both seemed out for his blood.

They drove south and thought about settling in Kansas, but then continued west in search of a new beginning and wound up in Phoenix, Arizona. Clara's sister, Hilah, spoke about it as though it were Shangri-La, even though the summers pushed past one hundred degrees, giving Wild Bill a legitimate excuse to stop off each day at the local bar for a cold one.

With what little money Bill saved, they rented a tiny ranch house on the street littered with empty forty-ounce beer bottles and dirty candy wrappers. There were a lot of kids running around with bad teeth, snotty noses, and poor toilet habits. The house lacked central air conditioning but had a rather large contraption sticking out from the side, whose only usefulness seemed to blow hot air. My sisters and I tied a sheet around it, creating an inflated bubble and transforming the whole setup into a makeshift fort. It was a magical place to spend a hot day shielded from the afternoon sun.

When Bill wasn't out looking for work, he spent his time sprawled across the couch with a beer in one hand and a Marlboro in the other, listening to Nat King Cole records while my older sisters and I put on skits for him. Being fourth in a line of five girls relegated me to the least glamorous roles—stepdaughter, mouse, dwarf, troll. My oldest sister was always the princess or queen, but it didn't matter since dad was too drunk or hungover to pay much attention to us.

I don't remember my father saying much to me beyond, "Sam, get me a beer," as he lay stretched out on the couch.

"Here, Daddy." At age four, I could count popping open a can of beer as one of my milestones.

Most days found my mother behind a scorching-hot iron getting Bill ready for the car salesman job interviews he claimed to be going to in those crisply starched shirts. It may sound like a cliché to say Dad came home more than once with lipstick on his collar, but it's true. My mother and father would fight about it until he'd convinced her it was just a pleased customer to whom he had sold an expensive car, and the commission money would flood in soon—and then, boy, would she feel foolish for accusing him of cheating.

Sometimes my father would disappear for days at a time. If not in the physical sense, he would escape to his fantasy world of chain-smoking and liquored-up conversations with Johnny Cash, who he claimed was his best buddy.

Mom traded in her gold, round spectacles for black-rimmed cat-eye glasses and now wore full skirts. She became a born-again Christian and joined a Baptist church, which infuriated Wild Bill. He wasn't interested in religion, attending church, or being saved by anyone but himself. He didn't understand why religion mattered to his wife. Having been brought up in a devout Catholic home, he especially couldn't understand why she didn't want to be Catholic. Dad preferred going to confession, saying a few Hail Mary's absolving him of his sins, then getting drunk to getting caught up in an emotional rally culminating in being dunked. They argued over everything, including the fact that my father kept a small statue of St. Francis hanging on his rearview mirror because, as a Baptist, she thought this was worshiping a false idol. The more religious my mother became, the more fights ensued.

After one particularly nasty quarrel, our dad disappeared for a few days, and my mother became very depressed. When he stumbled into the tiny ranch house inebriated, my older sisters were at school, so it was just my younger sister and me at home to bear witness to voices escalating past the volume on the small black and white television set. I considered turning up the volume to drown out the shouting but was afraid to move. From my vantage point on the couch, I could see my parents reflected in the sliding glass door. Mom was telling Dad he should have never come back when I saw him throw her against the wall, and she sounded like she was choking and flailing, knocking over the vase on top of the stereo console.

When Dad went to take a leak, Mom ran to where I was sitting like a statue on the couch with my eyes glued to the black-and-white TV. She looked straight into my eyes to deliver the message I knew in my heart meant the worst I could ever imagine.

"Run across the street to the Vonnes and tell them your parents are fighting and to call the police."

My tiny four-year-old legs hightailed it across the street. The sun was at such an angle, it turned my shadow into a much taller version of myself. It is my first memory of ever feeling needed. I kept repeating the words my mother told me to deliver to the Vonnes, but when I arrived at their doorstep, I panicked.

"My mom's fighting with my dad. I mean, my dad's fighting with my mom. Anyway, call the police!" I squealed as I burst into tears.

Mr. Vonne ran to the phone as Mrs. Vonne wrapped me up in her thick arms and took me inside, saying, "Now, now, dear, everything will be fine."

But in my heart, I knew it wouldn't.

My mother got a restraining order preventing Bill Butter from setting foot anywhere near the ranch house. Though court-ordered, it wasn't enough to keep our father away, and the constant fear of him stalking her made my mother wracked with worry for her safety and ours. It's no wonder she gained so much solace from the support she received from the church that had become her rock.

When Wild Bill showed up to yell at her from the alleyway, she would spray the hose at him over the fence and yell, "Go away, or I will call the police." In our sun-suits, my sisters and I hunkered down in the makeshift tent, the hum from the air conditioning blower drowning out their nasty confrontations. We all knew Wild Bill was no good. We heard it from our mother, we heard it from the church folks, and we saw it with our own eyes. But like anything abruptly spirited away, you feel its absence. I missed the smell of Dad's cigarette smoke and the sound of Nat King Cole playing on the stereo. The house became quiet, almost too calm.

Mom had to find a babysitter so she could get a job. She went through four or five candidates before settling on Margie, a heavy-set Native American woman, who, in short order, became part of the family. With Margie in charge, Mom had the freedom to go off to work without any worries; she knew her five little girls were safe in school or at home in her care.

Sometimes Margie went out for groceries or cigarettes, dipping into the big cookie jar on the kitchen counter where my mother kept the household money. I was four, and my baby sister was two, and when the others were at school, she would leave us alone in the house, but she always asked before she went out, "Can you be a big girl and watch your baby sister for a few minutes while Margie goes to the corner store? It's so hot out I don't want you girls getting overheated, so stay put."

I would turn my head away from the TV toward her and nod yes, or, if I felt afraid to be alone, I kept looking straight ahead at the television set and didn't say anything. Regardless, Margie's stiff shuffle walk could be heard crossing the creaky linoleum floor as the screen door opened and snapped shut behind her, triggering a rush of adrenaline through my body.

It might have been the hottest day of the year when I heard Margie opening the cookie jar and the jangling of coins tinkling against each other as she poured them into a brown paper bag. I could tell it was a paper sack by the rustling sound the coins made against it. I was watching *The Flintstones,* and a few pesky flies kept swooping down in front of my view of the TV. Their unrelenting buzz made me feel more tense than usual. I had a funny feeling in the pit of my stomach.

This day, Margie didn't ask my permission to go to the store. When I didn't hear the screen door snap shut but close without a sound behind muffled footsteps, I knew something was wrong. The afternoon sun rose high in the sky as my younger sister slept in her playpen, her thin blonde hair sticking to her face from the summer heat, and the small fan next to the TV provided little relief. I stood vigil over my baby sister all afternoon until the sun scooted across the floor the way it did when it was time for my older sisters to arrive home from school. Frightened and feeling alone, I wondered why Margie never returned.

When my mother got home from work and discovered the money was missing, she went berserk. She was angry about being stuck with five little girls in this small, dirty house married to a deadbeat husband, and she was ready to take it all out on me for not wanting to eat what she made for dinner. I had nothing to eat or drink all day, but I wasn't hungry.

"I have no patience for little girls who don't want to eat, so you can go to bed with no supper," she railed at me.

I climbed into my bed, shivering from head to toe and feeling it was my fault Margie made off with our money.

Our cousins were over to play, and when my aunt arrived to pick them up, my cousin grabbed her mother's hand and asked her to come and check on me. The sun was close to going down, but the house was still boiling. When Aunt Hilah entered the room, she saw the stacks of clothing, toys, and blankets my sisters and cousins had piled on top of my shivering body.

"Get me a thermometer. I think Pammy's ill." My aunt removed the stuffed toys and held my hand.

"She's just faking. She didn't want to eat the turtle soup I made for supper," my mother snapped.

"Just get me the thermometer, Clara ..."

My temperature confirmed what my aunt, a registered nurse, suspected. I had a fever hovering at 104 degrees.

"Get me a cold rag. We need to get Pammy to the emergency room."

I recall how good the cold rag felt on my forehead, but little else until I awoke in a hospital bed. The doctors ran some tests and discovered I had a kidney infection, most likely caused by inadequate toilet training, which at the age of one comprised being told to sit on the potty-chair until I pooped or peed and then given M&Ms as a reward. I don't recall using toilet paper much as part of this ritual. I'd sit on the potty chair, pull up my underpants, grab some M&Ms in my grubby little hands, and be on my way.

Lying beneath the bright lights of the emergency room, receiving intravenous fluids under a warm blanket, I felt safe. But once the fever broke, I went home in the same soiled underpants I'd arrived.

About three months later, Mom decided to pack all us girls up to take a train out of Phoenix and out of Bill Butter's life forever. The church helped my mother hatch the plan to go back to the family farm and held a garage sale where she sold every stick of furniture, every ashtray, and every Nat King Cole record in Wild Bill's collection. If it wasn't nailed down, it went to the highest bidder. Dad's prized stereo console fetched a pretty penny.

The journey would take over a week and would be difficult

with five little girls under the age of ten. But the options were slim, and this seemed like the right thing. Our grandparents, Pap and Gammy, could help take care of us. The farmhouse had plenty of bedrooms and lots of space to run around. It would be a haven from Wild Bill Butter.

The church deemed it essential to have us baptized to save our souls before we made the trek across the country. I knew that when folks got called up at the end of a service and walked single file on the red runner between the pews up to the altar, the preacher dunked them in a mysterious pool, and they'd arise dripping wet and gasping for air. I found it terrifying.

When the pastor called out, "Will the Butter family, please come forward to receive God's holy blessing of baptism?" I froze like an icicle clinging for life to a tree limb, hoping the sun would stay hidden behind a cloud. My mother was so caught up in the emotion of it all she didn't notice the skin beneath my skirt remained stuck to the pew as she carried the baby to the altar in her arms, and the three older girls followed like little ducklings. I rejoiced in thinking I might have the power to be invisible. There would be many times to come when I wished I could disappear.

One by one, I witnessed my mother and sisters dunked in the pool as the pastor repeated the words, "Upon your profession of faith and by the Lord's command, I baptize you in the name of the Father, Son, and Holy Spirit. Buried in the likeness of His death and raised in the likeness of His resurrection..." and so on. I remained stuck to the pew, unable to move.

I clearly remember arriving at the farm. The imposing clapboard house welcomed us, and we went running upstairs and downstairs, charging from room to room, exploring every nook and cranny as excited as though we were exploring a funhouse at an amusement park. The first floor had a large kitchen, dining room, living room, our grandparents' bedroom, and a sun parlor where Gammy grew plants year-round. Two different stairwells led to the four upstairs bedrooms and an upstairs kitchen. One of the stairwells had a banister. It was hard to resist sliding down the smooth, shiny black wood. I can still remember how the gentle evening breeze felt drifting through the screen door, laden with humidity, and how different it felt from the unforgiving arid wind of the Arizona desert. Most of all, I remember the first time my grandmother hugged me, filling my heart with hope. The long journey was worth that one hug.

Mom found a job in the reservations department at Allegheny Airlines, which several years later would merge to become US Airways. Pittsburgh was a bustling hub for the airline, so my mother worked very long shifts, earning a good paycheck, stabilizing our family. Every morning while eating Trix cereal, I watched my mother apply her makeup in front of a small, rectangular mirror that hung at a slant, affixed to a chain on the kitchen wall. She'd apply her red lipstick and smack her lips together, snap her purse shut, and be out the door before I'd wiped the sand out of the corners of my eyes.

The church thought they were delivering us from evil by getting us as far away as possible from Wild Bill. They didn't realize they were sending our family straight to hell—into the arms of the devil himself.

4
PRINCESS

As the maple tree leaves began to lose color, and I was turning five, my grandfather, Pap, introduced my sisters and me to a game.

Okay, girls, gather round. Let Pap Pap tell you the rules of the game called Tiger. You can hide anywhere in the upstairs or downstairs of the barn. But you can't turn the lights on. And when I catch you, you can't scream because then the other girls will know where the Tiger is. We'll keep playing the game until I find you all, or Gammy calls you in for bed."

The barn had an upstairs with two large haylofts, a granary room where the oat sacks were stored, a workshop area, and a large, open wooden plank floor. Two different swings hung from the rafters, and there were floor-to-ceiling aluminum sliding doors that let out to an area where the tractors parked above the corral. The downstairs had about thirty horse stables and plenty of places to hide, including a tack room. Pap growled, and we girls let out a scream and scattered to hide.

The first time we played the game, Pap found me hiding behind a large, metal oat bin downstairs. It was pitch black, and I couldn't see anything. It was a great hiding place, but he found me because I let out a gasp when I pressed my face into a spider's web. Growling like a tiger, he lifted me from behind the oat bin, put his hands down my pants and stuck his fingers up inside my panties like he was reaching for my heart.

"Now stay quiet, Honey Girl, or the Tiger will eat you alive," he whispered.

There was no need for Tiger to tell me to stay quiet. The thrust froze my mouth shut. It was the first time Tiger caught me, but not the last. Before long, he did as he pleased whenever and wherever he wanted whether the lights were on or off.

Winter passed, and the lilies of the valley began bursting through the thawed ground beneath the forsythia bushes. My grandfather summoned my sisters and me to assign us each a pony or horse according to our size. He felt it was time we learn to care for animals of our own. We were all so excited as we lined up for Pap to present us with our steeds. He hesitated a moment when it was my turn, and made a whistling sound through his slightly parted lips as he chewed down hard on a big wad of tobacco.

"Here, Pammy, this one's yours."

The pony, my grandfather gave me was Princess, a former show pony. She lost her glory when her left eye was kicked in, crushing the bone, causing the socket to cave in, leaving a small red fireball where her eyeball had been. The trauma made her shy away from almost everyone, so, her black coat was gray from receiving so little brushing. Kids from the surrounding suburbs would visit the farm for free rides for brushing the ponies, but no one was ever interested in Princess. She wasn't old and was still breeding, but her spirit seemed broken, like mine. Her damaged eye was the way my entire body felt.

Princess and I bonded right away, and I spent hours brushing her black coat until it was shiny again as she listened to me scheme up the future. As the years passed, Princess kept my spirit alive by listening to me sing songs from *Mary Poppins* and then *The Sound of Music*. Imagining myself as Maria running through the fields, I always ended by softly singing "Edelweiss," which I found difficult to get through as I choked back tears. The simple lyrics touched a place in my heart that still felt open. I could be like the edelweiss, small and white, clean and bright. I could look happy, and I could bloom and grow forever if only I could escape. I often imagined Princess and me galloping up over the hills and never returning.

When I started first grade, there were four Butter girls enrolled in Burkett Elementary School, and we all played the clarinet like our mother had when she was a girl. Because we were from a divorced home at a time and in a place where it wasn't common, folks looked at us with pity. We dressed oddly in clothes our aunt collected from the Salvation Army. The profound peculiarity was how optimistic we were despite our circumstances.

Each night, my grandfather, grandmother, mother, and the five Butter girls gathered around the kitchen table for a family meal prepared by Gammy. We'd bow our heads while Pap delivered a heartfelt prayer to God for giving him the strength and guidance to watch over these young girls. Our lives were now his responsibility because of that worthless, good-for-nothin' Bill Butter. His prayers were nothing more than a show for my grandmother to convince her he was a devout Christian and not an evil sinner, but I could see through his lies. I drowned out his voice with my prayers for deliverance from the evil grasp he held over me.

After dinner, my grandmother helped us clear the dishes before retiring to her bedroom to read. Pap liked to watch TV, notably *The Ed Sullivan Show*, on our old black-and-white set. Color televisions were coming into vogue, but Pap resisted wasting good money on such new-fangled things. My grandmother put sheets of colored vinyl over the screen—one red, one yellow, and one blue—giving it an appearance of color TV. When the announcer said, *"The following program is brought to you in living color,"* I believed I saw it in color. That was my grandmother's magic. She made me see things as they could be if I imagined them so.

Resting back in his reclining chair, Pap would start picking at its edges. He made a distinctive sound like a dampened whistle or a hiss as he released air through the gap between his dentures and pursed shriveled lips.

"Come here, Honey Girl," he'd say, summoning me to sit by his side in my thin nightgown. Duty-bound, I sat as motionless as a statue while he reached under my gown in search of the most delicate parts of my flesh.

The first time this happened, with a look of horror on her face as though she might be sick, my mother darted from the room. As time went on, she stopped reacting and kept her eyes glued to *The Ed Sullivan Show* with the rest of the family.

My grandfather told me I could never tell anyone anything because if I did, terrible things would happen to the whole family. Pap reminded me we were under his roof out of the goodness of his heart, and we'd have nothing if he kicked us out.

As I matured, Pap became harsher in the ways he touched me. If I tried to resist his fondling or kissing, he applied force, sometimes pinning me down by resting his forearm on my throat. I wondered if my mother knew Pap was abusing me. I felt estranged from her, which amplified my pain, but I felt the abuse I was experiencing was the way the world meant it to be. It became as commonplace as my chores like dusting the black staircase every Saturday or feeding the pigs or taking the trash out to burn.

Despite knowing it wasn't my fault that my grandfather was abusing me, I couldn't help but feel guilt and shame, which caused bouts of depression and made me want to hide away from everyone—not so easy a feat with four siblings. When forced to interact with them, I would play the consummate comedian so they wouldn't see the pain behind my eyes. I became skilled at hiding the truth and being able to make everyone laugh.

The sisters especially loved a ridiculous face I dubbed "The Frozen Seymour." Standing barefoot in the snow until my teeth chattered, I flipped my lower lip upside down in an exaggerated way as it turned blue from the cold. My sisters would laugh until their bellies hurt, and I would feel euphoric, if only for a moment as the icy snow numbed my senses.

Rummaging around the cellar or stumbling upon a secret attic, I found bits and bobs hidden away that I could recycle into something new and beautiful. I would take these treasures and re-style rooms while shifting the furniture around as it suited me when I felt bored or wanted to let out some nervous energy. The old farmhouse was a treasure trove of heavy antique credenzas, china closets, and buffet tables. I delighted in the family's gasps when they walked into a room I transformed, flabbergasted how I moved such heavy things by myself. It was an outlet for me and something I relished for how it made me feel both creatively and physically, and to alleviate my sense of boredom. Moving those massive antiques around like they were nothing more than doll-house furniture made me believe I could do anything.

As the years passed, the distinctive whistling sound my grandfather made as he was calling his prey triggered an intense fight-or-flight response in me. I felt as though I might jump up and push his recliner over, landing the old man flat on his back and vulnerable, then kick the living hell out of him. But I kept these impulses hidden. As I grew, the old man's control over me became stronger as I became angrier, bottling it all up inside.

The only person who made me feel safe, beside Princess, was my beloved grandmother, Gammy. She was a rotund woman whose full belly laugh was as welcome in my life as a cool breeze. She crocheted and watched soap operas, all while listening to me chatterbox away the afternoon. I loved picking blackberries with her in summer for her delicious homemade jams. We boiled the fruit on the old kitchen stove before adding the individual spices and ingredients. In the fall, we would turn these jams into homemade pies for Thanksgiving, and then again at Christmas time. With deep snow outside, the fruit tasted as fresh as the summer day it stained our lips and fingers.

One time when we were out picking blackberries, we came upon a shallow bunny's nest made from grass and fur in the meadow near the blackberry bushes. Had we not entered the blackberry patch on all fours, clinging to our baskets, we might have missed it.

"Pammy, look here," she said, as she carefully pulled back the messy grass. "This is a bunny's nest. Let's take a peek inside."

Sure enough, there were five tiny newborn bunnies. Gammy told me they were Eastern cottontails snuggling in the nest.

"Why did the mama make the nest out here in the open?"

"Well, the mama bunny is smart and makes her nest out in the open because most predators like to stay hidden. Just because the mama isn't here doesn't mean she isn't nearby. She will only visit the nest when she knows no one will see her. She probably sensed our coming up the hill, and ran close by for cover, hoping we wouldn't see. She's probably watching us right now."

I scanned the horizon looking for the mama, then watched the babies wriggle, as newborns do, before covering up the nest.

"Are you sure the mama loves the babies, Gammy?"

"She does. With all of her heart."

With that, we went off to pick baskets of berries, but her words resonated and filled me with trust.

There were times I wanted to tell Gammy about how much Pap was hurting me. What stopped me was an inner fear that she might already know or have some inkling of his insidious behavior. It seemed unlikely my grandfather woke up one day and became a pedophile. Confronting my grandmother, and learning she knew the truth might jeopardize my relationship with the only person I felt understood or cared about me. That was something I couldn't risk losing. Nothing good would come from sharing my darkest sorrow. I relished my time with Gammy too much to burden her with my problems.

One day, after being trapped in the granary with my

grandfather, I hightailed out, leaving him resting back on one of the oat sacks. I ran up to the blackberry bushes to crawl under them and hide. As I dropped to my knees, I saw the bunny nest and pulled back the loose grass. The five bunnies lay motionless in what was no longer a nest, but a shallow grave. Tears filled my eyes as I realized their mother must not have returned to the nest.

I picked myself up and ducked under the barbed wire fence, which ripped through my white blouse and into my flesh. Blood trickled down my back as I scrambled up over the field into the woods. Thrashing through the thicket like a hunted animal, I reached another barbed wire fence separating our property from the neighboring sheep farm. A large tree trunk, fuller than any I had ever seen standing in the woods, had fallen across the fence, extending into the sheep farm. It appeared to have rotted from the inside.

I climbed on top of the massive trunk only to discover the tree now had a new life—to provide a habitat for insects, rabbits, lichen, and mushrooms. I found a cozy place to sit atop a cushion of soft moss while I dried the remaining tears. Then, to my complete astonishment, a wood sprite presented itself to me. His skin was unique in its ability to adapt to his surroundings for surviving in the woods, which led me to name him Copy. Copy's eyes were soulful, and it seemed he knew everything I was thinking. After a while, Copy coaxed his sister out from hiding in the shadows. She hugged me tightly, and I named her Kissy. While most girls my age were confiding in Barbie dolls in the safety of their bedrooms, I was holed up in the woods, talking to imaginary wood sprites about how I could survive another day.

I confided my deepest, darkest secrets, including everything JD forced me to do. Though the wood sprites were powerless to prevent my grandfather from harming me, they were always there each time I needed them. They understood how conflicted

I felt and were the only ones with whom I shared my private shame. Over time, I spent more and more time with my wood sprite friends, because this was a secret place where no one could find me, and I craved being alone.

Maintaining my grandfather's approval seemed the only way to survive, but no matter what I did, nothing was ever enough. I would break my back cleaning the stables for him, but he would bark out, "You hung the pitchfork where the broom should be and the broom where the pitchfork should be. You're just like your father—I hated that man."

As his physical abuse escalated to include verbal abuse, I tried harder to please him, but it only made things worse. The more I wanted to please him, the more Pap sensed he was in control, and the more he became hell-bent on destroying my physical and emotional well-being, for no other reason than he could.

Time spent with my grandmother was my only respite from the ugliness. Besides picking blackberries in the summer to make jam, I loved hearing the stories behind her extensive spoon collection, which hung on an ornate rack in the dining room next to a wooden plaque with the poem "Trees" by Joyce Kilmer etched into it.

I memorized every word of Kilmer's poem and often recited it by heart to Copy and Kissy while nestled in the large, fallen tree trunk's moss where we met. It became a mantra, a prayer I would repeat in my head while encountering anything unpleasant, especially when it involved my grandfather. As unclean hands and the bristle of unshaven skin rubbed against the delicate flesh on my thighs, Joyce Kilmer's words lifted me out of the sadness, and into a place where I could see beyond the horizon. There was something out there waiting for me.

Gammy also shared her collection of rare coins with me. "This is one of the first minted United States pennies," she told me. "This could be worth a lot of money someday. And this one is a Confederate States half-dollar. This one here, it's not worth much now, I don't think. But it's from the 1800s, and here's one from the early 1900s."

"They're beautiful," I said, rubbing the cold metal against the flesh of my palms.

"I know how troubled you were when your babysitter stole those coins from your mother. It wasn't your fault, Pammy. You are a good girl. Bad things sometimes happen even to the best people. But nothing but good should ever happen to you. You are a good, good girl. You are blessed."

I wrapped my arms around her wide girth and squeezed her tightly as though I would never let go.

"It smells like those pies are ready to take out of the oven. Let's go check on them," Gammy said as I helped to pull her up from her recliner and raced to the kitchen.

It was spring, and I was eight years old when my grandmother left to attend her reunion at Slippery Rock College. I can still remember every detail of what she was wearing, including little pearl-cluster, clip-on earrings, and her distinctive dotted swiss, dark navy dress. Clutching her small suitcase, she stood in the shade of the leafy maple tree next to the springhouse, waiting to leave as we laughed and hugged.

"Please, Pammy, recite the poem "Trees" for Gammy before I go."

I recited the poem I knew by heart, but halfway through, my lower lip quivered. Tears welled up in my eyes, and a knot in my throat blocked the words from flowing. I tried my best to finish the recitation, despite my grandfather's making his whistling sound, which caused my skin to crawl. I couldn't finish, and rushed into my grandmother's open arms, crying like a baby.

"There, there, sweet child. No need to be upset. Gammy will be back in a week."

But after that day, I never saw my grandmother again. She had rheumatoid arthritis in her back and slipped while taking a bath at the college, kicking on the hot water faucet. Gammy was unable to hoist herself up in the slippery tub, and the scalding hot water gave her third-degree burns. The last I heard from my grandmother was a letter she wrote from the hospital. I have read and reread it so many times, and each time, it's as though I can hear her voice. I can feel her pain and can imagine how defeated she felt—she knew she was never coming home.

Ohio Valley Hospital
July 4, 1967
Dear Pammy,

I'm sitting up in the wheelchair, so I will try to write a few lines to you. You know it is over five weeks since I've seen you. I hope you are getting along all right. Did you enjoy your cousins' visit? I hope someone loaned Dale a pony when he wanted to ride. Dave and Diane probably were too big for ponies. You told Mom to ask me about the Barbie clothes I started to make. I am sorry, but I don't know where things were put. I will try very hard to get some things made for each of your dolls while I am getting through the convalescent stage. I hope it won't be too long, of course. I just wish I could get out of here. My right foot is not too far from being healed, but the left looks terrible yet. Your old Gammy just isn't much use anymore. Well, be a good little girl and help Mommy and Pap all you can. Lots of love and kisses to all, as ever your loving "Gam." Here is a quarter for being good.

Love, Gammy

I hid in a closet for weeks after my grandmother passed away. I was no longer able to sing my favorite songs, even to Princess.

BLIND PONY

Four summers had come and gone since I arrived on the farm. When the colors of autumn were at their fullest, and the sun rose later in the sky, just before dawn, Princess went into labor unexpectedly, so there was no vet to attend to her. I was there to comfort her and help coax the little filly into the world. Being the first person, she laid eyes on bonded me to the pony. I watched as the newborn discovered she could stand on her wobbly legs and instinctively nuzzle in to find her mother's milk. That morning, my life found a new purpose, something to keep me going— to love my new pony.

Her brown coat had a pale-white cast to it, reminding me of the morning mist, so I named her Misty. Using a wood burner, I carved a little sign with her name to hang above the stable.

The fall after Misty was born, I turned nine. I was out in the fields rolling bales of hay down Gobbler's Knob for loading onto a wagon to go back to the farm. It was a sweltering hot and humid day, and my grandfather demanded we work quickly as a rainstorm was brewing beyond the hills in the distance.

Rolling bales down to the wagon, I spotted three men riding up the hill in my direction. It was unusual to see riders I didn't know on Gobbler's Knob, so the three men made me curious. As they galloped closer, there was something vaguely familiar about the man on the white horse. Though I couldn't be sure, I thought it might be my father.

I hadn't seen my father since a failed attempt at visitation after our parents' divorce sent him screeching down Clever Road at 100 mph to drop off three of my siblings and me because our oldest sister didn't want to visit him on his birthday.

The men galloped up the hill to where I was standing. The man on the white horse wore a crisp white cowboy shirt and a white cowboy hat. I stood in the field mesmerized as he rode right up to me with his posse and said, "Girl, what's your name?"

"Pam," I said as butterflies somersaulted in my stomach. "I'm Pam."

"No, your name is Sam. You are Sam, and don't you forget it!"

Before I could take it all in, JD rode up, on his horse, Texas Rose, with a pitchfork in hand. JD stabbed Wild Bill in the chest, telling him, "Get the hell off my property, you son of a bitch, or I'll set the law on you."

When my father's blood seeped through the crisp white cowboy shirt, I chose not to look away. At least for a fleeting moment, I knew what it felt like to stand up to Jeremiah Davis Deemer.

5

RETURN TO SENDER

The dramatic encounter on Gobblers Knob between my grandfather and father made me romanticize Wild Bill. Seeing him unafraid of my grandfather elevated him to superhero status in my naïve and impressionable mind. I even fantasized about stabbing my grandfather in the chest the way he had stabbed my father. And I believed Wild Bill would come back for me.

Two winters passed since Misty was born. When the first buds appeared on the naked trees, it was time to break her in. It took a lot of perseverance as I worked each day to get the high-spirited pony to wear the harness and saddle. She bucked me off several times, but it made me appreciate her feisty spirit even more. She was teaching me a valuable lesson about life.

Before long, I showcased her obedience as we galloped up over the field, and by summer, I had a steed equal to those of my sisters. Graceful and lean, she was stronger and faster than any of their horses or ponies, and we reached the top of Gobbler's Knob before everyone else.

As the summer days stretched longer and we were harvesting the last of the peaches, nectarines, and root vegetables, my grandfather announced, "You won't be riding Misty anymore. That's your younger sister's pony now. She's too big for Dynamite, and you're too big for Misty."

Over the years that followed, I watched my younger sister grow from the Shetland pony, Dynamite, to Misty and then to a horse named Belle, while I remained stuck in time with the blind pony, Princess. There was nothing small, white, clean, or bright about me.

By ten years old, I knew what it meant to hate. The disgust I harbored in my heart for my grandfather was a load I would be burdened with until I could get free of JD Deemer's hold over me. I needed to stay strong.

Copy and Kissy helped me hang on to the belief that someone out there would save me. Although it was like dropping a penny into the dark abyss of a wishing well, hoping a wish would come true even though it felt futile, I couldn't give up on believing the day would come when the truth would set me free.

Every year at the start of school, I thought about going to the school nurse or a counselor and telling them everything. What kept me from doing so was fear my grandfather and mother would deny it, and they would lock me up for being crazy. I didn't dare speak out about any of it.

I did, however, make a few attempts at drawing attention to myself, hoping perhaps someone would look closer and discover the nasty truth.

In fourth grade, I pretended I couldn't hear during a routine ear examination at school. The technician turned up the tones so loud I thought my eardrum might burst, but I remained stoic and didn't flinch. Referred to a specialist in downtown Pittsburgh for further evaluation, they quickly ascertained I was faking. But no one seemed concerned over why I might be pretending to be deaf.

Mom was angry; she had taken a day off work, but I relished the time we had alone in the car. I fantasized we were going to do something special together. The entire car ride I wanted to bring up what was pressing on my mind, but I couldn't bring myself to tell her how much Pap was hurting me. There was an impenetrable wall between us. She couldn't hear what I couldn't say.

By the time I was eleven years old, I had grown tired of pretending I was living an ordinary life. There was nothing normal about it. I resented that the one thing I wanted from my mother, her protection from my grandfather, was something unattainable.

It made me not want anything from her. I hated getting gifts from her so much I would sneak into her closet where she hid the wrapped presents and delicately unwrap each gift labeled "Pammy" so I could see what she was giving me. With very little in my life I could control over, I wanted to withhold all of my emotions. I never wanted to be surprised and allow my pure feelings to show. In my heart, I knew my mother loved me, but sometimes I felt she would only love me if I kept the dirty secret we shared quiet.

After dinner, burning trash was a chore rotated between two of my sisters and me. I hated the smell of rotting food and the odor of burning sanitary napkins so much that I would gladly trade even the most physical chores such as slopping the hogs or shoveling snow to dodge this ritual. Even when it was freezing outside, the girl on trash duty would have to wait until there was nothing but glowing embers to ensure a stray spark wouldn't start a fire. However, during Christmas or birthdays, I was first in line to volunteer for trash duty as I knew the plume would be colorful. Also, paper burns quickly, leaving me to seize the opportunity to sneak around the house, peering into the windows to spy on my family. I studied their faces, their laughter, and their body language. What was it about me that was so different?

Before I turned twelve, my mother forced me to attend Bible school to prepare to get baptized. I never understood why I had to go to school to get baptized since my sisters never went before we left Phoenix so many years ago. I attended Bible school with Pastor Morford, an uninspiring man who made me despise everything about religion. I asked his advice, "How can I follow the Ten Commandments if one is to honor your father and mother when since as long as I can remember my mother taught me to only refer to my father as 'It?' Does that sound as though I am honoring my father to you?"

It seemed like an innocent enough question to ask, but in short order, Pastor Morford made a house visit to meet with my mother. I pressed my ear against the door leading into the living room from the hallway of the black stairwell so I could hear their conversation. He told her I was incorrigible and was upsetting some other kids in the Bible class. My mother told him she would speak to me, but she feared I had inherited the worst qualities of my father.

I heard every hurtful word she uttered about me except the truth. Whatever bad attributes I might have inherited from my father didn't compare to the fact I inherited a pedophile for a grandfather. My self-preservation instincts kicked in, and I kept my head down until my baptism was over. I couldn't expect Pastor Morford to understand that no amount of water could wash away the sins perpetrated against me.

My mother began sending me to visit with my Uncle Jim, who lived in Long Beach, California. He was now a Presbyterian minister but found his calling running a group called Inner-city Ministries, which took disadvantaged youth for nine-day backpack trips up in the High Sierras. The age requirement was sixteen, but being Jim's niece, I could attend the summer even though I wasn't yet twelve.

My entire family had been visiting Uncle Jim and his family in Long Beach for several years. We could fly to California for free because of Mom's job at the airlines. Uncle Jim treated us to many fun experiences from Disneyland to body surfing at Huntington Beach, where we made bonfires and roasted marshmallows. I was keen on the chance to hike in the mountains because it would mean getting away from my grandfather for an extended period. I would have stayed for the entire summer if it were possible.

I fell in love with the mountains where I felt unencumbered by my daily routine of dodging my grandfather and doing chores on the farm. The fresh air was like breathing in a clean slate each day, and Uncle Jim's daily sermons were uplifting and made me feel I could rise above the sorrow. I admired how he could touch so many young souls with troubled backgrounds. He had a way of connecting with kids; they felt comfortable enough to open up and share their experiences about everything from trouble at home to run-ins with the law. I listened, though I never felt safe enough around these older kids to share my inner turmoil. But Uncle Jim was intuitive enough to see through me, and he sensed I was holding back.

Each night in the mountains, he and I talked for hours as we tended the smoldering campfire, watching the tiniest of embers hang on, glimmering with light, and refusing to stop burning and shining. It gave me hope I, too, could hang on. We talked about my father and mother, how they got together, how much they loved each other, and what drove them apart. Speaking about the past with Uncle Jim was like turning a light on in a dark cavern.

On the second consecutive summer trip to the mountains with Uncle Jim, he told me how he saw Pap steal the tires from a man's truck and swindle people out of money. I sensed he told me these stories so I would know it was okay to talk about Pap in a less than favorable light. I suspected he knew I was keeping a dark secret about my grandfather that was eating me alive, but I felt too vulnerable and afraid to open up to anyone, even Uncle Jim.

Desperate to trust someone, I was scared that if I opened up, Uncle Jim would persuade me to bring it into the "circle of sharing" in front of two dozen other kids relaying their childhood traumas. I might be so humiliated and embarrassed; I'd jump off a cliff. I didn't want to die, but I wanted to show the world how far the abuse had pushed me. I often stood on the side of a steep ravine contemplating how easy it would be to step off. My problems would be over by making a final statement without saying a word. It seemed so much easier.

As much as I thought I kept my feelings hidden, I always felt Uncle Jim could see right through to my soul.

Weather in the High Sierras could be unpredictable. One

morning I woke up to snowflakes tickling my nose. Uncle Jim and the counselors rallied all the campers to pack up and get on the trail. While rolling up my sleeping bag, I felt a pang in my side, and I doubled over in pain. It felt as though I was being gutted like a fish. I was unprepared to become a woman that day and had no choice but to allow the blood to soak through my clothing as I walked on the trail alone, the snow covering the tracks behind me. I realized I was no longer a little girl, and there was no going back.

After returning from the backpacking trip, I felt braver and had a renewed sense of purpose and direction. But I still wasn't strong enough to stand up to my grandfather, and it wasn't long before his abusive behavior sent me running up over the hill, as it had so many times before, and into the woods seeking the solace of Copy and Kissy in our secret hiding place. Out of breath, I was about to collapse onto the fallen tree trunk but stopped when I saw a tuft of wool stuck in the barbed wire. I reached for the remnant, pricking my finger on the fence. Startled, I looked up to see the adjacent field littered with the corpses of dead sheep. Hungry wolves must have slaughtered them, leaving nothing but mounds of bloodied white wool strewn about the cold, hard ground of the impending winter.

I climbed into the fallen tree for shelter. The woods smelled of blood mixed with the rain, and moss, as red puddles formed in the field beyond the barbed-wire fence. I tried to summon Copy and Kissy, but they couldn't hear me through the now pelting rain.

I was at a tipping point. Either I had to bond with my mother and be honest about the pain I was going through—and she would support and love me—or I would need to run away. If things stayed the same, I knew I might be heading down a dark path leading nowhere, or might go mad or become a juvenile delinquent. If running away meant I could be proud to be alive and forge on, wherever that road might lead me, I knew the choice was at hand.

That year in school, we had sex education in health class.

What would happen if my grandfather were to corner me when it was my time of the month? Or worse, got me pregnant?

My mother was sorting laundry in the hallway leading to the sun parlor. I attempted to join in sorting the clothes, but it may have been easy to read that I had greater things on my mind, which my mother had a penchant for avoiding. Her guard immediately went up, and I could feel it.

"In health class yesterday, the teacher was talking to us about becoming a woman. And how, when this time happens in your life, you need to get more exercise and stuff like that—you know, because of your metabolism changes."

She glared at me and said, "I'll tell you what exercise is. You try sorting out ten filthy stacks of laundry and then lugging them up and down those cellar steps. That's exercise. So here—have at it." She kicked the laundry in the air, grabbed her purse storming out of the house, and got into her car. She took off, backward, down the red rock driveway as the tires spun, sputtering stones in the air.

I stomped up the black stairwell to her room, rifled through her lingerie drawer for the cigarettes I knew she kept hidden there. I spotted a piece of paper with an address in Phoenix, Arizona, and suspected it might be my father's, so I stuffed it in my pocket and snuck a few extra cigarettes.

Behind the bushes in the back of the house, I sucked a cigarette down to the filter. I dragged harder and harder on each puff, intending to make myself feel dizzy. I realized my painful choice was clear. All I had was my will and a determination to fight or succumb to being destroyed.

I went back inside to lug the piles of laundry down to the washing machine in the cellar. The basement was dark and dank. Although we now had gas heating, the old coal furnace remained along with the black soot, as did the old ice chest gifted to our family by a gentleman who boarded horses at our stables and owned a bakery up on Steubenville Pike.

Each week, as a gesture of kindness to my grandparents who had taken in six extra mouths to feed, he dropped off week-old baked goods deemed too stale to sell, and sometimes we girls would lift the lid of the ice chest, allowing a billowing cloud to blow out, smelling like January. When my grandmother was alive, she could hear the freezer lid close with a thunk from the living room above the basement and knew when one of us girls was getting at those pastries. Knowing Gammy could detect our sneaking into the freezer had been a deterrent.

Unaware my mother, too, could recognize the distinctive thunk, one Saturday, on tiptoes, I tried my best to sneak a pastry out of the freezer chest. As I exited through the cellar door to the yard with a frozen pastry shoved up under my shirt, Mom ran after me and grabbed me by my hair, twirling me around until the cake fell to the ground, and then spanked me as hard as she could in front of all the boarders.

Imagine, a week-old pastry causing such a fuss. Now, even though there was no one around to catch me, I had no desire for the freezer-burned delicacies; there was no room left for sweetness in me. Everyone around me was insane, and I wanted to retreat from them all.

There were some old wooden doors my grandfather allowed Lenny The Junkman to store in the rafters of the barn. Lenny lived in a small shack on the outskirts of our land, collecting junk for a living, hence his moniker. I was never sure what the connection was between him and my grandfather, but for years JD had allowed him to store odds and ends in the barn and the springhouse. I used the old wooden doors to make a secret room off the side of the hayloft, leaning them up against a beam and creating a small alcove behind. I brought pillows and old blankets and trinkets up there so I could hang out without being seen and smoke cigarettes in the hideout.

One evening, my sister and her boyfriend came up to my hangout room with a bottle of Mateus wine to share, but without telling me, they laced it with LSD.

I experienced my first acid trip before I outgrew my training bra. A kaleidoscope of colors spun inside my head, and the patterns, colors, thoughts, and ideas shifted and changed and rearranged each time I blinked. I hallucinated I could fly and almost jumped out of the hayloft window to get away from a rat wearing a top hat and carrying a white cane who chased me around the barn while my sister and her boyfriend disappeared, laughing, up over the hills.

Beyond terrified, I gathered whatever presence of mind I could summon, which told me the only safe place was under the covers of my bed. All I needed to do was find my way there without being caught by my grandfather. If I were to encounter the old man in this drug-induced state, there was no telling what might happen. My senses were acutely aware of every mouse in the house, every cricket outside, and the occasional owl's hoot. I could listen in on every conversation in each car as it drove past the briar bush on Clever Road. I heard each overripe berry drop and splat on the side of the road where my cousin, Donny, got hit by a car and died years before when I was two-years-old. I cursed Clever Road.

Safely ensconced in my bedroom, I burrowed under the covers as I heard my mother's footsteps coming up the stairwell. I lay still, holding my breath as she opened the door to see if I was in the room. Satisfied I was in bed, she closed the door behind her. I slowly let go of my breath in short bursts, straining to not gasp as the sheer curtains, blowing in the breeze of the open window, swirled around as if they might engulf and strangle me.

By approximately 9 p.m., I was peaking from the acid. Raw emotions and heightened senses pierced my skull, attacking every brain cell at once. By the time I started to come down at around 1 a.m., my mind was sharp, and I could imagine the vastest concepts with ease. I discovered a way to cope and gain perspective. I could tap into the Universe and see my destiny existing beyond the black hole. There was another galaxy of dreams ahead in the world. Maybe there was hope.

At about 4 a.m., I carted my bell-bottoms down to the cellar and washed the mud off before throwing them in the dryer so they would look fresh for school the next day. And as quiet as a mouse, I helped myself to not one, but two-week-old frozen pastries before going back to bed, hoping for a few hours of sleep before the alarm clock went off.

Over the next month, I gathered the courage and began writing to the mysterious address in Phoenix I presumed was my father's almost every other day. I would imagine what he thought when he read my notes.

One by one, the post office sent the letters back stamped RETURN TO SENDER. I kept writing to him because I found it cathartic, if only while putting pen to paper. Knowing he was out there somewhere, and one day we'd reunite, gave me the courage and fortitude to survive another day. By the time I'd received twenty or more letters back, I began to wonder if I had the wrong address. What explanation was there, except the one I dreaded most: that Wild Bill didn't want to hear from his long-lost daughter, Sam.

All I had to cling to were vague memories conjured up by old, black and white photographs of my sisters and me in our crinoline dresses mugging for the camera in front of his parent's house in McKees Rocks. Dad coaxed us to pretend we were drinking beers by posing us with empty 40s clutched in our tiny, dirty hands.

But in my bones, I knew it was only a matter of time before Wild Bill would send for me. I had to spend every day preparing to leave the farm forever. I would never give up hope.

6

OLD COINS

My grandfather's bedroom smelled of the old port he guzzled each night, horse manure, and chewing tobacco, which wafted into the sun parlor each time he opened his bedroom door. I had never dared to enter his room, but I remembered the tin filled with rare coins my grandmother shared with me to the delight of my overactive imagination. Now, those coins were going to come to my rescue and buy my ticket out of this place.

I already knew how to feel as though I was invisible when allowing my grandfather to behave toward me the way he did when he thought no one was watching. Having honed my invisibility powers, I felt brave enough to enter his room to search for those coins Gammy shared with me.

His liquor cabinet was behind a glass door affixed to the top of an old drop-down desk where he kept receipts, bills, and his checkbook. I pulled the wooden chair beneath the desk to the closet, where I had seen Gammy store the coins. Stepping up on tiptoes, I peered inside the top shelf. I reached toward the back, and my hand made contact with the tin can as my sweaty fingers grasped it, sparking memories of Gammy I had long since pushed aside.

I remembered the story of one coin in particular, and I became absorbed in looking for that specific coin when I heard the screen door slam shut on the front porch. Pap's heavy cowboy boots vibrated through the floorboards, causing the teacups in the dining room china closet to rattle. Every fiber in my being alerted me to abort the mission, but my body felt as frozen as the first time I'd encountered Tiger.

Tossing some of the coins back into the tin, I shoved it on to the shelf and, teetering backward, managed to climb off the chair and replace it at the desk, though askew. There were two entrances to Pap's bedroom, one door off the sun parlor and the other into the hallway of the black stairwell. Since he always entered his room from the sun parlor, I tiptoed as light-footed as possible for the door to the staircase, but as his footsteps came closer, I realized I couldn't make it out in time and ducked under the bed to hide. Lying as still as possible, I listened to his footsteps enter and then stop. I had forgotten to close the closet door. He closed it. I heard him open the liquor cabinet and guzzle some port straight from the bottle. He then shoved the chair under the desk. I worried he might have noticed it was at an angle. My heart raced in my chest as he sat down on the side of the bed and swung his legs up onto it with his boots still on.

My grandmother died about five years ago, and all that remained of her presence were dusty perfume bottles on her dresser and renderings of Pinky and Blue Boy she had painted by number, propped against the wall on top of the mantel. Surrounded by cobwebs, dust, and dirty socks, the stench beneath the bed sickened me, but the fear of being caught gave me the fortitude to lie straight as a board and remain calm and invisible in the presence of evil.

"Supper's here! I brought Kentucky Fried Chicken. Come and get it!"

Pap hoisted himself upright. I pictured him rubbing his balding dome as he pushed himself off the bed, took another swig of the port, and departed, closing the door behind him. I remained motionless for a few minutes before wriggling out from beneath the bed, shuddering to think of what might have happened if he'd caught me in his room. I was still shaking as I exited the door leading to the black stairwell, praying I didn't encounter anyone on the other side. Luckily, the family had all gathered around the kitchen table and were already digging into the buckets of chicken. Since Gammy passed away, Pap dispensed with the formality of a dinner prayer, so it was every girl for herself.

I bounded into the kitchen. "Oh great, Kentucky Fried Chicken!"

"Where have you been, Pammy?" my mother asked. "You're covered in dirt. Go clean yourself up."

As everyone was digging into buckets of chicken, I went to the bathroom, glad to have this quiet moment to gather myself. Then I realized: Mom must have bought Kentucky Fried Chicken because today was payday. With the family distracted, I clicked open her purse that she hung on the hallway doorknob and slipped a bill from the crisp twenties that stuffed her wallet. I bolted up to my room, climbed on my bed, and hopped up onto my tall dresser to shove the twenty-dollar bill into the ceiling lamp for safekeeping.

The next day I skipped school and hitchhiked to downtown Pittsburgh to see if I could pawn a few of the coins. It was the only way to know how much they were worth. There was no way I was about to enter my grandfather's room again if I didn't have to.

The pawn shops were seedy places, and I was an obvious target for getting picked up by a truant officer. I wandered in and out of a few of them until I came upon one where the old man behind the counter reminded me of Lenny the Junk Man.

"What can I do for you, young lady?" the pawnbroker asked.

"Well, you can give me top dollar for these coins my grandmother gave me before she passed. I know they're worth a lot more than you can probably pay me, but I am in dire need of money."

"Oh, are you getting ready to set sail on some adventure?"

"If only," I said, knowing full well I best keep things close to my vest. "My grandfather is ill. I need to get him some help." I said it with conviction, as those words could not be more real.

"Maybe you should come back with your mother or father? It

might be best to make a transaction such as this with—"

I cut him off. "My mother is dead, and I have no father. I need this money. Can you please help me? I'm in a real jam. And besides, you're the only friendly face I feel I can trust in this corridor of broken dreams," I blurted out, trying to sound grown-up and philosophical.

"How poetic you are. I never thought my store was in a corridor, much less one of broken dreams," the pawnbroker said with a chuckle. "How much money is it you need?"

As he was scrutinizing the coins with a magnifying glass, he tried to maintain a poker face. But I could tell he knew they were valuable.

"Two hundred dollars," I said with conviction.

"Will you take one hundred and twenty?" he asked, arching up one eyebrow.

I felt like I was in a scene from Oliver Twist and had come face to face with Fagin. I knew the amount was less than they were worth, but I was desperate to get out of there, so I agreed. When he turned to get the money, I artfully snatched back one coin.

He counted out the bills, and before he noticed there was one less coin, I took off down the street, happy with my haul. Now I knew these coins were worth money, just as my Gammy had told me they were.

I bought a donut from a small bakery, and I was enjoying it while strolling down the sidewalk when I encountered a man dressed in a burgundy jacket with skinny lapels and tight black pants, smoking a Salem cigarette outside of a shoe store.

"Hey, pretty lady. It looks like you could use some new shoes."

My white Keds were a yellowish-brown, with frayed laces. I looked down at my feet with embarrassment.

"Come on in and let me show you some of our new styles.

A beautiful woman like you deserves to have the best," he said as he flicked his cigarette into the gutter.

From floor to ceiling, high-heeled shoes stood at attention, awaiting a prospective Cinderella. A few women were strutting around checking themselves out in the mirrors, and the cash register was ringing up sales for other girls. I took in their scanty outfits, leopard prints, and paisley-patterned tops, and became self-conscious about my appearance. Babydoll tops were all the rage, so I'd found a maternity top among the Salvation Army clothes our aunt gave us and cut it high enough to show a bit of my midriff. I thought it looked stylish flared out at the bottom. But illuminated by the store's harsh fluorescent lights, it was apparent the edges were unhemmed and ragged.

"I will bring out a few pairs for you to try on, okay? What's your favorite color?"

"Black, I guess." But then I thought to myself; black is for Sunday school shoes. Glancing around, I saw a girl wearing a bright pink sequin top and blurted out, "Do you have anything colorful, like maybe pink??"

"You read my mind! I have the perfect shoe. What size are you?"

"Size seven, I think."

It was a while since I had purchased a new pair of shoes. My shoes were hand-me-downs from my sisters, already broken in and stretched to fit the foot of the previous owner.

The shoe salesman measured my foot and said, "You are precisely a size 7."

He disappeared into the back and emerged with an oversized shoebox. Lifting off the top, he uncovered a pair of pink, suede, six-inch platform shoes.

"Try them on."

I stepped out of my Keds, exposing my dirty socks. I felt

my face go red with embarrassment, but slipped my feet into the shoes and stood tall to take in my statuesque figure in the full-length mirror. With the extra six inches, I felt like a fashion model. The pink platforms even made my old jeans and maternity top look chic.

"How much are they?"

"You can't put a price on elegance. And you can't put a price on how far these shoes can take you. Remember what those ruby slippers did for Dorothy? Well, these shoes will get you a lot further than Oz."

The first grown-up decision I made in my life was paying $18.95 for those pink platform shoes. I clutched the bag close to my chest on the bus ride home, peeking inside along the way, giggling with excitement about how far I could go in these shoes. I got off the bus in Kennedy Township and hitchhiked just past the farm to sneak in a back way and avoid my grandfather's detection.

Once inside the house, I ran to my bedroom to hide the shoes behind some clothes in my closet. I thought the box would be the perfect place to store the letters I received "return to sender" from my father. Every day I waited for the postman to arrive so I could dart down the hill to the mailbox, hoping for a letter from Wild Bill. By now, there were dozens of letters marked "return to sender." I sat on the side of my bed and began to read through them.

When high school began, I felt conflicted. Part of me already felt gone, but another part of me secretly held on to the hope my life could have a special meaning. I was my mother's special daughter. Her protector, who could keep the awful things she experienced away from her. Together, we would defeat the evil that haunted us both.

To distract myself, I tried out for cheerleading. My mother seemed genuinely impressed at my dedication and warmed up to me, as cheerleading tryouts became something we bonded over, and I worked hard to master the moves. She proudly watched me practice and tried to give me pointers, which became what I lived for every day.

There were now only two children left in the house, my younger sister and me; maybe with less distraction, Mom could show me the motherly love missing in our relationship for so many years.

Exuberant doesn't begin to describe how I felt when my name was announced as making it onto the squad, even though it was only as an "alternate." Being an alternate meant I got to dress up for the games in my uniform and pass out flyers, but cheering in front of the crowd was contingent on one of the other girls being out sick. The first time I got to cheer, I was so excited to impress Mom. I could tell she was proud of me.

When Tammy, the team captain's family, announced they were moving out of town, the coach chose me out of the three alternates to step up as a permanent member of the squad. I couldn't wait to tell Mom.

She came home earlier than expected from work and walked into the sun parlor to discover Pap mounted on top of me with his pants around his ankles. I was crying and trying to get him off me. Tears were streaming down my face, but she walked right past us and ran up the stairwell to her room. Tobacco juice dribbled down his chin right into my mouth as my grandfather hoisted himself off me.

He said, "Now see what you've done?"

Repulsed, I grabbed my clothes, ran up the hill, and headed for the old tree trunk—Copy and Kissy's former home. As I ran, I saw my mother's stunned face as she walked right by me. Finally, she couldn't pretend to be blind to it anymore because she caught him in the act.

How could I even tell Mom about the good news I'd just

received about getting a regular spot on the cheerleading squad? We should have been going out for an ice cream cone at Dairy Queen, but I was running through the thicket, scratching up my bare legs and wishing I had never been born.

When we first came back to live at the farm, I was vulnerable and small. Like any smart pedophile, Pap chose the most natural target he could manipulate and gain control over. That target was me, and, at one time, had been my mother. I think that's why she and I were always at odds; I reminded her of her vulnerability.

I had always been looking for a secret place to hide. My grandmother once found me hiding in a crawl space beneath the black stairwell in a stack of old clothes.

"Pammy," she said, "Dark places like this are only for the cat to have her litter of kittens. Come on out of there."

I wanted to curl up into a ball and hide, black it all out. I didn't want anyone to see me. But my grandmother had been right. My mother didn't react to what she witnessed, and it made me realize it was time to stop hiding.

I was out of breath and trembling when I reached the familiar tree trunk crossing over the barbed wire fence. Copy and Kissy were long gone. Every remnant of the bloodied wool disappeared—buried in leaves, carried off by other animals, or dispersed by the wind. There was nothing left for me here, but I had nowhere to go.

The fourteen-year-old girl in me ached to dress up in the cheerleader outfit and cheer on the team, but jumping for joy was reserved for happy, well-adjusted teenagers. The abuse had finally defeated me.

The next few days were agony as my mother and I stopped talking and avoided eye contact. My grandfather moved out to the barn and refused to come into the house even for supper.

The coach called to tell me Tammy's family had decided not to move after all. But, since they had already given me her spot, it was up to me whether I wanted to give it back. I had lost my enthusiasm for being a cheerleader. Cheerleading had become the only connection I shared with Mom. Without her encouragement, I was no longer interested and decided to quit the squad.

I was walking up the stone pathway to the house after school when I heard the phone ringing off the hook. Bounding up the front porch, I swung open the screen door and dove for the receiver. Out of breath, I picked it up and said, "Hello, this is Pam speaking."

The voice on the other end of the phone said, "Sam, is that you? You ever been to Powder River? It's a mile wide, an inch deep. It's too thick to drink and too thin to chew. How 'bout it? You wanna come? Cause that's what I been hearing."

It was my dad, Wild Bill.

"Now, listen here... Write this number down. You call that number and tell my guy Mickey when you are coming, and he'll let you know where to go."

"Got it," I said, scribbling the number down, figuring one of my letters had gotten through to him at last. I was choking back tears of sorrow and joy wrapped together in one big knot in my throat and thinking, "I don't know where Powder River is, but it sure sounds better than here."

"Wait 'til I tell Cash my girl, Sam, is coming to town. You're doin' a brave thing. Like my buddy John Wayne always says, 'Courage is being scared to death and saddling up anyway.'"

A few days later, at dawn, I went out to the stable to see Princess. These days I kept as far away from the barn and my grandfather as possible. But faced with the reality of leaving the farm forever, I realized I would never see Princess again. I sang her "Edelweiss" for the last time as I pressed her soft nose against my face to dry my tears and said goodbye.

7

PINK PLATFORM SHOES

Bumping my way through the throng of unfamiliar faces at the Greater International Pittsburgh airport, I didn't feel like I was running away; I was on my way.

Passing by strangers, I tried to project confidence. I wanted to let go of the image of being a frightened, abused, fourteen-year-old teenage girl who dropped out of cheerleading. I was leaving my past behind to live with my father, my protector, my confidant, my savior.

My clothing style was unique; I was going for a Sgt. Pepper vibe, donning a high school band uniform jacket with a piece of tulle sewn around the bottom like a ballerina skirt that hung over my bell-bottom jeans. As I strolled past the blurred faces of fellow travelers, my long, silky, blonde hair flowed behind me as if in slow motion. I imagined they thought I was a model, like Cybill Shepherd.

Then I tripped and dropped my purse, allowing its contents to ping-pong across the polished cement floor, uncaring feet kicking its treasures out of reach. On hands and knees, I scrambled to recover as many tiny bits and pieces as I could of the life I was leaving behind.

The remnants of a charred twenty-dollar bill wafted through space. I remembered the day I stole it from my mother's wallet and hid it in the ceiling light. The heat from the bulb burned a good portion of the bill, now rendering it useless tender. I kept the frayed piece to remind myself how lucky I was I didn't burn the house down. When I dove and snatched it mid-flight, the edges crumbled further in my hand, underscoring how little I had left on which to cling.

BLIND PONY

My third-grade picture, lucky rabbit's foot, Bonne Bell lip-gloss and letters more precious than friendship—were all strewn across the airport lobby. One letter to my dad postmarked "return to sender" remained stuck between the pages of a journal of poems. A man handed me my wallet, which had about eighty dollars in it and a few of the rare coins stolen from the tin on my grandfather's shelf.

Dark ghosts and gray spirits shadowboxed around me as I proceeded toward the gate.

When the plane took off, it was pouring rain. Carole King's "So Far Away" came through the headphones on the in-flight radio, while my tears kept rhythm with the rain. Exhausted from the entire ordeal, I fell asleep before they turned the seatbelt sign off, and when I awoke, I found myself bumped over in Dallas for two hours until the next plane would take off for Phoenix.

Since my mom worked for the airlines and we could fly for free, I'd become accustomed to flying to cities only to arrive and take the first flight home. Flying was a past-time, the way one would hang out at a mall. So, though being stranded in Dallas was nothing new, the delay gave me time to think about the fact I was running away from home. There was still time to turn around and go back.

My legs felt strangely numb, and I couldn't lift my feet; then I remembered I was wearing a ridiculous pair of hot pink, six-inch platforms weighing almost as much as I did. The guy who sold me the shoes promised they would take me far, and I believed him, thinking somehow these magical shoes would transform me into the grown-up I needed to become. All the pink platforms had done was make me ache for the child I was leaving behind. It was beginning to dawn on me—there was no going back.

I pulled out the letter I'd sent to my father three months prior, and as I read the words, I wondered why I sounded so chipper. Did I think my father's love would be contingent on my being a happy and well-adjusted teenager? How should I act around a man I didn't know, and who knew very little about me? Should I tell him what I had been through these past years, or was it better to keep the secret hidden? Did he already know? I needed something to chew on while contemplating my future and bought a bag of black licorice at the airport store. I had a lot to consider. I felt frightened, leaving the only life I had ever known and fearful of what my future held.

An emotion surfaced with fury, causing me to chomp harder and harder on the licorice to the point I thought my jawbone might crack. It wasn't fair that my only option to escape the grasp of the warped hands of the man I despised was to run away.

When they announced it was time to board the flight to Phoenix, it was hard to shake off the feeling this was a colossal mistake, but it was too late. The plane door closed, and all I could do now was wait for another door to open.

Wobbling down the jetway at Sky Harbor airport, I put one platformed foot in front of the other, maintaining my balance as I tried to keep my expectations in check.

The rendezvous point we'd set up was at my dad's local watering hole, Dave's Tavern. Driving through the city streets, it all felt vaguely familiar, conjuring visions of my life before the nightmare of living with my grandfather began. I imagined a little girl in a pale blue nightgown running barefoot down the street with rose petals blowing behind her in the hot desert air, thorns pricking her tender skin.

I hadn't seen my father since I was nine years old, the day my grandfather stabbed him in the chest with a pitchfork. The scene had replayed in my mind so many times it had grown to epic proportions. Wild Bill had become almost Christ-like, dying on the cross to absolve all sins. The blood soaked his white cowboy shirt and splattered against the smooth coat of the white stallion as he galloped off, assuring me he would be back to seek revenge against

JD Deemer. But some sins you can't absolve or wash away. Or "return to sender."

I wondered if I should ask my father why he returned all the letters I wrote. Settling back, I closed my eyes and decided I wouldn't dwell on anything from the past. I went into such a deep state of meditation that the cabbie's voice startled me.

"Okay, this is the place. That will be five bucks."

I paid the fare and emerged from the cab, teetering even more as the pink platforms negotiated their way across the uneven parking lot. I imagined Misty standing up for the first time on her new legs right after she was born, and I found the courage to hold my head high. My bag was placed firmly on my shoulder; I clutched the small carry-on, pausing for a moment, wondering if the cabbie had dropped me off at the right place. Dave's was not where I pictured the reunion with my father would take place. I knew it was his local watering hole, but this was a hole in the wall, a dive joint. I swung the door open.

It took a moment to adjust my vision to the dimly lit bar. At 7 p.m., the sun had still not set, so Dave's was as dark as the old cellar and as cold as the freezer chest full of stale pastries. As my eyes adjusted, I could make out a pool table in the center, surrounded by a few torn-up booths and a bar. A small light illuminated the way to the restrooms, and a payphone hung on the wall near the door.

The old jukebox was playing one of Wild Bill's favorites, Nat King Cole's, "Smile"—so I knew I was in the right place. I paused a moment to listen to the words, blinking back tears. Intuitively, I knew Wild Bill wouldn't want to see Sam crying, so I headed to the phone affixed to the wall, pretending to be chatting up an old friend. My fingers traced graffiti on the walls, phone numbers, and hearts with initials engraved inside. Gathering my emotions, I waited for the song to end.

With my composure in check, I made my entrance and began

walking toward the man hunched over at the bar, who sensed I was staring at him as he swiveled on his barstool just enough for me to glimpse his profile. The next record dropped down on the jukebox, and a Waylon Jennings song played as a layer of cigarette smoke over the bar lifted.

It was him. Wild Bill. My father.

He barked out, "Gimme another V/O water tall, and hey Mickey…" He turned toward me with a twinkle in his eye and a broad smile, and nonchalantly announced, "This here's my girl, Sam."

Mickey said, "What will it be, young lady?"

"How about a Coke?" I replied as the corners of my mouth attempted to squeak out a smile.

My dad laughed and said, "Make it a rum and Coke."

I felt less like a long-lost daughter and more like I was playing a part in a film. Our exchange didn't feel real; it felt oddly scripted. Wild Bill didn't exhibit any affection or show any excitement about our meeting after all these years. He kept his emotions close to the vest as he bragged to all the bar cronies that he had three more blue-eyed beauties just like me. His buddies took me in with skepticism, as though this young girl coming to town might throw things off for Wild Bill, and they seemed protective of him. They were suspicious of me.

Among the men at the bar were the Estrada brothers—Lionel, George, and Carlos—who were lawyers and liked to gamble on the ponies. Wild Bill was their handicapper. They must have had some big winnings that day because Bill seemed in good graces with the Estradas.

They slapped him on the back, saying stuff like, "Wild Bill—there isn't a better handicapper than Wild Bill. Give us another round!"

When the Johnny Cash song "A Boy Named Sue" hit the rotation on the jukebox, Wild Bill launched into a colorful story of how his long-lost daughter, Sam, had inspired the song. He and Johnny had been out drinking and were driving through El Paso, Texas, while out on tour. He recounted the story as if Cash were in the room to corroborate every detail.

"We were both dressed in black cowboy outfits because, you know, I was the one who inspired Johnny to wear all black. And I was telling him about my girls I left behind, but not because I wanted to. It was that good-for-nothing JD Deemer that drove me out of my girls' lives. He put the law on me if I ever came around. But I asked Johnny, I asked him, 'Did I ever tell you about my girl named Sam? The prettiest thing you ever saw. Little blondie, eyes blue as a sapphire jewel. And I got three more like her, blue-eyed, and one, well, two with brown just like mine."

Bill took a moment to take a swig of his whiskey and continued. "Five little girls. Their momma packed 'em up and took 'em back to the farm. I guess she did right."

Lionel Estrada, the older and most sensible of the brothers, intervened. He remained calm while presenting the facts with a soothing sense of reason.

"Now come on, Bill, you taught John Wayne to ride a horse, you convinced Dean not to leave the Rat Pack. You invented the twist-off bottle cap. Not much of a father? Come on."

"I have been on a perilous journey of the heart ever since I left the girls with that son o' bitch JD Deemer."

Now he was addressing me. "But that didn't mean I wasn't thinking of you. I told Johnny I had a girl named Sam, and Johnny, he says, 'That ain't nothin. I got a boy named Sue.'"

After hanging on Wild Bill's every word, the Estradas and a few other cronies at the bar were so quiet it made the rest of the bar patrons also stop talking as if they were waiting for a cataclysmic event to occur. And then in unison, the entire establishment burst into laughter. It seemed they may have heard this story more than once, but it was a revelation to me, and if only for a tiny moment, time stood still, and I wished I could hold on to this feeling forever. I stood up in my pink platform shoes and hugged my father.

Wild Bill yelled out the order, "Give everybody another round!" And then he said, "You sure are a tall one," oblivious to the six-inch pink platform shoes which had brought me so far, just like the salesman said they would.

We clinked glasses, and my dad yelled out, "Hey Angie, this here's Sam, my girl I been telling you about."

Angie was a slim, brown-haired waitress who had been passing out drinks to the tables.

"Well, hello there, Sam. Welcome to Phoenix. You will love it here. Sun shines every day."

She scribbled out an address that would turn out to be my new home—the Tampico Apartments, about two miles from my new school.

"I'm gonna split soon; it's been a long day for me. But you'll be needing this." She handed me the key to the apartment. "Wild Bill's told me a lot about you, and I think we're gonna get along just fine."

I held the cold key in my hand as though it were a rare artifact. We never used keys on the farm. Now I would have something to hang on my lucky rabbit's foot. Although the rum numbed my senses, I grasped what had just transpired. This key meant I would not be staying with my dad. Maybe it was just a temporary thing until Dad could get things set up because my arrival was so unexpected. But over a few more rounds of drinks, Wild Bill opened up about his new family, comprised of a wife fifteen years younger than Dad, his step-son, and my biological half-sister.

My sister was only five years old when her mother, who had been one of his mistresses back in Pennsylvania, passed away from cancer. Dad went to great lengths to return to Pennsylvania to claim his daughter and bring her back to raise her with his new wife. She was ten years younger than me, making it easier for his new wife to accept than a runaway teenager. Dad made it clear I couldn't be part of his new family.

At around 1 a.m., we stumbled out to the parking lot. I was trying to process everything while Dad took a leak beside his car and handed me a crumpled-up bill.

"Here's a C-Note, Sam."

Cautiously unfurling the paper, I discovered a C-Note meant a hundred-dollar bill. I had never seen one before, let alone clutched it in my hands while I wobbled on the uneven pavement in those damn platform shoes. I felt dizzy from the rum but optimistic about my decision to leave the farm and move to Arizona to get to know my father even if it meant being on my own. Mostly, I was glad to have gotten as far away from my grandfather as possible.

Just as I realized I didn't know which direction to go, one of the Estrada brothers yelled out of his car window, "Hey, Sam... Over here. I'll give you a lift down Camelback to the Tampico."

Hopping in, I hoped I wouldn't throw up all over the car. I never drunk so much Coca-Cola in my life, let alone tasted rum. A part of me still believed my mother would come for me. To be honest, I thought I would have a few days in Phoenix, and then there would be some drama with my mother demanding to ship me back to Pennsylvania. I would put up some resistance, but ultimately, I wanted to go home. I clung to the hope that my act of defiance in leaving would be enough to shake things up and make my mother realize she loved me and missed me, and I deserved her protection; I needed my mom.

"This is the place," Carlos said as we pulled up in front of the Tampico Apartments. Still dizzy, I fumbled with the key in the door until it yielded, pulling me with it into the small apartment on the first floor of the two-story building. I set my suitcase down and felt around for a light switch so I could find my way to the bathroom. When I came out, Angie was standing there in a robe, waiting for her turn.

"I'm sorry if I woke you up, Angie."

"No problem, kid. Just need to take a piss. You can sleep in the bed with me, or you can sleep on the couch. But just so you know, I sleep naked. Can't sleep with any clothes on my body."

"I'll... The couch is fine."

There were no blankets, so I fell asleep, shivering with the air conditioning blasting above my head.

The next day, true to his promise, Wild Bill showed up at 8 a.m. to accompany me and my hangover to enroll in tenth grade at Camelback High School. I immediately felt out of place when I showed up the first day at my new school wearing those god-forsaken pink platform shoes. But even in flip-flops, I knew I would never fit in.

The subsequent days and years would prove there was no search party out looking for Pamela Sue Butter. Each passing day my mother didn't reach out to me or call me or show me she cared about my well-being chipped away another little piece of my heart.

Reality sank in. I would need to finish high school as soon as possible, so I could work full time to support myself. Dad fronted Angie my first month's rent, but I had to scramble to find a job fast. So, I went to the principal's office and asked if I could test out of some of my classes. I aced every exam and began taking correspondence courses to graduate early.

Every day after my morning classes, I hitchhiked to the mall to clock in through the employee entrance at JCPenney, where I got a job in the robes and lingerie department. It wasn't long before I discovered I'd inherited more from Wild Bill than just his thin lips and squinty eyes when I smiled. I also possessed an uncanny ability to sell anybody anything—or at least, I could say for sure, robes. If you walked into my department at JCPenney, it didn't matter if you were passing through on the way to another department, I was going to sell you something. I sized my customers up and put myself in their slippers.

"Diamonds and lingerie. Two sure-fire ways to a woman's heart," I would say to the men. "You just need a little something to put the zing back into your relationship," was another line I used to positive effect. I became part salesgirl, part relationship sage, and the robes and lingerie were flying out the door. Even the management seemed to take notice.

Over Christmas break, I took on additional hours and was working late one Saturday night when Wild Bill came sauntering into my department tipsy to pick me up so I wouldn't have to hitchhike home. I had scarcely seen him since he enrolled me in school, except slumped over the bar at Dave's or when he would occasionally drop by the Tampico unannounced on the way home to his new family. He'd beach himself on the sofa while I did my homework, and when he sobered up enough to drive home, he would down a can of beer before saying goodbye. To say it made me happy to see him, drunk and all, is an understatement. Seeing my father anywhere besides Dave's Tavern was akin to spotting a unicorn in the wild.

I asked him to meet me out in front of the store, but he insisted on following me through the employees' exit. On the way out, he stole two poinsettias. He thought it was hilarious to be running out of the JCPenney's with a poinsettia in each hand. Hightailing to the car and dumping the booty in the trunk, spilling dirt everywhere and breaking several of the stems in the process, filled him with adrenaline, and he couldn't stop laughing.

"What the hell, Dad? I get it—you feel you can take two damn poinsettias for no other reason than you feel like it. But it's not cool because I work here, and I need this job. Why the hell did you do that? Do you want to get me fired? Shit, Dad."

With complete disdain, I shifted my eyes downward and furrowed my brow as I slammed the car door shut. I was beginning to understand the highs and lows that came when rolling with Wild Bill Butter.

He launched into his John Wayne impersonation, "Ya been to Powder River? It's a mile wide. It's an inch deep. It's too thick to drink, and it's too thin to chew… Gimme a kiss. No lips. If you're a Butter Girl, you've got no lips."

I was so angry with him, but part of me felt exhilarated by his sheer cockiness. Even under the influence of God knows how many rounds of drinks at Dave's, Wild Bill still had enough charisma to charm away any negative thoughts.

He never taught me to ride a bike, bandaged a skinned knee, or comforted me over bullies teasing me for wearing Salvation Army clothes. But Wild Bill was my dad. And that was enough.

We both erupted into laughter as I wrapped my arms around him, breathing in the distinctive scent belonging only to Dad.

We burst into Dave's, singing a rousing rendition of "White Christmas," flanking the counter with the broken-stemmed poinsettias.

"Mikey… Sam and I thought you needed to get into the Christmas spirit at this place. Isn't that right, Sam?"

"Yes, we did. Is this my cue to jump up on the bar and perform a tap dance to "Jingle Bells?" Though playing along, I still felt angry at him for stealing the poinsettias.

"Do it," he said, egging me on.

We laughed and downed multiple rounds of drinks. When Wild Bill dropped me off at the Tampico Apartments, he leaned over to hug me goodbye and said, "I love you, Sam."

The next day when I clocked in at JCPenney, they asked me to leave. I emptied my locker, which included a lip gloss the same color as the pink slip inside.

8

RUMI TOLD ME

I got a lead on a waitressing job at an Italian restaurant not too far from my school. Because the restaurant served alcohol, and I was only fifteen, Angie let me borrow her ID. The restaurant owner, Joe, had more important things on his mind than checking to see if my hair and eye color matched the ID, and I got the job.

The place felt romantic and familial at the same time, with small tables covered in pink and green checkerboard tablecloths with matching cloth napkins that one might encounter on a picnic in Italy. The smell of homemade bread wafted from the kitchen, mixing with Joe's secret recipes that had been in the family for years. Most of the patrons were regulars, and it didn't take me long to realize the more I recognized them with a friendly greeting like, "Welcome back!" the more tips I earned.

I memorized the menu, recalling orders without even writing them down. The only tricky thing was to remember during working hours, my name was Angie, not Pam... or Sam. When Joe called out my name, and I wouldn't pay him any mind, he became frustrated and would call my name several times in succession, "Angie, Angie," escalating in volume each time, causing heads to turn in search of Angie.

"Yes, sir! What do you need?"

"What I need is for you to answer me when I call your name!"

"Oh, so sorry. I was just concentrating on remembering the orders, and I guess I zoned out."

"What does this mean? You zoned out?" Joe asked in his thick Italian accent. "Are you on drugs or something?"

"Oh, no, of course not, sir. This job means everything to me. I only want to focus on doing a good job for you and the customers, sir. I'm sorry."

Joe threw his hands up in the air and shook his head as he mumbled something in Italian on his way back to the kitchen.

There was a man, a regular, who sat in the same booth in my area every time he came in, who exuded an air of mystery with his long, curly dark hair and beard cut tight to his face but much fuller than just stubble. His strong resemblance to Al Pacino was enhanced when he wore dark aviator sunglasses even indoors.

The best part of going to work was when I saw him seated alone in the corner booth. Though we never spoke beyond the usual banter while I took his order, he always left a sizable tip. I wasn't physically attracted to him, just curious about whether he was a good guy or a bad guy because he almost seemed like a character in a movie.

"So, what will it be tonight?"

"Well, if I'm lucky, I'd like to be having a cocktail with you later this evening, Angie."

"How do you know my name?" I said, sounding paranoid. What if he's a cop like Serpico and he knows I'm a teenage runaway? I glanced around the restaurant for the exit doors.

"Your name badge kind of gives it away. I'm Stuart. Stuart Litvak."

Stuart mistook the look of panic on my face as though I might be insulted; he just hit on me. "I'm sorry, did I come on too strong?" he asked.

"Oh, sorry, no. What will it be, Stuart?"

"I'll just have my usual chicken parm."

"With extra sauce, right?" I smiled to let Stuart know I wasn't offended that he asked me out.

When I set his meal down, the thought of not having to hitchhike home at 10 p.m. made me throw caution to the wind and say, "If you're still up for that cocktail, my shift ends at 10."

At 10 p.m., Stuart's red Camaro pulled into the parking lot. Stuart rolled the window down and said, "Hey, Angie, over here, hop in."

The Camaro smelled of clove, and what looked like research papers cluttered the back seat. We drove along in silence before Stuart said, "I've been waiting a long time to ask you out. I wasn't sure you would say yes."

"What made you sure?"

"When you smiled at me today, I just knew."

He reached over and grabbed my hand in his, moving it in rhythm to the beat of the song on the radio—Ain't Nothin' Like the Real Thing" by Marvin Gaye.

I felt like a grown-up when we pulled up to the swanky bar; it was a lot classier than Dave's, though that wasn't difficult. We sat across from each other in a leather booth. The waiter appeared to take our order, and Stuart ordered a beer.

"I'll have a glass of wine," I said, with as much confidence as my fifteen-year-old self could muster.

The waiter replied, "May I see your license, please?"

Having imbibed cocktails with Dad at Dave's Tavern before this, no one ever asked to see my ID. It was dark in the bar, but I worried the waiter would notice my hair and eye color didn't match the description on Angie's. I immediately started to try to think up a quippy answer like the Clairol ad, *"Does she or doesn't she?"*

Thankfully, the waiter handed me back the ID and asked, "Red or white?"

"Oh, white, please."

Stuart and I sat across from one another for a few awkward moments waiting for our drinks.

"It's been a while since I've been out with a woman who got carded."

"Me too, I mean, it's been a while since anyone carded me."

"So, Angie, why did you say yes?"

The wine arrived, and I took a significant gulp.

"Why wouldn't I say yes? You're a handsome man. Plus, I'm a little shy, so I don't get asked out often."

"Why don't I believe you?"

"Why shouldn't you believe me?" I paused to take another sip of wine. "Maybe it's because you don't trust women. Maybe because you've had your heart broken a dozen times or so… Am I right?"

"You're a cool cat, Angie. I like you."

I could tell Stuart was trying to evade the question. My intuitive nature recognized a pain hidden behind his eyes, which is probably the reason he wore those tinted glasses. I sensed he didn't want to reveal his emotions, even to himself.

"Or maybe you are the one who's shy?" I quipped.

We made quite a pair. Stuart didn't want to talk about himself, and I had to be careful not to reveal too much about myself or risk blowing my cover. Instead, we engaged in a verbal tennis match.

"I'm a psychologist. In my practice, I treat people who might have some difficulties in their lives, including relationship problems, depression, anxiety… Those sorts of things."

"Sounds like you must be a very compassionate person. But what does it mean, you 'treat' them?"

"That's a good question. Therapy is about providing a safe place for patients to open up and talk about things. Sometimes, I try to find a way in by asking them a question about themselves just to get the conversation going. For example, Angie, what are you passionate about in your life?"

"I don't have time to be passionate about anything right now except for finishing school."

"I understand. College can be tough. Especially being around kids who aren't serious and are there for beer pongs."

I almost choked on my wine. While happy Stuart seemed to be

inferring I was a serious student, it should have been easy to read the sheer panic on my face realizing I almost revealed I was still in high school. I changed topics.

"How many patients do you treat in a week?"

"It varies, but I have about twenty patients I see regularly. Besides being a psychologist, I'm a writer, too," he added.

"What are you writing about?"

"As a behavioral psychologist, I am intrigued by the brain. Do you know most people only use twenty percent of their brainpower?"

"I believe it! If you look up dumb blonde in the dictionary, you'll see my picture."

"I doubt that. Where do you go to college, Angie? What are you studying?"

Now, here was another question that had caught me off guard from which I could think of no way to recover. I couldn't believe I hadn't even thought about figuring out a plausible backstory though I'd been Angie for over a month or more. The real Angie didn't go to college. All I could do was summon my Wild Bill instincts and try to redirect the conversation, a trick Dad had imparted to me over drinks at Dave's. He told me most people like to hear themselves talk, so if you ever find yourself in a jam, get the other guy talking about himself.

"My current focus is on art and marketing...but enough about me. Hey, have you heard the Buckingham Nicks album? I adore it. It makes me want to be a songwriter. To express yourself with music is a real gift."

"I haven't heard them, but I am very intrigued by what makes some people become artists. I am conducting a study of the right and left hemispheres of the brain. The left hemisphere deals with art, language, creativity, and instincts. The right side is for memory, attention, reasoning, mathematical ideas. The side of the brain that develops more determines the person you become."

"I guess I'm a lefty. I don't have a rational bone in my body, and I'm terrible at mathematics unless it involves counting cards at the blackjack table."

"Angie, you are one funny chick. I dig you."

I was fifteen and squeaking through high school. The cards I was counting were report cards until I graduated from high school, but I knew enough math to realize Stuart was old enough to be my father.

Stuart never asked my age, assuming I was at least nineteen since I had a drinking-age ID. My disguise allowed me time to embody the character of Angie and begin a relationship with him.

Over the next few weeks, Stuart introduced me to the Mensa Club and his religion, Sufism. We had many conversations about complex topics over peanut butter and jelly sandwiches at the kitchen table in the tiny house he shared with his four Bullmastiffs.

"Have you ever heard of the poet Rumi?" Stuart asked.

"No, I haven't, but I love poetry."

"You may find this hard to believe, but he was a 12th-century poet whose words still resonate today. He wrote about life and death in a way most people feel but can't put into words. I have read this book many times, and each time, I gain new insight into the meanings behind his words." Leafing through the dog-eared book, Stuart added, "I mean, I can open it at random and find a quote that reflects how I am feeling. For example, you asked me how I knew you would say yes when I asked you out a month ago. Rumi told me!" he said with a laugh. "I mean, dig this: *'Whatever lifts the corners of your mouth, trust that...'* See what I mean?"

With that, Stuart put his hands on my shoulders and gave me a gentle kiss. I felt awkward and out of my element, but also safe, which was the thing missing in my teenage life. When I entered his orbit, I never wanted to leave and began spending almost every night at his house.

Stuart often left the book of Rumi's poetry in the bathroom, so I began doing as Stuart did and opened the book to whatever page felt right. Rumi's beautiful words about forgiveness and loss inspired me. I began to realize how much hatred I harbored in my heart for Pamela Sue Butter. She haunted my life. I may not have realized it, but I was running away from myself.

Hundreds of books, along with dog slobber, covered the small living space of Stuart's house. But I discovered besides writing a book and running his psychology practice, he had joint ownership of the Camelback Sleep Shop and Waterbeds Unlimited with his partner, Everett. Waterbeds were at the height of their popularity, and Waterbeds Unlimited was the most well-known waterbed store in Phoenix. Sales were at a peak. Suggestive slogans were popping up on billboards around town: *"Two things are better on a waterbed. One of them is sleep." "She'll admire you for your car, she'll respect you for your position, but she'll love you for your waterbed."* The revelation this Al Pacino-like psychologist also owned waterbed stores was a paradox that made me even more intrigued.

I would randomly pick up and read the typewritten pages I found scattered about Stuart's home office. I read everything I could get my hands on as I became obsessed about why some people become creative, and some achieve at mathematics and science, while others struggle with everything. Was it possible to develop both?

I also became interested in learning about Sufism, too, but his religion was something he kept to himself. Although a psychologist and so well versed in reading other people, Stuart didn't like to share much about himself. Stuart was satisfied with compartmentalizing his life. I found him complicated and beautiful. He seemed wounded, like me. I even loved his slobbering dogs.

Though his practice included hypnosis to get people to stop

smoking cigarettes, he walked around the house in his underwear that was a size too big, puffing away on cigarettes that smelled like cloves. One day I asked, "Can I try one of those?"

He wouldn't share his religion with me, but he happily shared his addiction and handed me the burning Krakatoa Kretek clove cigarette. I inhaled the enticing, pungent, thick smoke, and exhaled, filling the room with a haze, causing me to cough. Then Stuart surprised me by asking an unexpected question.

"I noticed you sometimes ignore people at the restaurant when they call out your name. It's almost like you can't hear them, but I think you can."

I had become so invested in being Angie; it was a surprise he was even making this observation. So, I made up a story about being hard of hearing in one ear. I should have known better than to use this excuse since it hadn't worked in fourth grade.

When I wasn't expecting it, Stuart whispered something funny in my supposed deaf ear, and I laughed. He'd tricked me, and I wasn't happy about it. I should have just told him the truth, but before I even knew what I was saying, Wild Bill's daughter sprang into action.

"When I was young, I pretended to be deaf to get attention from my mother. It was stupid; I had no reason to do it other than I wanted the attention. I think I've formed a psychological block about it. So, when I want attention, I can't hear sometimes. Does that make sense?"

Stuart shot me a puzzled look and said, "No."

My little white lies were becoming part of who I was, which suited me. I didn't want to waiver in my story. Then Stuart presented me with a book entitled *Why Am I Afraid to Tell You Who I Am?*

"I think you should read this book, Angie. I think it might help you."

One glance at the book jacket told me this book would not

help me. When you're lying through your teeth to survive, you need more than a juvenile self-help book. I was using a fake ID to work and hitchhiking to get there and attending high school while carrying on a relationship with a man twice my age. And, to top it off, my crazy, alcoholic father might show up at any moment. I had a lot to deal with besides being afraid to tell someone about myself, and I felt insulted and just plain angry at him for tricking me. He was right—there was fear behind telling him who I was. But I realized if I told Stuart I was fifteen years old, he might want to end our relationship, and I didn't want to jeopardize that.

I stifled my teenage angst before responding, "Thank you, Stuart. I appreciate your thinking of me, and I assure you, I will read the book, and when I discover who I really am, you'll be the first to know." He laughed.

On a Wednesday afternoon, I was late for work for the third consecutive time because I had trouble hitching a ride. Joe had enough of Angie and her "zoning out" and fired me.

Maybe being a waitress wasn't my calling in life. I was better at sales, which I proved at JCPenney. I saw a NOW HIRING sign in the window of Waterbeds Unlimited, hitching a ride past the store. So, when I saw Stuart the next night, I broke the news about losing my job and asked whether he'd consider hiring me. Absorbed in watching the news about Watergate, it annoyed him I kept pestering him to hear me out.

"I'm an excellent salesperson. It's a trait I inherited from my dad. He can sell you the boots off your own feet."

"Angie, I'm not in charge of personnel at the waterbed store. Everett does all the hiring and looks for salespeople with a track record, so I don't have any pull on who they hire."

It sounded as though he was passing the buck. If Wild Bill had taught me anything, it was the ability to tell when someone was lying to me. It infuriated me and put me off seeing Stuart for a while. I was there for him when he was lonely and needed someone to make him laugh. I deserved a little reciprocity. But if he wasn't going to help me, I made up my mind to see if I could get hired at Waterbeds Unlimited by myself.

The next day, I walked into the store, determined to Wild Bill my way into a job. Waterbeds Unlimited was the ultimate boys' club. It even smelled like a locker room.

"I saw the sign you are looking for a salesperson. I'd like to fill out an application."

The guy behind the counter said, "We're out of applications. And anyway, the ad doesn't say 'salesgirl.' It says, 'salesman.' Big difference, little girl. But if you want to come in and lay down on a bed to try it out, I am happy to show you what you're missing." His sales buddy joined him as they both snickered and exchanged a few more lewd comments with each other at my expense.

"Thanks, but no thanks!" Humiliated, I couldn't think of a good comeback, so I turned around and walked out the door, wishing I had a cool car to screech away. It was a scorcher, with temperatures pushing over a hundred degrees. Only a crazy person would venture out on foot. Out of sight, I hitchhiked back to the Tampico Apartments.

Two days later, I got a job at Hobo Joe's Coffee Shop off Black Canyon Freeway located in a stretch of highway traveled by people either leaving town for Prescott or coming into Phoenix. Most of Hobo Joe's patrons were truck drivers fueling up on coffee doing a cross country run or guys sobering up before going home in no rush to get back to their families—like Wild Bill. When Angie told him I was working there, he became a regular fixture. That was the one upside of the job. I saw more of Wild Bill at Hobo Joe's than I had since moving to Phoenix.

Between school, my upcoming graduation, and hitchhiking back and forth to work at Hobo Joe's, I didn't have time for Stuart. When he called, I made up reasons I couldn't see him, and when I ran out of excuses, I stopped answering the phone or told Angie to tell him I was out. Stuart gave up calling after a while. I think he assumed I had lost interest, which wasn't the case. It was a monumental accomplishment for me to be graduating high school early, and I would have appreciated sharing it with him. I just wasn't sure how he would take the news about my lying about my identity and my age.

When the printed announcements for my graduation arrived, there was only one person I cared about sending it to, which was Mom. I wanted her to be proud of me and all I had accomplished.

When the big day arrived, it filled me with anticipation, wondering if my mother would surprise me and show up. "PAMELA SUE BUTTER," the principal called my name over the loudspeaker. This moment was the first time I was ever proud of my name. Beaming, I took in the vast crowd of people and remained hopeful my mother was out there in the sea of faces. When I exited the platform, I caught sight of Wild Bill yelling to me, drunk off his ass like a clichéd scene left on the cutting room floor of a bad B-Movie. But, unfortunately, it was happening in real-time and unedited. I would have to live with the memory of Wild Bill stealing the spotlight from me for the rest of my life. My eyes scanned the crowds searching for the familiar face I longed to see. But I felt relieved my mother was a no show, sparing her from witnessing her ex-husband make a fool of himself.

As caps flew up in the air across the football field, I clutched mine tightly, deeming it too precious to cast away. Kids were breaking off in packs to get drunk and pursue the ritual of toilet papering houses, an expression of their rite of passage. I went back to my apartment alone feeling unsatisfied, realizing the high school diploma that was so meaningful to me meant very little to anyone else.

9

GET ME PAM BUTTER

The unexpected benefit of working at Hobo Joe's was that it freed me from pretending to be Angie. I could be myself again and figure out who Pam Butter wanted to become.

While with Stuart, I had spent a lot of time exercising both sides of the hemispheres of my brain, trying to figure out who in the hell was Angie. But since Angie never really existed, it was a waste of time. Still, it made me sad I would have to say goodbye to the good qualities I came to love about being Angie. She was older and more sophisticated and surer of herself. She had never been abused as a child and had a family back in Pennsylvania who loved her. Pam Butter was still an abused, lost teenage runaway girl. I decided it was easier to make up a character than to try to come to terms with my authentic self.

"That's as far as I'm going this way. Sure glad I met ya," said the trucker who gave me a lift from Hobo Joe's. It was my lunch hour, but I had a job interview and was hoping I would get hired for this job and never have to go back to that greasy spoon.

"Me too, I said as I waved my ride on, grateful he had air conditioning, so my blouse wasn't clinging to my underarms. I was just a block and a half from the interview location, so I could walk the rest of the way, and stride in with confidence and nail this job.

Oasis Waterbeds had just opened; even the carpet still smelled new. It was on a stretch of Camelback Drive known as "waterbed row," so it was a straight shot from Waterbeds Unlimited and Camelback Sleep Shop.

The owner of Oasis, Amir, had a thick Persian accent and dark, bushy eyebrows and greeted me with an enthusiastic handshake. He was smart enough to know that anyone looking to buy a waterbed, including a custom frame and sheets, would compare prices and products between the three stores.

At the interview, I told Amir I loved sleeping on a waterbed and boasted about how at JCPenney I was outselling every other salesperson in the store. I knew I could do the same at Oasis. Amir was a savvy businessman who didn't need much convincing that hiring a young, attractive girl to sell beds made perfect sense.

"You are what I am looking for in a salesgirl. When can you start?"

"I can start today if you like. It looks like some inventory just arrived," I said, glancing at the colorful sheets stacked along the back wall.

"I could begin by getting the boxes organized, putting some linens on the showroom beds, and I think the place could use a good vacuuming. I forgot to mention I ran my Great Aunt's motel every summer growing up, so I'm excellent at making up beds and keeping things tidy." When I was nine years old, after my grandmother died, I spent a few weeks of the summer with my Great Aunt Sarah, who had a motel business. I was only stretching the truth a little, but it worked.

"Okay, you're hired! You can start today!" Amir said, pumping my hand while kissing me on both cheeks.

I didn't like people telling me I couldn't do something, so outselling the guys down the street at Waterbeds Unlimited became a personal challenge. I wanted to prove to myself that once I set my mind to do something, I could succeed, and I knew if I got the job at Oasis, it wouldn't be long before I would become the best salesperson on the block.

I filled out the job application using my real name, Pam Butter. After just two weeks on the job, Amir printed up personalized business cards I could use to write quotes on the back for my customers so they could do comparison shopping. I was sure I inherited my intuition from Wild Bill, giving me a keen insight into knowing which pitch line I should use to make the sale. "If you get a better price, I'll match it . . . or go lower." "This is the best price you will find. If anyone tries to say they're selling you the same thing for less, they're lying."

Within a month, Amir was having trouble keeping inventory in stock, and "waterbed row" was buzzing about a cute salesgirl named Pam at Oasis, who was outselling the boys' club at Waterbeds Unlimited. Even Stuart's partner, Everett, noticed the drop in their sales. I found out because after I made five or six significant sales in a row—all to people who had first shopped at Waterbeds Unlimited, I got an invitation to come to the store to meet Everett.

I had a moment of sweet revenge when greeted by their star salesperson, Danny, the same guy who had turned me away. He was a short guy with a Napoleon complex who did his best to intimidate me with his scowl. A man sporting a fake tan arrived, with over-processed, bleached, blond hair and blue eyes that popped like flashbulbs each time he blinked. It had to be Everett. He wore skin-tight, bell-bottom jeans; his overall appearance was that of an aging wanna-be rocker. Like Stuart, Everett was into Sufism and had an affinity for young blonde girls, as evidenced by his companion, who skulked into the office to wait for him.

"So, you are the chick who's been stealing our business?"

"What makes you think I am stealing your business? It's a free world. People can shop wherever they want, and people seem to prefer to shop at Oasis."

"But the guy who owns Oasis knows nothing about this business. We've been in business for years. We are the gold standard!" Everett's rebuff sounded more like a whine. "Why do you want to work at that Persian palace, anyway?"

"Who says you are the gold standard? The only thing golden about you is," hesitating a moment before saying, "your hair." I realized the comment I made about his hair was mean spirited, but it just slipped out. However, it appeared lost on this man whose ego took it as a compliment, so I kept going. "This carpet hasn't seen a vacuum in months, and for the record, burning incense is not a body-odor deterrent. From the inventory I see on your floor, you don't have as many quality pieces as Oasis. Why would anyone want to shop here? So why would I want to leave Oasis?" Everett was at a loss for words, and I seized his vulnerable moment. "But if you were to make me an offer to run Camelback Sleep Shop, I might entertain the idea."

Camelback Sleep Shop was a brand-new store about a mile down the road set up inside a small house so you could walk from room to room, getting lost in a fantasy world. I thought it had so much potential and a place where I could use my unique design sense and my obsessive, compulsive passion for rearranging furniture. I could style each of the rooms with a different waterbed frame, creating multiple looks. I envisioned playing my Buckingham Nicks album and dancing about the shop as waterbeds flew out the door.

"Well, that's an interesting idea. I will have to talk to my partner, Stu. He has the final say on these types of decisions."

I had never heard Stuart referred to as "Stu" before, and it almost made me laugh out loud. It was enlightening to catch Stuart lying about not having any say in the hiring decisions.

Maybe I would have to let him borrow, *Why Am I Afraid To Tell You Who I Am?*

"I could be the yin to Waterbeds Unlimited's yang." I knew that would get him.

He flashed his sparkling teeth—made even whiter by his preternatural tan—into a wide grin and said, "Okay... Okay. Let me set something up for you and Stuey." With Stuart's name going from Stu to Stuey in a matter of minutes, I knew I had Everett on Team Pam. But I wasn't entirely sure I knew the man I had been dating these past months.

Stuart set up an appointment to meet Pam for an interview at his practice toward the end of his business day. When I showed up, Stuart thought I might be stalking him.

He said, "Hey, Angie. It's nice to see you; it's been a while. I've been thinking about you. But I have a patient scheduled who will walk through the door at any moment..."

"No, you don't."

"Of course, I do. My patient will be here any moment," he said.

"You don't have a patient scheduled because your appointment is with me, or I wouldn't be here."

A look of terror swept across his face, as though it crossed his mind I had run down poor "Pam" in the parking lot in a jealous rage. Just thinking about it made me laugh out loud. The more I tried to suppress my laughter, the more terrified he looked until I blurted out, "I'm Pam!"

"What the hell are you talking about, Angie?" Stuart said, standing up in full confrontational mode.

"I know this might seem weird. And this might take a moment for me to explain, so may we both please sit down?" I asked as I pulled up a chair across from him. "You gave me Why Am I Afraid to Tell You Who I Am? Well, I'm not afraid anymore. I just graduated from Camelback High School. I used my roommate's ID to get the job where we met because I wasn't old enough to serve alcohol, and I needed the job because I'm a runaway. That's why I never responded to people calling me Angie because that's not my real name. My name is Pamela Sue Butter. I am sorry I lied to you, but at the moment, it felt like my only option. If I told you how old I was, you might tell the boss, and I feared I would lose my job. Or worse, maybe you wouldn't have taken me seriously or wanted to spend time together. I don't know what it's meant for you, but it has meant a lot to me. After I lost the job at Joe's, the only place I could find work was the Hobo Joe's out on

Black Canyon Freeway. Between hitchhiking to and from work and studying to graduate high school, I never got to see you, and I missed you. When I asked you for a job at Waterbeds Unlimited, it hurt when you turned me down, but I understood. So, when I saw a position open at Oasis, I went to the interview, and I got the job. And I am good at it, or your buddy Everett wouldn't have sent me over here to meet you, Stu."

There was a long pause. Stuart leaned back in his black executive chair and lit up a Krakatoa Kretek. He offered me one, but I declined.

"I can't believe you have the audacity to light up a cigarette in the very premises where you hypnotize people to quit smoking. I may be a liar, but you, Stuey, are a hypocrite."

Stuart chuckled, but he knew I was right. He continued to seem skeptical but said nothing until the silence made me feel like I was about to burst.

"Okay, so now that I've told you the truth, you don't believe me. I can see it in your eyes." I got up to leave but turned back to say, "Look, you have every right not to believe me. But I can prove it. Here."

I reached into my purse and pulled out my wallet. Though I hadn't yet passed the driving test, the DMV issued me a driver's permit.

"Here is my real ID. See? I am Pamela Sue Butter. Sixteen years old. I even have a car now."

Wild Bill had refurbished an old Chevy Nova with a Navajo-pattern interior and gave it to me as a gift to make up for embarrassing me at my graduation. He even had the car modified to put the stick shift on the floor because I was having trouble with it on the steering wheel. Still, Stuart said nothing.

"You know what? I am glad you turned me down for a job at Waterbeds Unlimited. It smells like boys who don't shower and makes me feel dirty, just walking into the place. Besides, I'm making excellent commissions at Oasis."

As I turned to exit his office, he said, "Hey, wait a minute... come back here."

I stopped, clutching my new Coach leather handbag.

"I think I like this Pam girl better than I liked Angie. And I liked Angie a lot."

Stuart must have been a good psychologist because he knew I was hiding something. But I expected discovering he had been dating a teenage runaway for over a year might have given him a reason to pause. However, we picked up where we left off, and I got the job running Camelback Sleep Shop, where I could play my Buckingham Nicks album to my heart's content as I had imagined. I also got to take care of a parrot, the store's mascot.

One day, Stuart's Bullmastiff dogs escaped from his backyard and went on a neighborhood killing spree, leaving a carnage of several beloved pets in their wake. Forced to move or put the dogs down, Stuart relocated to a ranch outside of the city. It was a peaceful retreat. I enjoyed being there, a break from the tiny apartment when I moved out of Angie's place after I graduated. But something was missing for me, making me feel restless, though I wasn't sure what it was. I was walking the grounds smoking a Krakatoa Kretek when it occurred to me—I was growing up, and Stuart was just getting older.

Before I had time to process this revelation, Stuart caught me off guard when he announced over breakfast that the timing was right, and he and Everett had sold the waterbed stores. The profits had been shrinking, and they were smart businessmen who knew it was better to get out when they could still get top dollar for the business.

I decided to leave Oasis, but Stuart knew I gave up job security for something unknown. It had been less than six months since I took the job, and Camelback Sleep Shop had already become my baby, and I took pride in the place. I realized he must have been thinking about the sale for some time, so his lack of confiding in me only underscored our lack of intimacy.

I felt no consolation from him when he added, "I'm sure you will be able to keep your job. Camelback Sleep Shop is doing better than Waterbeds Unlimited."

The new owner was an African American gentleman who wore thick gold chains, lots of rings, and colorful clothes. He had a tight Afro, and his overall appearance was suave and debonair. When he came to meet me at the shop, he flirted with me in a way that was a bit unsettling but sexy at the same time as we exchanged small talk.

Then he asked me, "Do you like being a sales clerk, pretty Mama? I mean a beautiful woman like you, stuck in a shop all day? You should be out there sharing your beauty with the Universe. You are a queen. You should be making over one hundred dollars an hour sitting on a throne, not holed up in this little fairytale world with a parrot that doesn't even talk and just shits all day. That damn parrot doesn't say shit. All he does is shit." He laughed out loud. "Are you the one who has to clean up all of its shit?"

"Yes," I replied, shifting my gaze downward. I loved having the parrot in the store. It gave the store its personality. But if I told the truth, I had become fed up with cleaning shit for a parrot that never talked.

"So, how can I make one hundred dollars an hour?"

"I have a business venture where men come to worship women like you. All you need to do is provide a little companionship to them. Talk nice to them. Maybe give them a massage? You know, a back rub with nice oils and stuff."

"Are these guys lonely? Is that why they need companionship? Where do I meet them? How much time do I have to spend away from the shop to do this? Because, you know, I am the one who has to look after the parrot."

"You just leave cleaning bird shit up to some other damn fool and listen to what I'm telling you." He pulled out a card embossed with shiny gold ink. "You think you can make it over to this crib at about seven-thirty tonight, have a glass of champagne with some of my girls, and you can find out what it's all about?"

"Okay, sounds interesting. I'll be there, but you aren't firing me from the Sleep Shop, are you?"

"Girl, why you even thinking about coming back to this place? If you like cleaning up bird shit that much, I'll give you the damn parrot because I don't want that shit machine stinking up my store."

I felt like I had nothing to lose. If I didn't go, the boss might fire me, anyway. I also had a feeling it wouldn't be business as usual at the Camelback Sleep Shop.

When I showed up at the address on the card, my heart sank to realize his "crib" was nothing more than a trailer parked in the desert alongside several others. I sat slumped down in my car as I took it all in, watching as a car drove up to a trailer. The door opened, and the guy stepped inside, glancing around first as though making sure no one saw him. Before long, multiple cars were coming and going every ten to twenty minutes. Guys who looked wealthy. Guys who looked like your typical family man. Truckers were pulling up in big rigs and greeted by scantily dressed girls with three-inch-long fingernails.

I became more and more uncomfortable angry at myself, falling for such a flimsy and sleazy story. This place was nothing but a whorehouse run out of trailers parked on a desert lot. And all it took to get me here was the promise of not having to clean up bird shit.

I swore at myself for being such an idiot as I turned the key in the ignition of the Chevy Nova. A big white Cadillac pulled up beside me. The boss stepped out, and I heard the gravel crunch beneath his shiny boots. It was a sound that lived in the recesses of my subconscious mind, and it terrorized me. I sat frozen. He knocked on my window.

"Now, why aren't you up in there?" he asked.

I rolled the window down just a few inches and mumbled out the words, "Well, I don't think this is quite what I understood from our conversation. I don't think this is for me."

"So, you want to clean up bird shit the rest of your life?"

He pulled out an enormous wad of one-hundred-dollar bills, the likes of which I had never seen.

"Or you want to count huns with me?" In quick succession, he peeled off a slew of bills and said, "Here, take it, it's yours. That is if you get your pretty white ass up in there like you promised."

He said it like there was an or else attached to his statement and sent a shiver down my spine. He stuck his hand through the window and held the cash in front of my face, so close I could smell the newly minted bills. Adrenaline rushed through my veins, and I could hear my heart pumping, realizing there was no way to negotiate my way out of this predicament. My Wild Bill instincts took over as I snatched the hundreds from his long fingers and hit the gas. Rolling up the window, I peeled across the parking lot, skidding on the gravel.

What little I knew of the man, something told me he wasn't the type to forget about this and let it go. Trying to keep the Chevy from careening off course, I kept my eyes on the rearview mirror. Convinced he was on my tail, made me frightened to return to my apartment for fear he knew where I lived. I thought about going to Dave's to find Wild Bill, but I worried if I told him what happened, he might show up with a gun and pop the guy's head off. I felt rattled, and the entire mess embarrassed me beyond reason.

Looking for somewhere to shift the blame, I thought of Stuart. Stuart must have known this man was not legitimate. How could he have exposed me to this creep with no warning? What kind of man puts his teenage girlfriend in jeopardy to get seduced by a pimp? All he said was, *"You can probably keep your job."* He never gave me the slightest impression the guy could be bad news. Comfortable I wasn't being followed, I pulled into a gas station, screeching to a stop in front of a telephone booth, to call

Stuart and vent my anger.

He picked up on the first ring. "Hello?"

"What kind of animal are you? I'll tell you what kind. You are a lecherous pig. How could you subject me to that pimp who bought your stores? You must have known he would be bad news for me. You are nothing more than a lonely guy who's as old as my father. You sicken me. I hate you, and I never want to see you again!" I slammed down the phone and cried. It felt good to let out the pent-up feelings I'd had about our relationship. Stuart only wanted me for sex, making him no different from the pimp who bought his store. How could I have been so naïve?

I got back in my car and lit up a Krakatoa Kretek. As I tossed the match in the ashtray, I noticed, stuck between the seat and the console, a flyer I'd received at Camelback Sleep Shop. It was an invitation to a waterbed convention in Scottsdale. A lot of manufacturers and retailers from California and the southwest were converging this weekend. I made the split decision to race across town, wearing the clothes on my back, to try to network connections from Los Angeles. I made up my mind that night I wanted to get the hell out of Phoenix. Lucky for me, I had the money for the price of admission clutched in my clammy palm.

The entry badge cost me $125. The convention floor was full of the latest waterbeds, frames, linens, and accessories. Wandering around the displays, I still felt shaken by what had just happened, so I was finding it challenging to focus when a handsome guy approached me, smiling.

"Overwhelming, isn't it?"

"What do you mean?" I asked, trying not to sound like a paranoid, fugitive on the lam.

"I mean all these people. I've never seen the convention attract this many vendors. They must be here to soak up the sun."

"Yeah, that must be it," I replied, trying my best to appear cool, calm, and collected as opposed to being on the run from an angry pimp.

"I'm Steven. I'm not here for the sun; it's too hot for me. I own two stores in San Diego, so I'm here to educate myself on the latest and greatest. And, if I'm lucky, squeeze in a little fun."

"Me too. I mean, I'm not from San Diego, but I'm here to educate myself. I'm Pam."

We strolled up and down the rows of booths while engaging in shop talk. I impressed Steven with my knowledge of the business.

After a while, he asked, "What do you say, Pam? Have you seen enough? Do you want to get a drink?"

Several martinis later, the encounter with the pimp that had led me here was a distant memory. I had never drunk a martini before, but the way Steven ordered them conjured visions of having drinks with James Bond. Drinks led to dinner, which led to an invitation back to his room, where Steven pulled out a crazy bong in the shape of a penis.

"Now that, I find amusing. Why on earth do you have a penis bong? You better tell me it's a gift from your girlfriend."

He laughed as he lit up a bowl. "I don't have a girlfriend."

I hadn't smoked pot since before I ran away two years ago. We took a few hits on the penis bong, and Steven began trying to kiss me, putting his hands all over me. I wasn't ready for an unfamiliar man to touch me, and my natural inclination was to resist his advances. But the stinging feelings I had about Stuart made me want to prove to myself I could do as I pleased. Between the martinis and marijuana, my defenses soon fell by the wayside.

The next morning, I awoke with a hangover and could hear the shower running. Steven appeared in the bedroom doorway to announce, "I have to go back to San Diego later today. But I would love you to come to see me soon. Would you like that?" I felt embarrassed by our spontaneous one-night stand when I woke up. It flattered and delighted me that Steven thought otherwise.

A trip to California sounded too good to be true. "Oh, and the hotel room is yours until Monday morning, so relax by the pool if you like. I wish I could stay with you, but duty calls."

Taking him up on his offer, I spent the next few days relaxing by the pool and enjoying room service on Steven's dime. Staying incognito at the hotel helped put distance between me and the encounter with the pimp.

Two weeks later, Steven sent me a ticket to join him in Newport Beach. When I arrived at the airport, he greeted me by sweeping me off my feet and into the air, before whisking me off to spend the week with him at his beach house. Steven bought me a cute, pink, one-piece bathing suit with ruffles on the butt and treated me like a baby-doll. He was an amateur photographer, so he took tons of photos of me frolicking on the beach. The cool ocean breezes of Newport were a welcome contrast to the blistering desert sun of Phoenix. Any space in my heart left for Stuart was making room for Steven.

While we were making out, the Crosby, Stills, Nash & Young song "Our House" came on the radio. Steven gazed into my eyes and sang every word with meaning. It was a touching moment, as my mind fantasized about what it would be like to put down roots with someone.

But as the week ended, so did the fantasy house, cats, kids, and happily ever when he let it slip this wasn't his house. Plus, Steven said he didn't have a girlfriend; he never said he didn't have a wife. And two kids.

Heartbroken, I was beginning to believe all men wanted from me was between my legs. He didn't even try to apologize, as if I should have guessed our time together was nothing more than kicks for him.

Anger, shame, disgust, betrayal—these were not the feelings that should burden a sixteen-year-old girl. Steven may not have realized how young I was, but regardless, it was no way to treat a woman. To be hurt, mistreated, abused: I accepted this must be my lot in life.

Arriving back at my apartment, I threw my purse down and flung myself across the bed. The contents spilled out of the bag, scattering tampons, coins, and business cards I'd collected at the convention. I could almost feel a thick skin growing around my heart. I wondered if one day, the thick skin would be the only thing left.

Exhausted from the emotional ordeal, I fell asleep, consumed by nightmares of a crazy pimp chasing me, my phantom boyfriend, and my daddy surrounded by broken poinsettias, laughing like a demented cartoon character.

I woke with a shiver from cranking the air conditioner up and began gathering the mess from my purse. Collecting the essentials first, I then started sifting through the receipts and mementos from my time with Stephen. I wanted to purge every single scrap of paper that reminded me of his face except for the cute photos he took of me on the beach. There were a few loose dollar bills, so I opened my Indian-engraved wallet to stuff them inside, only to discover five one-hundred-dollar bills tucked neatly inside the billfold.

I felt fury and disgust; this, I presumed, is what Steven deemed I was worth. I would have torn the money up if I wasn't out of a job. I missed Camelback Sleep Shop and the parrot that didn't talk.

With a void in the pit of my stomach, I spotted what could be my ticket out of Phoenix. It was the business card from Bruce, a friend of Steven's who lived in LA. After breaking my heart, Steven told me if I was serious about wanting to go to LA, I should look him up because he might take me in as a roommate for a while until I got on my feet. I sat on the edge of the bed staring at the card for the longest time before dialing the number.

"Hello, Bruce? My name is Pam. Your friend Steven told me

I should give you a call because I live in Phoenix, but I want to move to LA, and he thought you could give me a place to stay until I get on my feet."

"Well, hello, Pam! When would you like to come?" Bruce offered without hesitation. "I mean, please come and check it out before moving out here. Get the lay of the land."

It was clear Bruce wanted to sample the merchandise before committing making me feel like a cheap commodity, but I didn't care. I had more pressing matters than my self-esteem. I left for LA the next morning in a blind search for a haven with a stranger named Bruce. To say I had nothing to lose is an understatement. I hoped it might be a better option than what I was leaving behind.

10

A SEISMIC SHIFT

A limousine driver holding a sign with my name on it—PAM BUTTER—met me at the gate. He took the small carry-on, placing it on a cart as he escorted me through LAX before whisking me off to meet Bruce, my potential new roommate.

"Would you like to listen to some music, Miss?"

"Sure," I said, trying to sound cavalier though I was overwhelmed by the sights and sounds of Los Angeles. When I came to Southern California as a young girl to see Uncle Jim, the ride from the airport was on a freeway with nothing but cars to see. This drive was more intriguing and felt like a movie set complete with a colossal donut sitting atop a tiny store. "The Hustle" came on the radio as we flew down La Cienega Boulevard, gliding past oil derricks dotting the horizon that reminded me of the old oil rig on Gobbler's Knob. The sound of Princess galloping up the hill reverberated in my mind as I took in a place that formerly only existed in my imagination. Nighttime in Los Angeles.

When we turned off La Cienega onto Sunset Boulevard, my heart raced, and I couldn't hide my teenage enthusiasm. Gigantic billboards lined the streets, and when we turned onto Hollywood Boulevard, an almost carnival atmosphere permeated the air. I had never seen so many colorful people out so late at night, literally walking on stars that adorned the sidewalks.

Driving up Beachwood Canyon Drive, I spotted the Hollywood sign high above the hills as we snaked upward on the narrow streets. America's hit song "Sister Golden Hair" came on, and the lyrics seemed to fit the moment as we kept ascending higher and higher, and closer to the sign, so close I thought I could reach out and touch it.

The driver turned onto Pelham Place and came to a stop in front of a stunning, mid-century modern house supported by stilts on the side of a cliff. As I was about to ring the doorbell, Bruce flung open the frosted glass door and greeted me with a big hug as though we were old friends. The driver placed my small carry-on just inside the doorway, departing with discretion.

The view from the cliffhanger was expansive. Millions of tiny lights from the city masqueraded as twinkling stars. Bruce walked over to a bottle of champagne on ice.

"I heard you like champagne. Does Perrier-Jouet suit your palate?" Bruce asked as he popped the cork and poured the sparkling liquid into delicate crystal flutes.

"Mais, oui!" I said, attempting to sound continental. From what little French I learned in high school, I assumed Perrier-Jouet was French champagne, so a French response seemed appropriate. As the bubbles tumbled into the flute, blending with the city lights beyond, I wondered if I was in heaven.

Bruce was in his early 40s, lean and muscular, tan, and good-looking. He wore tight bell-bottoms with an untucked paisley silk shirt. His expensive-looking gold watch was loose on his wrist, causing him to flick it with a compulsive regularity, drawing attention to the fact it was a Rolex. His Coke-bottle-thick glasses gave him an almost cartoonish appearance, like a character from a Margaret Keane "big eyes" painting if they had worn glasses.

We settled into the sofa with our champagne. "So, would you like to do a little blow before I take you on a tour of the house?"

I couldn't stop thinking about was what was wrong with his eyes. Was he legally blind without those thick lenses? Could he see anything at all without them? Despite my insatiable curiosity, I didn't dare ask. It made me think about my blind pony, Princess. I wondered how she was and if anyone was brushing her soft, black coat.

"May I use the bathroom to freshen up?" I asked.

"Sure, right down the hall to the left."

When I returned to the living room, Bruce was already laying out several lines of cocaine on a mirror resting on a Noguchi coffee table. The jazz playing in the background reminded me of Stuart, and a wave of sadness came over me as I recollected our last conversation when I slammed the phone down on him. I wondered if he had any idea where I might be or if, in fact, he even cared.

I had never snorted cocaine but watched how Bruce did it, before breathing in a long, thin line of the powder, hoping the magical potion would turn off the memories swirling in my mind.

My eyes caught sight of a stack of albums propped up against the wall as I leaned over to take another toot. I read the cover of the top one and asked, "Is this Miles Davis playing?" The album read *MILES DAVIS Kind of Blue*. Bruce inhaled a long, thick line of coke, threw his head back, and said, "Man, you are too much. You are tight," which I presumed was a compliment. He ran his fingers over the mirror and rubbed the cocaine residue over his gums.

"Wow, man . . . A beautiful, blonde, blue-eyed chick who digs jazz and can recognize Miles Davis. Steven was right. You are the real deal. The total package."

Wondering what was so great about being able to read, Bruce's compliment did little to raise my self-esteem, and the cocaine only made me feel numb. I felt sorry for Bruce, and his blindness continued to dominate my thoughts.

In a little while, he showed me a small bedroom across from the master suite. "This will be your room," he said. It was a cute little guest room with a twin trundle bed pushed up under the window. The ceiling sloped, so the far end of the room was low, making it feel like the perfect spot for a small child. "Well, it's your room unless my kids are staying over. Those nights you will need to find somewhere else to sleep, which shouldn't be too hard for a beautiful girl like you. But otherwise, consider it your room. Just not tonight! Tonight, you are sleeping with me."

It was the first time he mentioned he had children, so I assumed he was divorced. It made me sad the way he sounded so nonchalant about having kids as though they were nothing more than possessions or temporary appendages, gone when he had no use for them.

He pulled me into his room, which had the same jetliner views as the living room, and pushed me down onto his waterbed.

"Ever slept on one of these before?"

Without thinking about it too much, I said, "Waterbeds have been my specialty."

"Not only does she love jazz, but she also knows how to fuck on a waterbed. I hit the jackpot."

I realized I needed to learn how to use my words more carefully. What I said was suggestive, and I was aware becoming roommates might come with certain strings attached, but I thought we would get to know one another first. I never imagined we'd be making out within twenty minutes of meeting each other. It didn't feel right. Sex was becoming something men expected of me, and I didn't like it. But if it didn't involve a matter of the heart, maybe just sex was okay.

When Bruce took his glasses off in bed, and I knew he couldn't see me, it was almost too intimate. Tears welled up in my eyes as I rode off into the night with the thundering sound of my blind pony, Princess, as we galloped up Gobbler's Knob, ringing in my ears.

Over the weekend, Bruce introduced me to the game of backgammon, which was enjoying almost cult-like popularity in Los Angeles. He told me about a private club called PIPS that held tournaments on the weekends and was all the rage. Though I had never played the game before, something about backgammon brought the two hemispheres of my brain together, as Stuart had described.

To win at backgammon, one needs strategy and luck. Bruce

reveled in the role of playing teacher, and I knew if I put my mind to it, I could learn the game and become a fierce opponent, which I hoped would amuse Bruce and help keep a roof over my head. We stayed awake until dawn, snorting coke and playing backgammon. I don't know if it was the game or the cocaine, but something made me intent on becoming the best.

By the end of the weekend, we sealed the deal. I was Bruce's new roommate. He sent me back to Phoenix to pack up all my stuff in the Chevy Nova and drive back to LA. Before leaving, I came across a backgammon rulebook sandwiched in a magazine rack between some old copies of *Esquire, Playboy*, and *Rolling Stone*. I figured Bruce was so proficient in the game he was no longer in need of it, so I slipped it into my purse. I'd study it cover to cover over the ensuing weeks before returning to LA, determined to impress Bruce.

Wild Bill had become almost non-existent since he gifted me with the Nova after graduation. When I quit Hobo Joe's and moved out of the Tampico into a second-story apartment, it was as though I moved to Pluto. Dad was too lazy or too drunk to climb the stairs, so he stopped coming by to sober up on my couch on his way home. I was beginning to understand what drove my mother away as I started to recognize the traits I had inherited from him, some of which I hoped to at least keep in abeyance. But despite our lack of closeness, it was important to me that we part on good terms. I left word with Mickey at Dave's Tavern to have Wild Bill call me. A few days later, the phone rang.

"Hi Sam, what are you up to?"

"Ummm... Nothin'. How 'bout you?" I asked, trying to sound casual.

"What's that, rustling?"

"What rustling?"

"Sounds like rustling paper. You aren't packing, are you?"

I stopped packing.

"Now, why would I be doing that, Dad?" Trying my best to avoid a confrontation over the phone, I asked, "Can you meet me for a drink?"

"Well, you better not be leaving town. I mean it, Sam. Don't even think about it!"

I couldn't believe my ears. I only wanted to see Wild Bill and say goodbye, and now he was interrogating me and threatening me not to go. And how did he know I was leaving, anyway?

"You know what, Dad. I am leaving town. Why the hell not? What do I have to keep me here in this hot hellhole? The privilege of seeing you every so often at your convenience, only to listen to you wax on philosophical about nothing but drunken-ass bullshit? I want more for my life, Dad. A father would have been enough to keep me here. But that's not you. You are Wild Bill, the gambling drunk who doesn't give a damn about me."

I slammed down the phone. It rang off the hook throughout the evening, but I didn't answer, listening to my Buckingham Nicks album while I kept packing because, despite my conviction to leave Phoenix, I didn't want to give Wild Bill even the slightest chance of talking me out of it. By midnight, the phone company would switch off my phone for good, and reconnecting with Wild Bill would become strictly on my terms.

The next morning could not have come soon enough. After hustling all the boxes to my car, I put the key in the ignition, adjusted the rearview mirror, and with a deep exhale, turned the key. But the Chevy wouldn't turn over. I tried it again. And again. I called the nearby ARCO station and spoke to a mechanic who showed up in a tow truck with jumper cables. I became anxious as he tried in vain to turn the engine over but couldn't.

"I don't understand! The car was just overhauled and had been working fine. It must be something small. You think you can fix it?"

"I can try," he said, wiping sweat from his brow. It was still early in the day, but it was already hot enough to fry an egg on the car, and I could feel the skin on my arms burning along with my temperament. The mechanic hitched up the Chevy, and I climbed into the tow truck, smelling of gasoline, oil, and body odor. But it was the familiar stench emanating from the open bag of Beechnut Chewing Tobacco on the seat between us that made me cringe.

Once at the shop, after checking the car out, the mechanic delivered the news.

"Well, it's something small, all right—Sugar granules. Someone put sugar in the gas tank. This thing is dead as a doornail. They loaded enough sugar into this car to do some serious damage. You can fix it, but you'll need to clean out the fuel tank and the carburetor, and there's no guarantee we can get her back on the road."

"Him. The car's a him. Is he really dead?"

Though I couldn't believe it, I didn't have to guess who sabotaged the Nova. How could Wild Bill be so heartless? It was clear I wasn't even on his radar, and he didn't care about my welfare when I left a message at Dave's for him to call me. All I wanted was to say goodbye. Why did he need to destroy the one nice thing he ever did for me?

The mechanic let me use his phone to call Bruce to explain I had car trouble.

"Let me talk to the mechanic," Bruce insisted, putting on his best macho demeanor to impress me.

The mechanic took the receiver. "Look here; someone put sugar in the gas tank of your girlfriend's car. Whoever did this might have an agenda against her leaving town."

That was all Bruce needed to hear. He sent me a ticket so I could come right away, and even organized a mover to collect my possessions from the mechanic, who said he'd store them for me at his shop until they arrived. The movers wouldn't be able to deliver them to Los Angeles until they had another load going that way in two weeks or more because the shipment was too small, but I would be fine for a while without them. As for the car, I told the mechanic I would get in touch with a guy named Wild Bill, who would take care of collecting it.

When I got to Sky Harbor airport, I called Lionel Estrada's office and screamed into the phone, "Tell Wild Bill he's a real asshole, okay? And let him know he can pick up the Nova at the ARCO station down the street from my old apartment since it means so much to him."

"Sam, calm down. What's going on?" Lionel asked.

"I'm moving to Los Angeles. I haven't spoken to my father in months. And then he put sugar in my gas tank so I wouldn't leave. He's a heartless creep who doesn't want me in his life, so I'm moving on."

"Sam, maybe Wild Bill had a reason for not wanting you to take that car out of state? You think about that?"

"Oh, because he probably stole it, and it's a hot car? Silly me for even stretching my imagination for a moment to think it might be because he loved me!"

Now I was steaming mad, so why was I crying? Leaving my father behind—with all of his baggage—was like giving up an old teddy bear. You know it's just an object, incapable of comforting you with its tattered fur and missing button eye, but it's something you cling to, even though you know it can't give anything back.

I went to the ticket counter, and the one-way ticket to LAX was waiting for me. Bruce believed a jealous lover was to blame for loading my gas tank with sugar. I was too embarrassed to tell him the culprit was my father.

When I arrived at Bruce's house, I noticed a plaque on the bedroom door that read, "Pam's Room." It felt odd, considering it was his kids' room, but I appreciated he was carving out some space for me to feel at home.

Bruce loved having my company, and it felt good getting a

fresh start in LA. He worked long hours every day, so he didn't like to go out much. He preferred to get coked up, pour himself a drink, and play backgammon with his new roommate before taking a downer and having sex, which became our nightly routine.

On Saturday, we started playing after lunch and were still doing coke and playing game after game when the sun rose above the Hollywood sign on Sunday morning. When I started winning, I realized Bruce was a sore loser, so when I got tired and wanted to go to bed, I let him win; he would only stop playing if he were the winner.

Bruce's needs were simple. Sex, cocaine, and winning at backgammon. My needs became much more complicated after he told me I would need to find alternate living arrangements on the nights his kids stayed over. When Bruce made this comment when we first met, I guess in the back of my mind, I thought if worse came to worse, I could always sleep in the Chevy Nova. Now, without a car, I was beginning to realize I would need to figure out a strategy that would satisfy Bruce's needs while quickly plotting my exit.

Bruce dropped me off in his forest-green Jaguar at the Beachwood Café at the bottom of the hill at Beachwood Canyon, where I studied the Want Ads and could take a bus to wherever I needed to go. Since the Manson murders, folks stopped picking up innocent-looking teenagers hitchhiking. I applied to at least twenty places with no success, mostly because most establishments served alcohol, and I was too young.

Bruce was footing the bill for everything, including the cocaine we were snorting every night, and I was a good distraction for him; to keep his mind off feeling guilty for leaving his wife and kids to fulfill his midlife crisis. Bruce wanted a girl for sex and to show off on his arm around town once in a while. But he could become bored with me at any time, and I knew he wasn't thinking long-term and would only keep me around while the novelty lasted. After only two weeks, I was already feeling tension brewing between us. It was challenging to read a person I didn't know well, but there were some signs, and the feeling was mutual.

"I have a buddy who knows the modeling agent Nina Blanchard," Bruce said one day. "You should try to get in to see her. She's building a stable of Los Angeles models, and I think you might have a decent shot to get some modeling work. Do you want me to see if I can get you an appointment?"

"Thanks, Bruce. If you think I have a shot, I'll try it, but I'm not sure I'm model material. I'm camera shy. Anyway, I heard about a hostess job at the Beverly Hills Polo Lounge, which pays well. I have an interview today at four-thirty."

"Wow! That would be perfect for you. I might be able to come back and pick you up to drop you off there; I'm meeting someone in Beverly Hills later today but won't be back until late. At least you would only have to take the bus back."

"Sounds great. And thank you, Bruce." I got up from the couch in his bedroom, where he was already snorting coke though it was only 9 a.m. I was heading to the kitchen to get some coffee but stopped with my back still turned as he continued saying the exact words I knew would sooner or later be spoken though I had hoped I would have at least a few more weeks to prepare.

"I mean, I love having you stay here, but I expect you to pay your way, and I also need to be sure you can find a place to hang out every other weekend when I have my kids here for sleepovers."

I grimaced before turning around to see him rub cocaine residue over his gums while adding, "Don't worry, honey. You will do great in this town. You're the best fuck I've had in a long time."

His comment hurt me. It made me feel like a cheap whore and set me off. He was the one who was so eager to bring me here under the pretense I could have a place to stay until I got on my feet. I had only been in town for less than two full weeks, and half of the time

I spent lying on my back across his waterbed. Exactly how did he expect that would help me to get on my feet? I could feel my cheeks get hot.

"Is that supposed to be a compliment?"

Bruce looked paranoid, and not just because he was high on cocaine.

"What?"

"Think about what you just said to me. You said I'm the best fuck you've had in a long time. Am I the best fuck you've had in twenty years? Twenty-five years? You were in a marriage for over twenty years, right? Are you comparing me to some girl you fucked in high school? Is that why you left your wife? Her pussy's not tight enough for you anymore?"

I wanted my words to hurt Bruce as much as he hurt me. But I knew from the look on his face I might have gone too far. I had to turn things around, or risk being kicked out on the street.

"I'm just playing with you! You better believe I'm the best fuck you've had, but I can't take all the credit. You know it takes two to tango."

I reached over to hug him, and he ripped my robe off and threw me across the waterbed to have sex, as the waterbed rolled like a wild wave in a storm. After sex, he snorted another couple of rounds of blow before taking a shower and leaving for work.

On the way out, he said, "Pam, here's some money for cab fare to get to your interview. I'll be back late. Catch you later."

He drove away in his Jaguar with the radio blaring Paul Simon's "50 Ways to Leave Your Lover." It was so loud I could still hear it for several minutes as he sped his way halfway down the canyon. The sting of our exchange resonated, and in that instant, I felt repulsed by everything about Bruce, especially his relationship with me.

Cruising down Beachwood Canyon Drive in a cab to the Beverly Hills Hotel, I felt thrown off my game and knew this interview was probably an exercise in futility. Still, it was an excuse to have somewhere to go, and I wanted to see the inside of the storied hotel.

The cab stopped for a light at Crescent Heights and Sunset, and I noticed a waifish looking girl with long, curly hair playing a recorder for tips. She looked happy, and I felt envious of her blissful life. She was doing what she loved, playing her instrument in the LA sunshine without a care in the world. Maybe I was missing the point of what my life could be?

The cab continued down the strip and pulled up to the valet at the Beverly Hills Hotel. I paid the fare and walked up the carpeted steps as a doorman opened the heavy glass door, welcoming me inside. Smiling with gracious appreciation, I made my way to the powder room to check my makeup and put on a touch of lipstick before announcing to the front desk I was here for the interview.

The woman behind the counter asked me to wait a moment and disappeared behind a door.

When she returned, she said, "I'm sorry, Miss. The manager tried to reach candidates yesterday to let them know we've filled the position."

"That's okay. It happens. Please keep me in mind for anything that comes up in the future."

I was turning to leave when I spotted the legendary Polo Lounge. I meandered over and peeked inside before building up the courage to take a seat at the bar. Within minutes of my sitting down, a well-dressed, handsome man asked if he could buy me a drink. I hoped I wouldn't get carded as I just turned seventeen, and the drinking age in California was twenty-one.

"Why, thank you so much. A glass of champagne would be lovely."

"I'm Dave. I'm a film producer. What's your name?"

"My name's Pam, but my dad nicknamed me Sam. All of my family have crazy nicknames, like Wild Bill, and Skinny, and Pinky." I laughed before adding, and then there's *Dickey*."

Dave chuckled.

"When my dad told Johnny Cash, he had a girl named Sam, that's how Johnny got the idea for 'A Boy Named Sue.' And, you know, Sue's also my middle name."

"You don't say? Sounds like something out of a movie!" Dave relished the story and asked, "Can I call you Sam? You look more like a Sam to me than Pam. Are you an actress?"

"No, but in this town, it seems the only way to make your way through a day is to act your way through it. So, I'm catching on."

"Well said, Sam!"

I loved hearing Dave call me Sam, but it made me miss Wild Bill.

We had a couple more rounds of drinks and exchanged fun repartee about topics ranging from Pennsylvania winters to high school sweethearts. When the subject of backgammon came up, I surprised and delighted Dave when I told him I knew of the game.

"Sure, I know how to play a bit," I answered with a sly smile.

"There's a club two of my buddies own called PIPS. I was planning on heading over there tonight. You want to swing by with me?"

"I've heard of PIPS. Sounds fun... Why not?"

We left the Beverly Hills Hotel in Dave's black Mercedes and pulled up to a roped-off entrance. The club was exclusive, charging annual dues of as much as a thousand dollars.

The doorman waved Dave in, and he waltzed me along into the epitome of glitz, glamor, and celebrity. The club included a dining room, a discotheque, and a backgammon room with custom-made tables and mirrored walls. So many beautiful people were hanging out playing backgammon and dancing. I became obsessed with the built-in backgammon tables, and as I settled into a spot next to Dave, I vowed I would one day have an exact replica made for the study on my estate.

Dave began playing, mindful to explain the moves he was making and the strategy behind them. We ordered dirty martinis, which, thanks to Steven, I learned I should nurse for as long as possible lest I'd find myself under the backgammon table by the end of the evening.

"Excuse me, which way to the ladies' room?" I asked while popping an olive into Dave's mouth.

Dave motioned, "Just down there and to the left. Oh, and here you go, Sam," he said, handing me a fifty-dollar bill.

I didn't understand why he gave me a fifty-dollar bill to go to the bathroom, but it seemed awkward to ask, and the bathroom had become an urgent matter, so I darted toward the illuminated sign.

I opened the door to discover this powder room was like none other I had ever seen. Every kind of pricey perfume and lotion, breath mints, and chewing gum were laid out for the guests to enjoy gratis; cigarettes, too, and even deodorant presented with elegance in crystal bowls and on fancy trays. An African American woman dressed like a French maid was handing fresh towels to each woman after washing their hands. I stood there, taking it all in before remembering my kidneys were about to burst, and almost didn't make it to the toilet in time. When I exited the bathroom stall and approached the washbasin, the woman was waiting for me to wash my hands so she could present me with a crisp, linen hand towel.

Out of the corner of my eye, I spotted a tip container covered in lace stuffed with five-dollar bills, quite a few ones, and some quarters, but I didn't see any notes of value even close to the fifty-dollar bill I had stashed in my purse. Do I ask this woman for the change, I wondered? Then it occurred to me; Dave gave me the fifty-dollar bill for her. I placed it in the tip container, and she smiled and said, "Bless you."

I walked out of the bathroom, feeling like I was just handed back my self-esteem. So many people had been out to take things from me my entire life. But I wanted to become part of a new food chain that was giving and loving. If I could provide this woman with enough money to feed herself and her family for a week after playing backgammon for a few hours, I knew I would be okay.

Dave and I played until we shut the place down and not counting money given to me to go to the powder room, I earned over $300 in tips from my backer just for blowing on the dice before each roll to bring him luck and suggesting a few winning moves.

When we pulled up in front of Bruce's house, it was late. Even though I never considered I might have a curfew, I hoped Bruce wasn't waiting up for me. It was the first time I'd stayed out so late, and I was too high and happy to face him.

As the Mercedes sat idling in front of the house, Dave said, "This was a blast. You catch on fast, Sam... I don't want to sound too Hollywood cliché, but you should consider acting. You're a natural raconteur."

"I don't know about acting, but I sure hope I see you around PIPS. Next time I'll play against you, so be prepared to lose. I fear you've created a monster, Dave!"

"Here's my card, Sam. Call me anytime. Hope I'll see you around."

Dave handed me his business card along with some free passes to PIPS. I thanked him as I closed the door to the Mercedes and blew him a sweet kiss.

When I went inside, I was relieved to discover Bruce wasn't home. I gazed at the view, appreciating the moment. Everything felt different. It was the first time I'd taken in the Los Angeles skyline for my sheer enjoyment. Not as a prop in Bruce's living room, trying my best to look sexy against the cityscape while blowing lines of coke with a guy having a midlife crisis. I took it in as Pamela Sue Butter, who was born, survived, and was now looking out over the entire city of lost angels as one of them. I felt less alone. If I existed, other people like me must be out there in this city.

I went to bed for the first time in "Pam's Room." It felt lonely and strange because Pam's room was on the second floor of an old clapboard farmhouse in Pennsylvania. This child's bedroom on Pelham Place was a far cry from being mine. I buried my face in the pillow, wondering what had become of my former self.

Bruce came home early on Saturday morning in a bad mood. I suggested we go out for breakfast at the Beachwood Café. It impressed Bruce when I paid for the meal.

"So, I guess the fact you have some money in your pocket means things are beginning to work out for you in Los Angeles," he said. "Good girl."

The way Bruce said the words "good girl" gave me the impression he thought the money I picked up the night before must have been from some rich guy I slept with, and I had to stifle my anger at his insulting insinuation.

"I guess you could say that. Yes, things are working out."

I didn't dare tell him I was partying with celebrities, playing backgammon at PIPS, or having an unbelievable lucky streak. Bruce had never been to PIPS, and it would have made him spit with jealousy.

The following week, I went to the appointment at Nina Blanchard's. I waited in the reception area surrounded by magazine covers of beautiful women, my already low self-esteem shrinking by the minute. I could feel the sweat from the hot bus ride clinging to my blouse, and considered bolting out the door when her assistant announced, "Ms. Blanchard will see you now."

I brought along a couple of photos taken by Steven in Newport Beach, and Ms. Blanchard commented on what a darling pink bathing suit I was wearing. That was the first and last compliment I received before she gave it to me straight.

"First, your nose is too big and asymmetrical and much too

bulbous. You don't have any lips. I mean, with the right makeup, we could get around that, but there isn't enough uniqueness to your face."

I could feel my face making involuntary contortions and twitches as Ms. Blanchard detailed my every imperfection.

"Don't get me wrong; you are quite a pretty girl even though you have crooked teeth. But you are too flat-chested and not tall enough. If you were short and had big boobs, maybe we could do something with you. But even five-foot-seven is short for a model, and you are just plain flat-chested."

I sat up straighter to appear taller and thrust my chest forward as if to make her question whether she had missed something.

With her glasses resting on the tip of her nose staring at my chest, she quipped, "There is nothing we can do about that unless you get your boobs done. Here's a telephone number for an outstanding photographer. Maybe you should give him a call. He's a talented guy, and he can make anyone look beautiful. He shot Marilyn Monroe before she was famous, which he likes to bring up, but don't let him con you into thinking you're the next Marilyn. It's a very competitive business, and I don't want you to get your hopes up. You're very cute. I wish you a lot of luck."

I couldn't help but admire Nina Blanchard and accepted every insulting comment she made about me with grace because I agreed with her. I realized I didn't belong in front of the camera. But being in her office, surrounded by professional photographs, made me think how cool it might be to be behind the camera.

"Who's next?" she asked.

I left the modeling agency feeling deflated but also inspired. Rather than hopping on a sweaty bus again, I walked down Hollywood Boulevard while mulling over the meeting and considering my other options. A blister was forming on my right foot from the strap rubbing on my heel. Walking barefoot seemed like the best option until I realized I was standing in front of Musso and Franks. Bruce mentioned the restaurant to me several times, going on about how many celebrities and big Hollywood hotshots ate there, and promised to take me one day. At that moment, I felt every promise I ever heard was empty, so it was time I started making some promises to myself.

To get off my feet, I pulled open the heavy door, greeted with a much-needed blast of air conditioning. Spotting the bar, I made my way there to order a drink. If there was one thing I'd learned from the few short weeks of being in Los Angeles, it was that even though Nina Blanchard didn't think I had what it takes to be a model; I was pretty enough not to get carded. And another thing: pretty girls in Los Angeles never had to pay for their drinks.

Before the bartender acknowledged my presence, a handsome guy in a smart-looking suit sat next to me and—bingo—offered to buy me a drink. I remembered Wild Bill's sage advice, *"If it's your last hundred dollars, buy everybody in the place a round of drinks, and you'll drink for free for a month!" I wondered, what would Wild Bill think of Sam now, drinking for free just because men believe she's irresistible? The thought of it brought a lightness to my mood.*

"Thank you. I'll have a glass of champagne."

"I'm John. I'm an agent. Are you an actress?"

"I'm Pam, but everyone calls me Sam. And no, I'm not an actress, but it seems everyone else in this town is. Is being an actress more attainable than being a model? Because I just left Nina Blanchard's office, and my self-esteem is still recovering. She pointed out every flaw I have and some I didn't even know I had," I said with a nervous laugh.

"Flaws are what make actresses more beautiful. Flaws make a woman more unique."

His words gave me comfort. Even though I didn't have aspirations of being an actress, it was hard to hear such harsh criticism about my looks. Soon we were enjoying appetizers, and I had forgotten all about the Nina Blanchard meeting. Even the blister on my foot stopped hurting.

When I returned from the restroom, John said, "Quick, finish your drink, and let's head over to the Frolic Room. They have a great happy hour, and we'll make it just in time."

It sounded like a great plan as I gulped the last of my champagne. While waiting for the valet, I felt queasy and flushed. The buildings shifted and were tilting as though about to topple down on to Hollywood Boulevard.

"John, I'm feeling a bit... Are you hot? I feel like my legs are..."

"Yep, it's a hot night," he said before removing his tie and unbuttoning the top two buttons of his shirt.

The wide lapels loosened gave him a more casual appearance. As if in slow motion, I got into his car before being engulfed by the neon lights of Hollywood Boulevard.

Sunlight streaming through slats in the blinds woke me up from a deep trance. Taking in the surroundings of a dumpy hotel room with the TV set droning in the background, I realized I didn't make it home last night. I got up to use the bathroom to discover John was not in the room. For a moment, I thought he might have gone out for coffee, but when I went to get dressed, I couldn't find my clothes. They disappeared along with my shoes and purse.

I sat on the side of the bed, feeling like I was on the verge of a panic attack. I remembered going to the bathroom at Musso's and returning to the bar to finish my drink. The last thing I remembered was getting into his car. Everything after that was a blur. I felt hungover. I saw a used condom on the floor, and I felt ashamed. How could I have let this happen to me? Angie warned me about men who will drug a girl's drink just to have his way with her. I was too trusting. I was angry at myself and wanted to cry. Then my self-preservation instincts kicked in, and I felt grateful to be alive.

A pack of matches I found in an ashtray had the address of the hotel, which I figured was at least three to five miles from Bruce's house. How was I going to get back there with no clothes or shoes? I assessed my reality and came up with only one option. I would have to make my way back to Bruce's wrapped up in hotel bath towels. I couldn't call Bruce or let him know this happened. I was too embarrassed. There was no one else to call.

So, I wrapped a towel around my body and one around my head turban style and stepped outside into broad daylight barefoot, at first, running from tree to tree and bush to bush, trying to keep undercover. But when I reached Beachwood Canyon Drive, I realized the more I walked with confidence, the more I projected the appearance of being a girl who was taking a stroll down the street to a friend's house for a dip in the pool.

Looking at my shadow cast by the sun, turban and all, I kept repeating to myself, "I am on my way to a swanky pool party. Can't wait to sip the sweet champagne awaiting me as I drift across the pool on an inflatable the color of a pink flamingo." If I could stay calm, I would make it back to Pelham Place.

Putting one foot in front of the other, I walked down Beachwood Canyon Drive. Silent wings beat inside of me. Memories of my childhood came flooding through, pounding the membranes of my cerebral cortex. I heard a marching band in the distance and the smell of romance in the air. A football game is in progress. Teens are kissing in the back of the snack stand, or under the bleachers. Wet panties shed, and cheerleaders are raising their skirts, all for the love of the game. A boy I had a crush on yells out, "Butter my balls, Butter." And I lose the 660-yard run despite being the favorite to win.

There was no pool party, no champagne awaiting me, no pink inflatable. The millions of butterflies flitting about in my stomach were the only thing keeping me going, for I felt like my heart had stopped beating three blocks ago. Pink Floyd's album *Wish You Were Here* reverberated in my mind, orchestrating my every move. My body felt as if it was moving in slow motion as it slogged through the hangover.

I still believed kindness existed in the world. I even felt today could be the day I would rise above my fears. Fear of being alone. Fear of being in love. Fear of trust. If I could hold on to the belief there was goodness in the world, I knew it would manifest in my life. I told myself this experience was a momentary setback. It was something to test my faith in humanity and myself.

Almost home.

Out of breath, I reached the top of the steps leading straight up the hillside from Beachwood Canyon Drive to Pelham Place. The pavement was hot and seared my flesh. I darted from one patch of shade to the next. Just 100 yards more to go, and I would find safety at Bruce's house in Pam's Room.

At last, I reached the front door, but the key was in my stolen purse. I hopped the fence in broad daylight, hoping a neighbor wouldn't see me and become suspicious. I walked around the house until I was outside Pam's Room, where slats of glass comprised a small window. Left unlocked—most likely, my fault—enabled me to remove enough slats to slip inside. I fell to my knees with exhaustion. All I wanted to do was get under the covers and sleep away this nightmare; grateful Bruce wasn't home.

Bruce came back later that evening, and I told him I wasn't feeling well. He left me alone, never asking where I'd spent the night before.

When the truck arrived, after almost four weeks of waiting for it, with all my possessions, it was a revelation for Bruce. He thought the unique way I styled myself with thrift store hand-me-downs was all on purpose, that my "poor little rich girl with a chic hippie vibe" aesthetic was all by design rather than a lack of money.

What emerged from those boxes told the story of an adolescent girl who ran away from home with very few worldly possessions, little life experience, and condensed high school education. The only books were about Sufism, a book of Rumi poetry, and *Why Am I Afraid to Tell You Who I Am?*, I kept for sentimental reasons.

The only furniture was a small side table handcrafted out of dried cactus branches, and a circular glass top it could no longer support. It was a relic from the Camelback Sleep Shop that broke apart in transit.

I had very few clothes, a small box of photos and other mementos including my graduation cap, some mismatched dishware, a coffee maker, and those cursed pink platform shoes. A cherished box full of letters marked "Return to Sender" addressed to my dad was among the treasures, some sheets, towels, and a comforter I didn't have time to wash before leaving.

As Bruce and I unpacked the boxes, they revealed I had nowhere to turn, and he was a married man with two kids going through a midlife crisis. Whether or not Bruce wanted to, he woke up to the truth he was still avoiding: What the hell are you doing with a teenage runaway named Pam Butter when you have a wife and two children?

Bruce picked up the box of letters addressed to my dad with the smiley faces and kisses on the envelopes and asked, "How old are you?"

I tried to maintain the pretense of being older than I was. "I wrote those a long time ago. Those letters are just sentimental treasures I should have thrown out by now," I lamented, pulling the box out of Bruce's grip, knowing my birth certificate was hidden, nestled beneath those letters. I never felt more alone or vulnerable.

"It appears some of my things are missing," I said, feigning outrage. "The movers must have brought the stuff I wanted to trash instead of my good things."

Bruce seemed unconvinced but said nothing.

"I don't feel like obsessing about it right now. Let's have some champagne and get this weekend started early."

Soon Bruce and I were partying, snorting coke, and playing backgammon as though nothing had happened. We went to sleep together on his waterbed until the waterbed made a sudden wavelike rhythmic movement as the little cliffhanger flapped up and down, and shook us awake.

"It's an earthquake!" Bruce yelled.

"What should we do?" I cried out, terrified.

It wasn't a significant quake, but seemed to go on forever, followed by several aftershocks. It was the final epiphany for us both. He belonged together with his wife and his children. I think it hit him his daughter could one day end up like me, in bed with a stranger. Bruce jumped out of bed and called his wife and kids to make sure they were okay. I could hear him on the phone.

"Don't worry. Daddy will come right over, and we'll go out for pancakes."

When Bruce came back into the bedroom, I had already put on sweatpants and a t-shirt. I knew the earthquake brought with it a seismic shift in our relationship, and it no longer felt right to appear naked in front of Bruce, with or without his glasses on.

"You won't be able to stay here anymore."

"Okay."

"I'll give you some time to figure it out. You are a wonderful girl, Pam. This experience has opened my eyes to so much. I will help you in any way I can to thank you for helping me to see things straight. You've opened my eyes to see what I've been missing out on with my family."

I was glad I opened Bruce's eyes. I flashed back to the innocent days of the first summer I rode Princess. There were multiple times Princess shied from something unexpected and threw me off her back on to the ground. We had to get to know each other and trust one another. If I could handle Princess, I could handle Bruce.

Bruce took off in the Jaguar to meet up with his family,

leaving me to think about my next move over coffee. I spotted a few lines of blow left on the coffee table from the night before, so I got high and stepped out into the glorious Los Angeles morning sunshine on the terrace overlooking Beachwood Canyon.

How could such a beautiful city be so cruel and uninviting? Ever since arriving in Los Angeles, I seemed to be out of luck: I couldn't find a job. I'd had my best clothes and shoes stolen along with my Coach purse. About the only positive was the night I won money playing backgammon at PIPS.

Then I remembered the passes Dave had given me to PIPS, which I had hidden along with some cash and my birth certificate under the mattress in Pam's Room. It was time to put them to good use. I'd go there tonight and impress the club with my backgammon genius. It's hard to lose when you've got nothing.

I might have helped Bruce see he belonged to his family, but he more than paid me back by teaching me the art of winning at backgammon. Most of the people who joined the club did so less because they loved the game and more because it was the chic thing to do. It was a place to be seen and to network. There weren't many players who were as knowledgeable about the game as I had become, so they were easy to beat.

After a few nights of hanging out at PIPS, I made as much as two thousand dollars just for playing backgammon . . . And winning. It was like shooting at fish in a barrel. After the first roll of the dice, after the opponent's first move, I would figure out how I would beat them. It was as if a doorway to a part of my brain opened, and I could see every move played out before it happened.

I became a popular fixture at PIPS. There were plenty of girls more educated and wittier and far more sophisticated than me, not to mention more beautiful. But they lacked one thing. They didn't know how to gamble like Wild Bill's daughter. Not only did I never lose, when I was high on cocaine, I could also spin a yarn like nobody's business. When I was high, sage pearls of wisdom flowed through me as I swam on a stream of consciousness, people asking me for advice as though I were a soothsayer tapped into the untold secrets of the Universe. While playing backgammon, I discovered a place I belonged and felt inspired and loved. All I needed to do was keep on winning.

By the time I ran out of the complimentary passes gifted to me by Dave, I was part of the scene and didn't need a pass. The doorman waved me in, past the velvet rope as though I were a regular. Bruce let me keep my things at his house until I moved to a permanent address, but I was no longer his burden or responsibility, leaving him free to repair his broken marriage. I knew it was time for me to plant some roots in LA and get an apartment, but I was enjoying being footloose and fancy-free with no regular job. Anyway, what kind of job could I get that would pay me in one month what I could make playing backgammon in one night? Plus, I was meeting some fascinating people from all walks of life—a writer, actors, famous musicians, a depressed director, and a few financial wizards—all of whom seemed to enjoy my company and I theirs. It was like a semester at an elite college where the cost of admission was to party and play backgammon.

One night, a prominent man asked me to accompany him to Paris. He was looking to make a significant purchase of a property there and thought it was a novel idea to take me along. I realized that not only did I not have a driver's license, but I also didn't have a passport.

"I wish I could go, but I have some things I have to take care of here," I said.

"What could be better than going to Paris, ma chérie?" he teased. "Have you been?"

"Oh, yes, many times. J'aime Paris. And I adore you for the asking. But I'm sorry, my calendar is full next week. We could pretend we are in Paris tonight, though," I flirted. "Let's get a bottle of the finest French champagne and imagine we're in

Grand Paris."

Off we went to his sprawling mansion in Trousdale Estates above Sunset, where we danced the night away to Edith Piaf, Jacques Brel, and Francoise Hardy, drinking champagne and snorting coke into the early morning light.

The moment left a strong impression. Note to self: must get a passport, tout de suite. I could only hope the opportunity to go to Paris would come my way again one day, and next time I would be ready.

A few nights later, at PIPS, I ran into my new friend Adam, who was engaged to be married to a socialite still in college back east. His relationship status kept me from making a move on him; the attraction was mutual. Were he not spoken for, there were nights I think he would have jumped me right in the backgammon booth as the fact I beat him every time we played made him crazy.

"You're a magician or some kind of weird, witchy woman. I don't know how you do it. You never lose," he said one night, exasperated after I pummeled him game after game. "You're like Wonder Woman or some backgammon superhero. Hey, I've got it—you're *Backgammon Girl.*"

"Well, I try to give you pointers, but your problem is you don't trust me," I pointed out as he shoved wads of cash to me across the table.

"Adam, this is crazy! I can't accept this much money from you. It doesn't feel right."

Even though he seemed to have an endless supply of cash, I felt legitimate guilt that I kept beating him, only to have him raise the stakes higher.

"Okay, I'll tell you what. Instead of paying my debt to you in cash, I'll introduce you to a guy who knows Bernie Cornfeld."

"I'm fine with whatever, but who the hell is Bernie Cornfeld?"

"He is only the brightest financial guru in the city, and

everyone in town is in his Rolodex. It could be an excellent move for you, no pun intended. Bernie can give you an entrée to Hollywood like nobody else. And your backgammon skills will impress the hell out of Bernie. Trust me; he'll love you. Forget about renting an apartment. Bernie might even invite you to live at his mansion. He lets a lot of chicks live there for free."

Later that night, Adam introduced me to Bernie's friend Jack.

"Bernie will love your ass," Jack said in a somewhat monotone voice that sounded ominous and frightened me. "He'll want to photograph that ass. Here's the address. I'll tell Bernie to expect you on Wednesday at twelve-thirty. Cool?"

I snatched the card. The address read, "Grayhall Mansion." Always up for an adventure, it intrigued me. And, I figured, who knows... I might even get a free place to stay out of it.

"Tell Mr. Cornfeld to be expecting me!"

11

IN COLD BLOOD

Squinting to block out the high-noon Los Angeles sun, I waited for a Yellow Cab to pick me up at the intersection of Crescent Heights and Sunset. Across the street, I watched the bohemian girl playing her recorder on the corner, surprised by how many cars stopped to give her tips.

When the cabbie pulled over to the curb, I said, "Grayhall Mansion, please. It's at 11—"

He cut me off. "I know where it is. Get in."

"Thanks so much."

"So, I guess you're new in town?" the cabbie asked.

"And what makes you say that?"

"You have a funny accent. Where are you from?"

"I'm from nowhere. You ever hear of the Beatles' song "Nowhere Man"? Well, I'm from the same place he is. The only difference is, he doesn't have a point of view, and I do. I have a point of view on just about everything. Go on, ask me anything."

The cabbie glanced up in the rearview mirror and chuckled. I could tell because of the way his eyes shined and wrinkles formed around them. We sat in silence for a bit as the taxi snaked along Sunset Boulevard, weaving in and out of traffic, before entering the residential section of Beverly Hills near the intersection of Sunset Boulevard and Whittier.

We drove past a Smokey the Bear ad, and he asked, "Want a cigarette?"

"Why thank you, don't mind if I do."

The cabbie flicked his lighter multiple times with his thumb. "Damn lighter's busted. You have a light?"

"Sure."

Rifling through my purse, I found the pack of matches I'd picked up the night before at PIPS. After lighting the cigarette, he offered me, I handed them to the cabbie.

"Ah, PIPS. Have you been there?" asked the cabbie caressing the coveted pack of matches.

"I guess you could say I'm a regular... I'm known there, you know. People call me Backgammon Girl."

"You don't say? So, are you like a celebrity or something?"

"No, just lucky!"

"Lucky? How do you mean?"

"I was born lucky. Plenty of luck factors into winning at backgammon, which is why I never lose. How long before we get there?"

"Have you ever been to the mansion before?"

"No, I haven't."

"Have you ever lost at backgammon?"

"No, I haven't."

"Ah, come on! You're pulling my leg. Everyone loses at least once in life," the cabbie said, sounding philosophical.

"Not me. So, have you ever been up there?" I asked.

"Sure. I've been up there a bunch of times. Lots of parties going on. Lots of celebrities. Trees surround it, so you can't see it from the street, but it's just up ahead."

We rounded the next bend, and my wide eyes caught the first glimpse of the magnificent quarry-face stone exterior standing as majestic as a medieval English manor. It sat atop a promontory like an enchanted fortress draped in vines and shaded by trees. Since arriving in Los Angeles, I had been inside some spectacular homes, but nothing came close to Grayhall Mansion.

I sank further into the seat as we made our way up the long Cinderella driveway and pulled to a stop in front of the formal entrance. The water in an ornate fountain sparkled like 10-karat diamonds in the summer sun, blinding me as I fumbled around my purse for the fare.

"Here you go. And keep the change. Oh, and for what it's worth, I have lost. I've lost a lot. Just not at backgammon."

Our eyes locked for a moment.

"Stay lucky, Backgammon Girl," he said. I watched the cab disappear beyond the trees.

Taking in the façade's grandeur, an unexpected wave of sadness cast over me like a cloud in front of the sun, taking me back to the Pennsylvania farm I left behind. In my idealistic memories, the dilapidated old farmhouse was every bit as majestic as the mansion. There were fireplaces in every room, but they boarded them up long before I lived there. The porch was decrepit and falling apart from the weight of the heavy snowfall of seasons past. Inside the weathered, dark green door, a black stairwell graced the entryway, and a sparkling, strawberry colored chandelier hung above.

I felt stuck in my childhood memories when Bernie Cornfeld, the owner of the mansion, appeared from seemingly nowhere, greeting me by name though never introduced. Wearing a little tweed cap, he was somewhat reminiscent of an elf or a munchkin, not good-looking in a classic sense but with an artful charm.

Though I picked up on a con man's scent, it only served to make me more intrigued. He exuded warmth and carefree enjoyment of life that comes from acquiring a lifestyle to which most can only fantasize.

"Let's go inside. I have some champagne waiting for us, Pam."

Waltzing me across the black-and-white marble floor of the imposing foyer with oak inlay and muted frescos gracing the walls, we entered a ballroom of baronial proportions. The carved and stenciled ceiling imported from Spain was elaborate in detail and made it difficult to bring my attention back to eye level to accept the champagne flute Bernie handed me.

"Here's a toast to having an amazing photoshoot," Bernie said as he clinked my glass.

"Photoshoot?" I asked.

"I can't resist photographing a beautiful woman."

Before finishing my first glass of champagne, I was stark naked, holding a bunch of grapes above my head in the middle of the Cinderella driveway. Cars and limousines were pulling in and out; wealthy men were coming to hang out with the bevy of beautiful women lounging by the pool. No one seemed to pay much attention to the impromptu photoshoot and my exposed bottom as if it was an everyday occurrence.

Out of the blue, Bernie asked, "Are you more into guys or girls?"

I tried to think of an ambiguous answer to pique Bernie's curiosity. At seventeen, I knew already that sometimes the less you say, the more attractive you become. It took little more than the mere raising of an eyebrow to elicit Bernie's histrionic response.

"Oh, *do* tell me more," he prompted, and I suspected his vivid imagination was busy filling in the blanks as he fired off more shots with his camera.

"You remind me of a Botticelli painting," Bernie gushed as I attempted to strike different poses. "I am inspired to shoot you like Botticelli's famous 'Birth of Venus' because you have a kind of Renaissance body and hair. Venus was an exceptional goddess in that she could arouse men to want her, but she also stimulated and inspired their minds. You have the same quality, and if I can just capture that essence on film, we will have something. It could mean a deal with Penthouse, and for you, my dear, the key to this town. You'll have men lining up around the block just to buy you a drink."

It reminded me of the now infamous pearls of wisdom served up by my father, that seemed to be haunting me, *"If it's your last hundred-dollar bill, buy everyone in the bar a drink, and you'll drink for free for a month."* What advice would Wild Bill have for me now as I found myself stark naked in the middle of the driveway to a famous mansion in Beverly Hills, California, posing nude for the prospect of having men line up to buy me drinks?

I was trying my best to look as demure and sexy as a goddess who has just been born from the sea, when Bernie asked, "How old are you?"

While I may have appeared as innocent as Venus, I was savvy enough to know my current under-age status might cause an abrupt end to the photoshoot. I didn't want to disappoint Bernie, Jack, Bob, or Botticelli, so I did my best to change topics—a skill I relied on for survival since I ran away three years ago.

"I'm flattered I remind you of Botticelli's famous painting," I said, imagining how an actual Botticelli painting might look. "But isn't it a bit cliché? That could be any number of girls. You know, at PIPS, I'm known as Backgammon Girl because I never lose," I said, trying to spark Bernie's imagination. "Few girls are lucky enough to say they never lose. Why don't we do some pictures with a backgammon board? Do you play?" I asked, already aware of his devotion to the game. I hoped this diversion would allow me to get inside the mansion and out of the view of every passerby.

"What a splendid and original idea for a spread. I can see it now: 'Meet Backgammon Girl.' Let's go into the library," Bernie said as he made an about-turn and led me, naked and barefoot, inside the mansion through the broad glazed door graced with ornate iron screens. I followed, attempting not to appear self-conscious with one arm across my chest and one hand grabbing my privates.

"I have a beautiful backgammon board set up in here. Do you visit PIPS a lot?" he asked.

"Often enough to have earned the name Backgammon Girl, rarely enough to get bored with the place."

"Do you get bored often?"

"Only when I'm with boring people. But you're not boring," I said with enthusiasm, happy to be getting my naked body into a less visible and vulnerable place.

Once inside the mansion walls and enjoying more champagne, I felt more comfortable being Backgammon Girl instead of someone pretending to know how a woman in a Botticelli painting would behave.

It was clear Bernie loved shooting photos as he fired off multiple shots while coaxing me into different poses, some of which I wasn't sure whether they were for art or his entertainment. I made him laugh with my trick of blowing on the dice before rolling—something I picked up from my dad.

He asked, "Does it work? Does it bring you luck when you blow on the dice?"

"Of course, it works. It builds up the anticipation, and everyone gets more excited. That excitement builds positive energy around the roll."

I could feel his lens zooming in on my lips as I puckered up to blow. When the light streaming through the window began disappearing behind the trees, Bernie called it a day.

"Okay, Backgammon Girl, that's it. It's a wrap!"

He set the camera down on the antique credenza and turned to pour the last glasses from the champagne bottle for a final toast to our impromptu photoshoot.

"There's a little corner bedroom upstairs, off to the left of the library, where you can get cleaned up. Follow me. There's someone I want you to meet later, so I hope you will stay for dinner tonight."

Bernie beckoned me up a little stairwell to a bedroom with an en-suite bathroom and handed me some towels that were about an inch thick and soft as sheep's wool, then he disappeared back down the stairs. I turned on the shower, stepping under the fine mist of warm water. The goat's milk soap had a fresh scent that mixed with the honeysuckle on the breeze drifting in through an open window. When I stepped out of the steamy shower, I dried off with the fluffy white towel, and I wrapped myself in a crisp white robe.

Growing up on the farm, I always dreamed of having a shower just like this. During rainstorms, I often stood beneath the rusted gutter, to endure freezing water, while twirling and splashing about in my pretend world of luxury. In the farmhouse, there was only one bathroom for eight people, and we all had to share one tub of water. By the time it was my turn to bathe, the water was cold and dirty.

Combing out my long blonde hair, I heard Bernie bounding up the small flight of wooden stairs. He entered the room clutching Truman Capote's book *In Cold Blood in his stubby little hands.*

"Here's a book I think you should read, written by the one and only Truman Capote. It's a great piece of literature filled with eloquent prose—what they call a 'complex triple narrative.' One minute you're on a journey into the lives of the murderers, then the victims, and then you're all wrapped up in the people whose lives were circling them in this tiny rural town in Kansas. It's Capote's masterpiece, and the best part is, it's all true. Do you like true stories?"

Overwhelmed by the surroundings and the champagne, trying hard to disguise my Pittsburgh accent, I blurted out, "I don't know. I don't like to lie."

Then Bernie asked me a question that offered me a way to escape painful memories of the farm. "So, what part of England do you hail? Not in London? Newbury Park?"

Without a moment's hesitation, I blurted out, "That's right!" wondering how on earth this man-about-the-world would think my Pittsburgh-ese was a British accent.

It was a natural leap for my mind to fantasize about the beautiful life I had in Newbury Park. However, I had never been east of Pennsylvania, let alone across the Atlantic. I seized the moment as an opportunity to become someone new. I could become anyone I wanted—even someone without a painful past.

Before I had time to blink, Bernie continued, filling in details about my life as if he were Gammy painting by numbers.

"Not only am I very astute at detecting accents, but I also understand something about women, which few men can claim. I understand their essence. I can pick up on a woman's pure soul through her eyes, her sense of herself, and her level of confidence. You are a confident, self-assured woman. But—and this is important—you don't seem to know your worth. You must find your worth. You must own it. Don't let anyone define what you are worth. That's for you to know and for them to discover when you are ready."

Reaching into his pocket, Bernie pulled out a wad of cash held together by a shiny money clip and peeled off a few hundred-dollar bills.

"Here's a bit of mad money. Consider it an advance for the Penthouse spread. Go shopping in Beverly Hills for something nice to wear to dinner tonight," he said, reminding me of Wild Bill.

Bernie led me through the mansion's massive front doors, back to the Cinderella driveway where several limos parked. A driver was soon opening the door for me, with instructions from Bernie to drop me off at Rodeo and Wilshire to go shopping. Back when I'd been hitchhiking on Black Canyon Highway in Phoenix to get from high school to work at Hobo Joe's, I dreamt of having a driver. But I never believed I would one day be heading for Rodeo Drive in a limousine that still had that new car smell.

I settled into the backseat as dreams of skipping through English gardens on my way to high tea played out in my mind while I contemplated my worth. What did Bernie mean by that? Did he mean in dollars and cents, or was my worth the sum value of my experiences?

My life had been a blur of memories since running away, and I was still coming to terms with the fact I could never return.

The years I spent growing up on the farm had left me feeling worthless. Maybe I could change all that by becoming somebody new. The new me could be worth something to someone. In England, there could be an entire family who wished me well and valued my life, who knew my worth, who couldn't wait for me to return for the Christmas holidays so they could spoil me with fig pudding and presents and take me for a ride in a horse-drawn sleigh.

The limousine pulled up in front of Bonwit Teller, and the driver mumbled something in his broken English, bringing me back to reality. He stepped out of the limo to open the door for me. Emerging like a celebrity from behind tinted windows, I waltzed in through the glass doors and entered a fantasy world.

Until that moment, the only shopping experience that came close was Joseph Horne's department store—a well-respected institution in downtown Pittsburgh, in a seven-story building at Penn Avenue and Stanwix Street. When I was twelve, a Joseph Horne's security guard caught me shoplifting a floppy sun hat while exiting Horne's, the tag dangling down ala Minnie Pearl. I took the bonnet for no other reason than I liked it, and I wanted to fit in with the older girls I was with, who were shoplifting. They brought me along to be their "mule," considering me too inexperienced to pull off the actual heists. After they stole a bunch of items, we met in the bathroom to transfer the stolen goods to me. When the security guard picked me up, I had a miniature silver clock, a pair of elegant leather gloves, a scarf, makeup, and some other odds and ends hiding in pockets, down my pants, and in my training bra. The other girls abandoned me when the officer escorted me to a back room where the interrogation went on for over an hour.

Grateful, they didn't search my body to discover the stolen merchandise, it took every ounce of nerve I could muster not to crack. After trying to reach my mother by phone, the officers let me go with a warning never to return to Joseph Horne. They would send a letter to my mother, notifying her of the incident. I sat in the shade of the lilac bushes each day as they bloomed, waiting for the mailman so I could intercept the incriminating notification of my crime.

Bonwit Teller smelled of new leather and expensive perfume, a magical assault on the senses. Closing my eyes to take it all in, I conjured the smell of leather from the horse saddles mixing with the fragrant scent of lilacs in the late summer breeze.

The sales lady asked if I would like to sample a cologne. My eyes scanned the sparkling cases and glistening counters before landing on a small bottle. There it was, a message from the Universe, sure to transform me from a little lost girl into a woman of substance: a perfume called "Worth."

"May I sample this one?" I asked, pointing at the French perfume by Je Reviens.

"Certainly."

She sprayed a small piece of paper and waved it in front of my nose. I took in more than just the cologne's aroma. I breathed in hope, excitement, and all the good things coming my way. It was a new identity of someone with value and purpose. A character who had committed no sins and lived a respectable life filled with infinite possibility. A life I deserved. A life worth something.

In my best British accent, I said, "I'll take it."

I floated out of the department store on a billowy cloud of Worth with a bag full of free samples, and a silk scarf still bearing the tags followed me out of the store. Old impulses die hard.

The scarf had a pattern with horses on it and a lovely gold border. When I returned to the mansion, I wrapped it around my torso and tied it at the neck to fashion a glamorous silk top, which I wore to dinner with my bell bottoms.

"What impeccable style you have, Pam. You look exquisite this evening."

I smiled, delighted that Bernie approved.

The evening's guests arrived and enjoyed drinks in the gathering room with impressive Corinthian columns flanking the entryway. At the center was a massive stone fireplace where a roaring fire created patterns of dancing light across the room.

The party reconvened for dinner into the octagon-shaped dining room. It featured a ceiling imported from a castle in France, displaying beautiful oil paintings depicted in the center of sculpted medallions.

At one point, Bernie commented that the gold in my makeshift top complimented the dining room's 24-carat gold-leaf walls. It was hard to fathom there was more gold covering the walls of that dining room than in most jewelry cases of the poshest Beverly Hills jewelry stores. At least, according to Bernie.

Seated across from me was a British actress named Charlotte, who made me feel like Eliza Doolittle. She was ten years older than me and a lot more sophisticated. I could hear some of the gentlemen seated around the table whispering amongst themselves about the nude cover she appeared on for one of the popular men's magazines. Her impeccable style and lovely face belied her biting sense of sarcasm, and she possessed an endless supply of nasty put-downs and amusing anecdotes. But it was her lilting British accent that made me shrink further into my seat. She made me feel like a phony. Her presence was so commanding one might have thought the entire dinner party was being thrown in her honor as she dominated the conversation and the attention of everyone at the table. At least the men.

Charlotte pushed the food with her knife onto her fork in an elegant way as she enjoyed small bites of fish mixed with steamed vegetables. Observing her sleek way of commanding the cutlery made me realize what poor etiquette I developed growing up in a family of five kids. I learned to grab what I could and eat as fast as possible so that I could get my fill. I began trying to push my food around like Charlotte. Flustered, I gave up in favor of enjoying the champagne that flowed as if from an endless spring.

Later in the evening, everyone at the dinner party retired to the patio and other areas of the mansion. Charlotte, flanked by two men dressed in colorful attire, approached me.

"So, you are the Backgammon Girl Bernie mentioned? I think you're cute, but I wouldn't want to play you. At backgammon, that is. I find it quite boring. Perhaps we could find something else to amuse ourselves."

"It's not boring at all once you understand the strategy behind winning. I'm happy to give you lessons. Backgammon can be—"

"Shhhh..." Charlotte put her finger to my lips, silencing me. "Let's find a quiet place."

We found a path to a secluded part of the garden, where we sat beneath a trellis of roses. Charlotte pulled a mirror out of her jeweled handbag and laid out some lines of coke to pass around our entourage. She tugged me close and writhed her hips next to mine in a suggestive dance. She kissed me, at first in a gentle way, and then with robust enthusiasm, as her two male companions also made out.

A dignified looking man swooped in on us and whisked Charlotte away. I could hear her laughter echoing across the patio as they disappeared inside the mansion walls, leaving me sitting beneath the rose trellis feeling awkward and alone. I figured the cocaine was making me a bit paranoid, so I headed for the powder room to gather my emotions.

As I made my way there, Bernie came up behind me and clasped my arm, saying, "There is someone I'd like you to meet, but first, please fix your face, my dear."

Ducking into the powder room, I looked in the mirror to observe my face randomly smeared with Charlotte's bright red lipstick, giving me the appearance of a little girl who had been trying on her mother's makeup.

Emerging from the powder room, I was fresh-faced but self-conscious, wondering if anyone except Bernie had seen my clown-like appearance moments before.

"You are even more beautiful without makeup, Pam."

Bernie gave me a broad smile and caressed my cheek before leading me across the patio to a rather tall man who sat next to him at the dinner table.

"Ibrahim, this is the young lady I was telling you about."

"Nice to meet you," I said.

"Pam, why don't you take Ibrahim up to your room where you can have some privacy and get acquainted with some small talk?"

I wasn't sure how to react to Bernie's referring to the room at the top of the small stairwell as *my* room. But I was grateful to have a place to stay that was a better solution than Pam's room at Bruce's house. Plus, at Bernie's, I wouldn't have to worry about getting a car or passing my driver's license test with limos at my disposal. And who wouldn't want to live in such opulence?

So, without thinking about it too much, I held my arm out for Ibrahim and said, "Shall we?"

"Yes, I would like that very much."

The man with the foreign accent followed me up the wooden stairwell to my room.

"I think that's a funny expression—small talk," I told Ibrahim as we entered my room.

"What do you mean?"

"Well, I mean, what makes talk small?"

"Maybe small talk is just what one needs to lead to big kisses," he said as he gave me a gentle push, laying me down on top of the bed.

"You remind me of Omar Sharif in Funny Girl," I giggled as we disappeared beneath the luxurious cotton sheets, dancing to the rhythm of cocaine, champagne, and cognac. I wasn't into making out with this stranger; in fact, his pheromones repulsed me, but I wanted to be held and feel safe. So, I gave myself to the moment, which lasted for the duration of the night. I floated in and out of reality, as though dangling from a thin thread. I felt lost and frightened, consumed by night.

The cawing of a big, black crow awoke me early the next morning, but I remained still, pretending to be asleep. I didn't want to see Ibrahim in the light of day, and I didn't want to make more small talk. I felt hunger pains through the remnants of champagne and cognac from the night before. I wondered why I hadn't eaten more, feeling silly about having been so insecure about my culinary etiquette.

Numb and void of emotion, I remained in a state of suspended animation reliving the events of our night of passion. The night before, I pictured silhouettes of angels dancing upon the ceiling in the moonlight, not disconnected bodies lying beneath the covers at a loss for words.

The night before, I imagined we were running in the wind with reckless abandon, his hair flying wild, and a broad smile on his face. I wanted him to be my fantasy hero — someone who could make me forget about my troubles.

In the morning's light, squinting my eyes to watch him dress, I saw his head was somewhat bald, and I couldn't wait for him to leave. Was this how men thought about me when I was the one skulking out at the crack of dawn?

I had been leaving PIPS to stay over at a different man's house almost every night for the past month, but somehow those encounters felt unlike what transpired last night. It had been my choice to go with them. Last night's encounter was not by accident or spontaneous. It was an arrangement for me to sleep with this man I didn't know, and odds were I would never see him again. It made me feel empty and used, even though I was fully aware that I had put myself in this position.

I lay motionless; the stranger would soon roll out, and disappear like the morning fog. The bed shifted, and I could hear the jangling of his belt as he pulled up his trousers. Some coins escaped his pockets, bouncing across the wooden floor into the cracks of the floorboards. A few fell onto the soft rug or disappeared beneath the bed. He tried to retrieve them, but his breathing got heavier as he bent over, so he left them there. I heard him descending the wooden stairwell in his socks. When his feet met the landing, he slipped on his shoes and continued across the marble floor to the front door. Then his car engine broke the morning stillness, and he departed down the long driveway.

Confident I was alone, I opened my eyes to take in the morning sunshine pouring through the cracks of the wooden blinds. I flipped over the side of the bed, my long, blonde hair tousled and hanging down as I stretched for the fallen coins.

Hoisting myself back upright with the loose change clenched in my fist, a shaft of light illuminated a note addressed to "Pam" on the antique dresser. I slipped out from beneath the covers and unfolded the letter. It read, "Thank you for an enjoyable evening." Resting beside the note was a Cartier watch, a tank style with a rectangular face and a little, gleaming sapphire adorning the dial to wind it up. Sapphire is my birthstone, and I had always wanted a ring with a sapphire stone, but a watch would more than do.

I felt timid as I fastened the watch to my wrist. I had never owned such a beautiful piece of jewelry, but I couldn't help but consider the irony of being given a timepiece, for I knew the clock was ticking. I just turned seventeen years old and had no job, no place to live, and no family. Perhaps Bernie was right. Maybe all I needed to do was to discover my worth.

I wriggled into my bell-bottoms, pulled my hair into a ponytail, and applied a dab of Worth perfume before emerging from Grayhall Mansion alone. The sun was warming up the earth beneath my feet as I ambled down the streets on foot toward the Beverly Hills flats, wondering what the day might bring.

12

CROSSROADS OF THE WORLD

The best part about the open invitation to stay at Bernie's was I didn't have to rely on strangers for a place to stay, and I didn't need to commit to paying rent. And because Bernie never locked the mansion doors, I could come and go as I pleased without interacting with anyone.

However, I knew the longer I stayed at Bernie's, the longer it would take me to find my real purpose, my worth. I was aware the scene at the mansion wasn't who I was at my core. I had much higher aspirations than lounging by the pool all day and playing backgammon and attending fancy dinner parties with famous people. I wanted to figure out how could I win at life.

Still, it was a charming and seductive lifestyle and one that felt convenient. Notable patrons at PIPS considered me a lucky charm, and wealthy men paid me to hang out with them and give them pointers or play their turn. Men who could spare a one-hundred-dollar bill or more to tip the bathroom attendant lavished me with compliments, champagne, caviar, and cocaine. I felt safe at Bernie's. At least for the time being.

One night, Adam showed up at PIPS with a buddy from New York who considered himself a professional backgammon player. Adam was high on coke, eager to have me play against his pal—almost giddy waiting for Backgammon Girl's embarrassing fall from grace. Not being able to have sex with me or beat me at backgammon made Adam more determined to have some conquest over me. My loss to Thomas would fulfill his greatest fantasy, which was to see me lose.

Adam spread gossip around the club with the regulars, that tonight would be epic because Backgammon Girl would meet her match. A small group began forming around our table as Thomas and I started playing. We were moving around the board at the same pace, but after a while, Thomas pulled ahead.

"I want to double the stakes with the doubling cube," he said, giving me a sideways look as though I wouldn't know what he meant.

Using a doubling cube brings a higher level of strategy to the game because the doubling cube can be a weapon when well-played. Once one player has the cube, only that person can use it, and their odds of winning go up. They have a formidable advantage because they can use it to either end the game or double the pressure on their opponent.

I studied the board for a moment. If I were Thomas, I would have waited to see what my opponent did with their next move. Odds were he made the call as a bluff to challenge my expertise with the game—or to see me sweat and back me into a corner where I would make a strategic mistake. I studied the board, and from where I sat, if Thomas didn't have the doubling cube, the odds were in my favor to win. According to the rules, if favored to win, it permits you to redouble and gain possession of the cube. This move is called a "Beaver."

At this point in the game, I felt it could go either way, but I had to calculate my chances and call it because there was no way I would let him hold on to that cube.

"I call a Beaver," I said with a sly tone.

"What the hell is she talking about?" Adam said with a nervous chuckle.

His buddy Thomas wasn't laughing, and everyone within earshot leaned in. The pressure was real.

Thomas replied, "She just quadrupled the stakes with her Beaver."

"With her beaver?" Adam acted hysterically now. "I know she's hot, but how can she use her beaver to quadruple the stakes?"

Thomas wasn't laughing. After his next roll, it was clear who would win.

"She got me. And she quadrupled the stakes with her beaver," Thomas said. "She got me with her beaver."

No one in the room except for Thomas and me seemed to know what the heck he was talking about, but the idea I had just won with my beaver made the entire place go crazy and erupt into chaos as Adam began throwing bills in the air.

"Does anyone want to play Backgammon Girl? She's out of our league!!"

I walked away with $3,000 in my pocket from one game, which was more than enough to rent an apartment, get my life organized, and begin planting some roots. But that could wait until tomorrow. The night was young, and Thomas led me like royalty to the bar for a round of drinks. In a while, we headed back to his suite at the Beverly Wilshire, where we partied until the wee hours.

When I woke in the morning, Thomas was in the shower. I reached for my watch to see what time it was, only to realize my Cartier had stopped ticking. I figured the battery had died, and since the Cartier store in Beverly Hills was close by, I would head over to replace it.

At around noon, I bid farewell to Thomas and sauntered over to Cartier on foot and presented my watch to a well-heeled woman behind the counter.

"I'd like to have the battery replaced, please."

The woman examined the watch and said, "I'll be back in a moment."

I scanned the glistening cases of jewelry, diamond bracelets worthy of a princess, engagement rings with impressive stones waiting to grace the hand of a woman deserving of becoming someone's wife. I began wondering if I would ever meet someone with whom I could share my life. My overactive imagination conjured visions of pouring coffee for my husband while he read the paper on a rose-covered terrace, enjoying champagne poolside and an evening bubble bath. Without warning, the woman re-appeared from behind a wall with a short, bald man who got right to the point.

"My dear, we cannot replace the battery because this is not a genuine Cartier watch. This timepiece is a forgery, a counterfeit. Where did you gain this imitation?"

I could feel my cheeks turning pink, then crimson red. Would they arrest me?

"May I please ask where you gained this watch?"

I was without words. The watch was a forgery, a good one, but a fake all the same. Now everything felt fraudulent and deceptive. The relationships I floated in and out of were like imaginary characters who had no real identity other than to play a pretend role in my life. It was as if I had seen behind the curtain to discover the Wizard of Oz was just a man, and the characters who led me down the yellow brick road were without a heart, courage, or substance.

After gathering my thoughts, doing my best to emulate Charlotte's accent, I said, "I bought it from a street vendor. Foolish of me, I know, to trust a stranger. I will ask my boyfriend to confront the vendor if we can find him. Will you please return it to me?"

"As you wish. And may I suggest to you, young lady, to not be so trusting."

Beyond humiliated from being scolded by the short, bald man, I turned to leave, but when a security guard came to escort me out of the store, it was a walk of shame. I shoved the watch into my open purse and swore never to wear it again. My face burned, and tears pooled up in my eyes, blinding me as I stepped outside and onto the sidewalk of Rodeo Drive, hoping I wouldn't run into anyone I knew. I could never look upon the stone walls of Grayhall Mansion in quite the same way again, and my journey on the path of that life ended for me right there in the Cartier store.

Even if it meant leaving behind the stolen scarf from Bonwit Teller and the bottle of Worth perfume, I decided I never wanted to return to the mansion. I had discovered an important truth. Everything in life is replaceable, except for one's pride.

Walking toward West Hollywood, I felt determined to find a small apartment to rent with the money from my backgammon winnings. I needed to get my life under control, find a respectable job, but I couldn't think on my feet.

I realized I had become wild and undomesticated, living a gypsy life—coming and going from Bernie's. But even the thought about settling down in a cozy home with a dog and a cat, not to mention a person, would cause me to panic, pick up and run away. It's not that I would want to leave. I would have to. The very idea of being settled, I found unsettling. I believed I didn't deserve these things. I felt secure and comfortable getting what I needed on the fly—no commitments.

At the next phone booth I saw, I called a cab to take me to the Old World Restaurant. I was hungry and hungover. Thomas and I polished off four bottles of champagne the night before accompanied by nothing but blini with caviar and Crème Fraiche, which now seemed like an eternity ago. As the cab sped down Santa Monica Boulevard, I glanced back at Beverly Hills in the side view mirror, glad to be leaving it behind.

Old World was in a landmark building—an iconic semi-circle that jutted out from the tip of where Sunset Blvd. and Holloway Drive intersect kitty-corner to Tower Records. It was the only place I could think of to tell the cab driver where to go.

I had been on my own for three years now. But entering the Old World Restaurant alone, asking for a table for one reminded me how alone I indeed was in the world. I suppose that's why I allowed myself to get so seduced by the glamor of Bernie's world and the nightlife at PIPS. I was trying to fill a void, and I wanted to belong somewhere to someone. Yet somewhere in my tangled-up heart, I felt at peace being alone. Tired and broken, I wondered if I already overstayed my welcome here on the spinning planet. I watched the cream swirl on top of the poured coffee the waitress had set down in front of me. The soul searching for my future ended abruptly with the voice of a man with a British accent asking me if I was alone.

"Might I join you for a coffee?"

His hair was dirty blond, and he had a beard like Stuart, although fuller. He wore a crinkled shirt with the sleeves rolled up and cream-colored linen pants. Despite looking as though these were the same clothes he slept in, he had a confident air about him. I didn't relish the company, but I didn't want to be alone, either. So, I gestured it was okay, inviting the man who bore a slight resemblance to the best-looking Bee Gee to sit down.

"I'm Sam," I said before realizing I had never introduced myself before as Sam—the name my father had given me—without telling the whole story about Johnny Cash. It was the defining moment when I decided I never wanted to refer to myself as Pam Butter ever again.

"Sam . . . That's a cute name. Is it short for Samantha?"

"My dad named me Sam," I answered, wondering how the name Samantha might suit me, the way one would consider a new pair of bell-bottoms.

"I'm Eugene. And I don't know who named me that – but I have always wished I had a proper nickname. So, Sammy, what do you do?"

I knew full well he was asking what I did for a living. If I had learned anything in Los Angeles the past few months besides not leaving your drink unattended, it was personal value relied on status. So, I decidedly dodged his line of questioning, hoping it would make him less interested in me so I could return to being alone.

"I like to go horseback riding. How about you? Do you have any hobbies?"

"I'm lucky. My work is also my hobby. I am a photographer. You're quite pretty. Have you ever been interested in modeling?"

"I have it on proper authority from Nina Blanchard, that I am too fat, my nose is too big, my teeth are too crooked, and my breasts? What breasts? Oh, and I'm too short."

"Well, what does Nina Blanchard know, Sammy?" he chuckled.

Just then, my omelet arrived, so I said, "Nice meeting you, Eugene, I don't want to sound rude, but if you pardon me, I'm quite famished."

I heard Old World omelets were every bit as spectacular as the smell of the steam wafting up from the dish in front of me. I took in the aroma while wondering what gave this stranger the idea to call me "Sammy." Before I could decide what I thought of it, Eugene ordered an omelet, making it clear he had no intention of leaving. Just as it arrived, an older gentleman Eugene referred to as Ivan, his "associate," showed up and joined us for a cup of coffee.

"Ivan, this is Sammy. She's from England and rides horses."

In the cab ride to the Old World, I had decided I would turn over a new leaf. I knew claiming I was British was a dumb idea and had determined to be myself. But I hadn't realized how much I now embodied the character I had pretended to be these past months and wasn't even conscious of the fact I had been speaking with a British accent to Eugene since he introduced himself. So, I had gone from British Pammy to British Sammy.

"Nice to meet you, Sammy."

Ivan's accent was foreign but not British.

I was cursing myself I hadn't ended this British charade because it took too much focus away from the more practical matters I needed to pursue like getting a decent job and a roof over my head where I didn't wake up with nightmares or hangovers.

The two men conversed in a language that sounded like Russian.

I was confused about how a British man spoke fluent Russian. The conversation between them was animated, and I felt alienated and uncomfortable. I fidgeted and looked around, wondering if I could find a graceful way to leave. What if they're Russian spies?

I noticed a man wearing dark sunglasses and a black beret. He had long, curly hair and a beard. He'd been staring at me since our arrival, jotting notes down in a black notebook. He must have consumed eight cups of coffee while biding his time, accepting re-fill upon re-fill, taking his gaze away from me only every so often to jot down more notes. I wondered if he was with the FBI on a stakeout of the Russian spies. Was I getting ensnarled in some mess? That's all I needed.

I felt my heart beating faster and faster in my chest, inching me toward a panic attack. I ran away from a mother I loved to a father who turned out to be a complete fool. Drugged and raped, busted for Cartier contraband, and now I was mixed up with Russian spies?

Sweat was moistening the hair on the back of my neck and began collecting on my forehead and palms. I thought I might be on the brink of losing it when Eugene resumed speaking in English.

"I'm sorry. I was telling my friend here all about you. We both think you are beautiful and were wondering if you would be interested in letting me take some pictures of you."

"It seemed like a lengthy conversation to say only that. What type of pictures? I told you, I'm not a model."

My suspicions about the Russians made me feel defensive. I also wasn't keen on repeating the modeling experience at Bernie's.

"I shoot for some of the most prestigious men's magazines in the world — Lui in France, Quick, and Stern in Germany. And Mayfair in England is my biggest client. You've heard of Mayfair most likely, right? Why don't you come up to my studio," he said, "and let's talk about it? Let me write the address down for you."

Eugene took a pen from his pocket and jotted the address down on a napkin. The man in the black beret paid his tab and sauntered across Sunset making his way to Tower Records. I felt foolish I had mistaken a man who looked like a starving artist for an FBI agent on a stakeout of those Russians.

I wasn't sure if I should tell Eugene I didn't own a car, and I didn't want to go with him. But I felt like I had nothing to lose. If Eugene and his accomplice ended up killing me, somewhere in my tangled-up heart, I felt at peace with that.

"Can I ride over with you?"

"I would love you to accompany me."

When the valet pulled Eugene's white vintage Cadillac around, I saw there was a tripod and other camera gear in the backseat, which put me at ease.

On the way to his studio, I revealed I had some photos taken already for Penthouse.

"I think the photographer who shot me has an exclusive with me for Penthouse."

"That's fine," Eugene said with assurance. "Although I shoot for Penthouse, they're not my biggest client."

"But I don't think I'm attractive enough to be a model, and if I can be candid, I didn't enjoy having my photograph taken. Especially without clothes on."

"You might surprise yourself if you sit for me. The way I photograph women is more akin to the way a painter paints them."

"You mean like Botticelli?" I asked.

Eugene let out a chuckle, and I could feel my cheeks blush with embarrassment for how silly it sounded.

"No, I mean, the way a painter captures a woman off guard. I look for those moments when you're not feeling self-conscious when you're unaware. I capture your essence—a moment like a painting. I didn't mean an actual painting."

As we drove down the boulevard, I sat with my hands folded in my lap, aware of my posture. Clutching my new Chloe handbag, my guard was up, but I didn't want it to be. I was numb from what happened at Cartier, and it was hard to hide my sadness. I tried not to show it, but my emotions were raw. I felt so torn apart, as though I might never put the pieces back together. At every traffic light, I thought about jumping out of the Cadillac. I questioned my sanity about being in the car with a stranger and over four-thousand dollars in my purse.

When we arrived at Crossroads of the World, feeling insignificant, I gathered up every piece of myself I could pull together to climb the stairwell leading up to Eugene's studio. Reminding myself, I had nothing to lose.

A pristine white backdrop adorned one corner of the room. Odds and ends—pieces of furniture, articles of women's clothing, and other props—lay strewn about the place. Ivan was already there making tea.

We sipped tea and ate McVittie's biscuits while reminiscing about England. Well, at least Eugene was reminiscing. I was pretending to be a girl without a painful past, who had an exciting future ahead—a girl I wanted to become.

"I am so glad I've met a sensible English girl with a proper upbringing," Eugene said. "These American girls have no soul. There's no depth behind their eyes, which makes it challenging to photograph them. When I spotted you at the restaurant, I knew you were different, and it didn't surprise me in the least you were British. Americans are spoiled and don't understand a thing about life."

"I can't say I disagree with you," I said as I thought to myself, *"And you have no idea how different I am."*

Later, in the early evening, Eugene took some photos of me, with my clothes on, but still a little sexy. The way Eugene moved and threw himself into the process was more soulful and less technical than Bernie. He exuded a sadness about him making me feel empathy towards him. As he was shooting me, he asked me various personal but funny questions, which made me smile and laugh in a way I hadn't for a long time.

"So, Sammy, what can you not live without?"

"Champagne, chocolates, and clean sheets!" I let out a giggle.

"That's the smile I was looking for!" Eugene said as he snapped away.

"Oh, yes, I almost forgot. I lost my ID, so I need to get my California driver's license as soon as possible. Can't live without that—at least not in Los Angeles."

"I'll take you if you like. I can't think of anywhere I'd rather be than the California Department of Moving Vehicles if it means I get to spend it with you. You are a delightful person, Sammy. I'm so glad we met."

With that, Eugene set his camera down and announced, "Let's call for a pizza!"

It seemed like eons ago since I had pizza, and I ate half of the pie. Then, I fell asleep, nestled under a worn woolen blanket on an overstuffed divan that looked out of place in the sterile studio environment. I felt safe being in a space that was creating an illusion by design and felt at home among props and fantasy clothes. Curiously, to me, it seemed more real than Grayhall Mansion.

Eugene sensed I had nowhere to go but never pried me for information. In his profession, he met many inexperienced girls like me, who appeared lost or misplaced. However, I remained steadfast about not letting him discover the frightened girl hiding inside.

Over the next few days, I learned Eugene and Ivan were speaking in Czech, having escaped from Czechoslovakia after the Soviets invaded during the Prague Spring. Eugene went to England, which is where he honed his British accent. He now carried a "stateless" passport. Ivan was Eugene's sidekick/talent scout, always on the lookout for girls to recruit for Eugene to photograph.

One of the unexpected benefits of hanging out with Eugene was he abhorred cigarettes, and cocaine was not his vice. Since arriving in Los Angeles, I had been partying hard almost every day. It became apparent how much time I spent hopped up on cocaine, which made me crave cigarettes and altered my better judgment. It felt good to slow down and become calmer and more clear-headed. I thought I could organize my mind's compartments again and started searching the listings for an apartment.

True to his promise, Eugene took me to get my license. After two tries, I passed the written exam, but I was unprepared for how different driving in California would be from Phoenix and failed the driving portion—five times. Eugene helped me laugh it off, chalking it up to learning how to drive in England on the opposite side of the road.

"I guess you have no choice. You are stuck with me, Sammy. But not to worry! I don't mind being your chauffeur."

I discovered Eugene had one vice—vodka, which he could consume at an alarming rate without seeming the least bit intoxicated. I figured it was something he grew up with from his mother country, so it didn't seem unusual. Hard liquor never appealed to me, and I was enjoying my new sobriety.

Eugene went out to run some errands one afternoon and came back to surprise me with a set of crisp, white 400-count cotton sheets, some champagne, and a box of chocolates.

"The sheets are for your new apartment, and the champagne and chocolates are for us to enjoy tonight!" he said, popping the cork.

Later that evening, after we'd consumed the champagne, he began downing vodka shots before opening up to me about losing the love of his life just a year before.

"Her name was Carole Augustine. She was perfection—everyone wanted to shoot with Carole. Her star was just beginning to rise as the face of the Manikin Cigar adverts. She was only twenty-four years old when she died, and we were planning to marry…"

"How did it happen?" I asked before realizing the question might be too personal. "I'm sorry, Eugene. That was insensitive of me to ask. You don't have to tell me if it's too—"

"She was on a photoshoot in Algarve, Portugal, and she vomited in her sleep and asphyxiated herself. They found her in bed at a villa near the fishing resort of Portimão."

He teared up at the memory, and I comforted him as best I could.

"She's buried in a cemetery in Golder's Green, back in London. It's been a while since I've have been to her gravesite. I miss her," he said, laying his head on my lap as he sobbed.

I brushed his long, blond hair away from his tear-drenched face, wondering what caused Carole to throw up in her sleep but couldn't bear to ask Eugene any more questions about it. It seemed he spent every day since her death feeling the agony of missing her. I could relate to losing someone you love. I missed my mom every day.

Now I understood the connection between us. Eugene was a wounded person like me, and this brought out my mothering side. Fate had brought us together so I could take care of him. I was "stateless," just like Eugene, ripped from my homeland, never to return.

13

LONDON CALLING

Ivan stopped coming around because I took over his job of recruiting the models. It was easier for pretty girls to relate to an affable British girl their age than to a gray-haired gentleman with a thick Czech accent. I soon knew my way around Hollywood and could spot the girls who just arrived and were looking for a way to get into the business. I got my rap down pat and could convince them to trust me.

"I work with a photographer who is an amazing artist. He'll make you look beautiful, you'll make some money, and you'll get some great photos for your portfolio. You can't even get a meeting with an agent without some good photos in your portfolio."

Referring to the day, Nina Blanchard cut me down to size and convinced me how unworthy I was, always broke the ice. I took great pride in helping girls who were new to the town by getting them a paid gig because I knew firsthand what a scary place Los Angeles could be. By giving them some work and some advice about how to stay safe in Los Angeles, I was helping them and also getting my self-esteem back. It delighted Eugene to no end that I could solicit the cream of the crop, some of whom would most likely have never gone along with Ivan. He presented me with a small Nikon camera to show his appreciation and promised to teach me the art of photography.

I also began styling the shoots and scouting the locations. All those years on the farm turning Salvation Army hand-me-downs into creative outfits proved excellent training. I shopped the thrift stores on Melrose and could put together great looks with used clothing and various bits and bobs and remnants of fabrics.

Eugene and I worked around the clock; for the most part, I kept him on an even keel and wouldn't allow him to break out the vodka on the set as Ivan did. He could get very prickly toward the end of a shoot, but I helped him stay focused by keeping the momentum going until the end. I also always made sure he would include a few professional-looking "headshots" of the girls they could use in their books.

Before I could find an apartment, Eugene and I became lovers, and those 400-count sheets ended up on the bed we shared.

Bruce had graciously agreed to store some of my things until I could find a permanent address, so I stayed in touch by calling him from time to time. As happy as he was to hear I had found a job I liked, didn't compare with how delighted I was to hear he was moving back in with his wife and kids. He was looking to rent the cliffhanger at Pelham Place, and Eugene and I needed a larger place to live, so we went to see it. We rented it the same day with my backgammon winnings as the deposit. I had it all—a great job as a stylist and set designer and a romantic house above the city with a man who adored me. Now, with a permanent address, I made it a point to apply for a passport—I wanted to travel the world at will. It arrived four weeks later, and I felt for the first time in a long while I was finding stability in my life.

One of my favorite albums was *That's the Way of the World* by Earth, Wind, & Fire, and the song "Reasons" had become the soundtrack to my life. I blasted it over the stereo and danced like Isadora Duncan with naked abandon on the wooden terrace that hung out over the canyon. The angelic voices lifted my spirit to soar among the clouds. I could fly, and I wasn't even high. I was the happiest I had ever been in my life.

Another month passed, and everything seemed perfect until one day, for no reason, Eugene turned the stereo off, threw my yellow robe at me, and said, "Cover yourself up, woman!"

"What's going on? Did someone complain the music was too

loud?" I asked with concern.

"No. I'm complaining. I'm sick of your frivolity."

A pattern had been emerging with Eugene that I had been trying to deny. The happier I was, the more it irritated him even to be around me. The better I became at the job, the less satisfied he was with me. Just when I thought I found some balance in my life, Eugene's unpredictable mood swings tipped the scales. We made a good team. But Eugene's overblown ego was getting the better of him. He was used to the models looking up to him. Now, they were looking up to me, and he didn't like it. He wanted to be the center of attention, and he missed the praise he received from models grateful to him for their lucky break. He missed being able to get drunk while shooting and have sex with whichever model he wanted. He felt tied down and didn't want to be part of a team. At his core, he was a lone wolf, and he felt trapped. On the set, he began making irrational outbursts in front of the girls about my incompetence.

"Sammy, what are you doing? Don't put that silk there! I wanted it over there!" he barked one day.

His comments not only did little to make him seem more important than me to the models, but he also frightened them.

"I'm sorry, Eugene. You're right. It looks better where you had it. Are you ready for Abigail now? I have her dressed," I said as I turned to escort the next model on to the set.

"I'm ready," Eugene mumbled.

As soon as he saw her, he began yelling again. "I can't shoot her in that getup. What is this? The Moulin Rouge?"

"Well, what would you like her to wear?"

"I will find something. Just… Just leave and let me work through this set. You and I are not on the same page."

Abigail looked at me with big eyes as if to say, "Please don't go."

"Okay, I'll organize the back room and leave you guys to it. Let me know if you need me," I said, giving the model a reassuring glance.

"When I say leave, I mean leave, Sammy. Go. I can't work with you bustling around here," he scowled. "Get out of my space."

His words stung because I thought we were in this together. I raised Eugene's game by recruiting the best models and working hard with limited funds. I couldn't believe how unappreciative and disrespectful he acted toward me. His ego wouldn't allow a woman to show him up. I grabbed my purse and left the studio, knowing full well Eugene was most likely pouring himself a glass of vodka.

I sat down on the steps around the corner from the studio, opened my book of quotes by Rumi, and flipped through its pages looking for a sign. I read the words, "It's your road, and yours alone. Others may walk it with you, but no one can walk it for you."

I began contacting photographers in town to see if I could find other work as a stylist. Eugene had helped me discover a career path, but it was apparent our paths were diverging. Or perhaps we were just spending too much time together. Maybe we could stay together but not work together. Sharing the cliffhanger made things more complicated than when we were hanging out together at his studio. I put most of my winnings from backgammon down as the deposit but I couldn't quite afford the rent on my own, and I didn't want to go back to PIPS. I considered finding a roommate and asking Eugene to move out but couldn't find the courage or heart to do so. I knew Eugene was a complicated man, and I understood his insecurities. Most of all, I felt sorry for him over the death of Carole, and I realized he must be tormented by her death even more than I thought. It seemed there was nothing I could do to make him happy. But that didn't mean I wanted to give up on him.

When we first got together, drinking had made him laugh and appear jovial. Though I empathized with his loss, it was difficult when he got drunk and shut down. He spent some nights at the studio, which was fine by me, though I would find myself wracked with worry about whether he was okay. I felt afraid he might fall and hurt himself when he was drunk or, worse, attempt to drive home.

One night I had a nightmare taking me back to when I was about ten years old, and my grandfather fell ill and was in the hospital. At first, my older sisters and I worked together to take care of the chores. But after about the second week, my sisters came up with excuses , and I was on my own to take care of twenty or thirty horses, a half dozen pigs, cats, dogs, and chickens. Every morning, I fed the horses their oats before letting them out to pasture. Once home from school, I cleaned out the stalls, threw the hay bales down from the loft, broke up the hay bales, put the hay in their mangers, let the horses back in and fed them their evening oats, and then started all over again the next day. Cleaning the stables for thirty horses was no easy task for a grown person, let alone a ten-year-old girl.

Wheeling loads of horse manure in a wheelbarrow along wooden planks out to the edge of the manure pile and then hoisting it over the side of the heap was the hardest part. One rainy day, the wheelbarrow's weight took me with it, and I went tumbling down to the bottom of the manure pile, getting knocked out by the thrust of it hitting me in the head.

When I came to, the rain was pelting down on my face, and I found myself in a puddle of decades-old cow manure mixed with fresh horse manure and rats rummaging through the waste. I don't know how long I was out, but nobody came looking for me. I wondered how long it would have taken for someone to find me if I had died in the cow manure that day.

I woke up the next morning with a clear realization from the previous night's horrible dream. Nobody from my family was looking for me now. They had never been. For all they knew, I was dead in a ditch somewhere. I hoped they thought I died. I never wanted to see them again. Because seeing them would mean Pam Butter still existed. And Pam Butter had died.

Eugene came home and announced, "My stateless passport is up for renewal, so I have to go back to England. I think we should give up this house and stay in England for a while. Sorry to spring this on you, Sammy. It's been weighing on me for some time, and I've meant to discuss it with you."

What a dilemma it was to decide whether this was the right timing for a natural break from Eugene or whether I should follow him to England, a place I had only dreamed about and pretended to have lived, a place I longed to go. Maybe he would be different in England, and things between us would get back to the way they had been. Perhaps it was fate? Or was it fate to use this opportunity to leave him?

My better judgment told me this was a natural breaking point in our relationship, and the best thing I could do for myself was to let go. I got up from the couch and went into the small kitchen to boil some water for tea. Eugene followed me.

"I don't know, Eugene. You and I haven't been getting along so well. Perhaps we need a break from each other. Why don't you go to England and get yourself sorted, and we'll see where things stand when you're back?"

"What d'you mean, Sammy?" He placed his hands on my shoulders and stared into my eyes with sincerity. "I know I can be a bit of a boar, but I need you. We're a team. I can't do this without you. I love you," he whispered, sounding like the old Eugene. "I have been dreaming about having you by my side in London. You'll see. Life will be wonderful for us in London. People know me there, and I'm respected. I don't know why we didn't leave sooner. I've been unhappy here for a while, which has been causing me to drink too much. I admit it, and I've taken out my frustrations on you. I apologize, Sammy, and I promise, if you come to England with me, things will be different. I promise. Let me make it up to you."

The plane ride to London was awful. Eugene got drunk and was obnoxious to the stewardesses while I tried my best to keep things from going off the rails. It was worth it, though, when I looked out the window as the plane prepared to touch down at Heathrow Airport. I had fantasized about the green hills and trees in the English countryside, and now, there they were.

An old, black taxicab hummed its way along country roads giving way to city streets, and then my wide eyes took in the red phone booths, the bobbies, the street signs, the pubs. It was all just as romantic as I envisioned.

Our new home was a one-bedroom flat in Hampstead near Chalk Farm, where the mother of Eugene's deceased girlfriend, Carole, lived.

I learned how to navigate the London Underground with ease and loved the new freedom I had to travel from place to place unencumbered by the need for Eugene to drive me everywhere in his old Cadillac. London lifted my spirit, making me feel confident and in love with life again.

Being in a place where no one knew me felt like a fresh start. But for Eugene, the opposite appeared to be true. Memories of his beloved Carole rendered him prone to fits of weeping. We made regular visits to see Vera, Carole's mother, and her old auntie who lived in a run-down council flat. During each visit, Vera would make a pot of tea and bring out the stacks of photo albums and shoeboxes containing hundreds of photographs of Carole, one of the most beautiful women I have ever seen. We would pour over the cover shots of numerous international men's magazines and talk about her for hours on end.

There was one photograph of Carole holding a white dove, with her curly black hair loosely twisted into a top knot. Each time Vera came upon the image, she would break down in a puddle of tears, and Eugene would give her some money, and we'd leave and not speak for the rest of the evening. We'd been in London for about a week when Eugene insisted we visit Carole's grave at Golder's Green cemetery. He fell apart and wept for over an hour, hugging the gravestone. I knew that day nobody could ever replace Carole.

I resolved to make the best of it and acclimate to my new surroundings. I did whatever I could to make things hum along, which meant getting busy with work. Working in London was a big contrast to Los Angeles. Recruiting the girls was a much different process because they all seemed to have agents. Once in a while, I met a girl on the street who I approached, but we mostly began working with professional models. Most girls were excited to work with Eugene because their agents told them he was the best photographer based on the work he had done with Carole, and the fact that he discovered her.

Eugene began drinking earlier in the day. He would stop by a pub and have a few pints of lager before returning to the flat when he pretended to be sober before pouring himself a glass of vodka.

After the first month, we were in London, it became evident Eugene was cheating on me. We would be shooting a model, and out of the blue, he'd ask me to run an errand to get something for the shoot.

"Sammy, could you get me some grooming scissors?"

It was always something he knew might take me some time to find. I'd oblige and would take my time, so I'd be sure not to enter the studio at an inappropriate moment. Part of me was beyond caring. I knew I should never have gone to London with him. I knew our connection had run its course, but he'd been so intent on wanting me to come, I believed him. I felt guilty because a part of me felt selfish. I wanted to go to London for the experience, and I used Eugene to get there. It didn't make me proud of myself. Eugene, meanwhile, was using me as an obvious crutch to get over Carole.

Eugene rekindled a decade-long friendship with a Russian guy who went by Angus, a purposefully non-Russian sounding name. They would stay up until late at night drinking vodka and ruminating over Dostoevsky, which emphasized Eugene's conflicted complexity. On one particular visit, Eugene started a diatribe about politics.

"So, Angus," Eugene began, after throwing back a few shots. "How come you, a socialist, live in the West like a baron with all the comforts and money and resist calling yourself a capitalist. Is it spiritual corruption that leads you toward hedonistic behavior? The condition of man is determined by what he expects from it, and that is the genealogy of culture. And we all carry our culture in our subconscious mind…"

Angus shot an uncomfortable look at me before Eugene continued.

"The way we carry our bacilli, viruses, and such, the symptoms of our culture we experience in our behavior and our expectations."

Angus shot me another look across the room as if to say, *"He's crazy."* He slowly got up from the chair he sat in for the entire evening, sipping vodka and puffing on a cigar while listening as Eugene continued to ramble on about capitalism and fascism.

Angus put on his fedora and grabbed his coat, saying, "It's late. I'm tired. Eugene, my brother, it's time to let it go. You have a beautiful girlfriend who I am sure wants nice things to have a nice life. You need to move on from the past. Thank you for your hospitality, Sammy."

With a tip of his hat, Angus bid farewell, leaving me to coax Eugene to bed or let him spend another night passed out on the couch.

I knew I couldn't understand how he viewed life after having lived a life under communist rule and how that affected him. It was true; I wanted a comfortable home and aspired to have beautiful things; did that make me a "capitalist pig?" Moving to London seemed like a dream come true. But when I looked around our tiny apartment in the night's context, I realized Eugene and I had different needs and aspirations. The flat was spartan with four piss-yellow walls, no television, just a few possessions he picked up from the house of his dead girlfriend's mother; among them was an old radio, half-melted as a result of being placed on a hot radiator. He sat in front of that melted radio every night with a glass of vodka. I hated how the twisted plastic looked but feared to ask him to replace it, as I had the impression it reminded him of Carole.

I thought back to the innocent time before we became lovers when I said the only things I needed in life were champagne, chocolates, and clean sheets. When I crawled into the bed alone, I was still hoping there might be a future with Eugene if he could heal his pain.

Despite Eugene's drinking and sulking, we were productive, and working together could still be fun. We did a slew of photoshoots for magazines Quick, Stern, Club, and Mayfair. I became well respected around town as a photo stylist and got exclusive deals for my shoots from Janet Reager, a specialty lingerie shop, and made connections with other hip stores on the King's Road.

Passing by the Royal College of Art in Kensington, I would walk the campus grounds for inspiration and pretend I went to school there. A painter from Sweden named Jon stopped me one day to ask if I would sit for him as a model, and I shared I was a stylist.

"What type of styling do you do? Is it high fashion?" Jon asked.

"It's for—dare I say—men's magazines, but it's all very tasteful. The photographer I work with is a genius."

"Well, if you've got nothing against the naked human form, maybe you'd like to pick up a little extra cash? Fine arts are looking for a new model."

"How do I apply?" I was so excited I couldn't contain my enthusiasm.

"You just did. Can you make it next Tuesday at eleven-thirty a.m.?"

I couldn't believe my luck. I would get to go to a real college and learn about art. Sure, I would have to sit there naked and motionless. But my eyes and ears would be wide open, and I would get to hear the lectures and see firsthand learning in a college. This modeling job was a dream come true for me. I juggled my time and kept it a secret from Eugene because I didn't think he would approve of my disrobing in front of the students. Then I got a lucky break.

When I returned to the flat one day, Eugene announced, "Sammy, I need to go to New York for a month for a big assignment from Club. I want you to sit this trip out. It will cost too much money for us both to go."

We weren't getting along, and I had my suspicions he might be having a rendezvous with another woman. But I didn't care because I was jumping for joy to be in London without Eugene around. I could go to the modeling sessions at the Royal College of Art and not have to hide my aspirations for higher learning.

After he left, I sat for two different classes—one in the morning and one in the afternoon. It was like receiving free education, and I was getting paid a stipend to boot. Maybe I could put enough money together to get a flat on my own before Eugene even returned. I was sure I could network at the college and meet other photographers for work. I felt motivated to be free of Eugene and start a new chapter.

When I was disrobing for the class one day, I noticed my breasts were tender and seemed more sensitive than usual. I dismissed it, thinking I must have miscalculated my time of the month.

A week later, I had an intense craving for chocolate milk and went to the canteen to buy a carton. After two sips, I threw up everything in my stomach. I was pregnant.

14

TRAA DY LLOOAR

The chemistry Eugene and I once shared had waned, and a baby would fix nothing between us. On the contrary, I knew it would make things much worse. My hormones were raging and playing tricks on my emotions and judgment. How did this happen? How could this happen? Why now? I thought about not telling Eugene and running off to have our baby on my own. But after thinking it through and a lot of soul searching, I made the mature decision Eugene had a right to know. If there was even an infinitesimal chance he wanted our baby or wanted to be part of our baby's life, I had no right to deny him.

When Eugene returned from New York, I broke the news. I knew from the moment the words left my lips; it was a mistake I would regret for the rest of my life. He responded as though it was a mere inconvenience, like missing a train by saying, "Well, that's most unfortunate."

When I pressed him to express how he felt and what he meant, he clammed up, saying, "I'm going out to the pub."

It must have been late when he returned to the flat and fell asleep on the couch because I could tell he hadn't slept on his side of the bed when I woke up the next morning. Pouring myself a cup of tea, he startled me when he came bounding into the apartment, clutching a box of croissants. Standing in my underwear and t-shirt, I went back to the bedroom to grab my robe out of modesty while he yelled out loud enough for me to hear him.

"Sammy, I got a call to visit some friends on the Isle of Man. Would you like to tag along?"

One minute he doesn't want to talk to me and now he wants to take me on a trip. I knew I should get in to see a doctor about the pregnancy, but I didn't want to bring it up. I entered the kitchen where Eugene had placed the teapot on the small table and put the croissants on a plate.

"I'd love to!" I said as I poured us each a cup of tea.

Until now, I had only seen the college nurse the day I discovered I was pregnant. But all I cared about at that moment was trying to work through things with Eugene.

"How long will we be staying?"

"Can't say for sure. A few weeks, I guess," Eugene answered before assuring me, "You will love it there, Sammy!"

We set sail on a small vessel that tossed about the Irish Sea like a tiny bath toy. All the while, it sank in; I was carrying a life inside me. My seasickness made the morning sickness all the worse. Eugene seemed unfazed as we passed through rainstorms that seemed to be following us from the coast of Liverpool to the small island.

When we finally reached the Isle of Man, we went to a pub to meet up with Eugene's friends.

"What will it be, miss?" the barkeeper asked.

"I'll just have some water," I said.

"Ah, come on, now. You must be ready for a pint after your journey. Here on the island, we only brew the best."

Without hesitation, Eugene blurted out to the entire group, "Sammy can't drink any alcohol because she's pregnant."

Everyone at the pub raised their glasses and began chanting a local song of good wishes. I was slightly embarrassed, but I also felt joyous. I thought somehow Eugene's heart had softened, and he was warming up to the idea and wanted to keep our baby. Though cautiously optimistic, I felt a glimmer of excitement.

"Ah, think about having the baby here," said an old man. "The baby could be a native Manx-man, last of a dying breed. There aren't too many young people left who want to bring up their offspring in the genuine ways of the island. Being a native-born

Manx-man would make the baby special, give the baby a real legacy, you know. Raise 'em up to be bilingual."

I became caught up by the idea and romanced by the language, which resembled Scottish Gaelic and Irish. Within a few days, I could put together a few short phrases. I fantasized Eugene's plan was to abandon me here among these lovely green rolling hills and happy people, whose mantra "traa dy llooar," meaning "time enough," seemed to suit my unborn baby and me. Here, in this beautiful place filled with friendly faces and warm gestures, time seemed to slow down. I could be free to deliver our baby in peace while Eugene maintained his bachelor-photographer image in London. That would suit me fine, I thought. He could come to visit the baby anytime he chose. I would get a job on the island, and we would live out the rest of our days in peace.

When the day came to return to London, Eugene was in such good humor; I believed everything would be okay. We had been there for almost three weeks, and things had been pleasant enough. I was waiting for when he would break the news that he was leaving me behind. But it soon became apparent he had no intention of doing so.

My stomach was still as taut as a drum, but a little protrusion was taking shape. When I touched it, I could feel a connection, but I remained wracked with worry that Eugene didn't share these feelings, even though he acted as though everything was fine. I suppose I was bonding with my baby and developing "mother's intuition," making me sense something was not right with Eugene.

As the boat pulled away from the dock, heading for the open sea, Eugene unceremoniously broke the news to me that he had arranged for me to have an abortion when we got back to the mainland.

"I don't understand! Why were you going around telling everyone I was pregnant?"

"I was just doing that for a show. What did you expect me to do, woman? Let them just think you were fat? That I was in love with a fat girl?"

His words hurt me and made me feel worthless. He grabbed me by my shoulders and looked me straight in the eyes. "You can't believe bringing a child into this world is a good idea for you, and I know for certain, it's not for me."

"But what about our baby? Maybe our baby wants to be born."

"Are you daft? The baby—if you can even call it that—can't decide about our lives. I demand you to get an abortion."

Eugene's words ignited a hormone-fueled rage of hysteria in me as I pulled myself away from him. I wanted to run away, but there was nowhere to go except to jump overboard into the choppy sea. The little boat tossed us about the cabin. As I slipped out of his grasp, Eugene lunged at me, slapped me across the face and pushed me down.

Then he kicked me twice near my stomach with his combat style boot. It took my breath away. I couldn't believe what was happening. Eugene seemed to have gone crazy, and I feared for not only the life of our child but also for myself.

I pushed him away and ran to the deck. It was dark and raining. Waves were lapping up over the railing, and it was very slippery. Eugene ran up after me. He grabbed me and threw me against the ballast. That was the hit that told me I needed to run from this man at whatever cost.

I turned around with tears in my eyes and said, "Go ahead. Do whatever you must. Throw me over the deck. Just make it quick. I don't deserve your torture, and neither does our baby."

It was as though Eugene had been in a trance and was coming out of it, not realizing how hard he hit me.

"Sammy, I'm sorry... I didn't mean to hurt you," he wailed above the sounds of the waves crashing against the boat, the rain pelting down.

"I don't believe you. I stopped believing in you a long time ago."

I walked past Eugene, feeling an eerie sense of calm like one gets after a storm though the rain had not yet ceased pummeling the small boat at sea. Inside the cabin, I curled up in a ball and clenched my eyes as my insides turned upon themselves. Getting pregnant wasn't something I consciously wanted for myself. But now, the realization my baby could be so quickly snatched away made me feel a sense of attachment I didn't know was possible. I buried my face into the pillow in tears, trying to reconcile why my mother didn't want me.

When we docked, my clothes were still wet, and I was shivering from head to toe. Before I could figure out what was happening, Eugene was admitting me to a hospital nearby. He had already made the arrangements. Without so much as a goodbye, he left me there, alone in my sorrow.

I was so angry at myself for giving in to him as my insides cramped up. Why couldn't I stand up to him? On the boat, I felt so fierce I could have thrown him overboard. But now, I felt like a hostage, being held against my will. When I put the pale blue smock on, I felt resigned to the fact, I was losing our baby.

They put me under anesthesia to have a procedure, and I had a vision of my mother. She was dressed in the cutoff shorts she was wearing the day she met my father. Her tight braids and short bangs framed her lovely face, and the gold-rimmed glasses kept slipping down her nose. I realized she was about the same age then as I was now. She wanted to be my friend.

She said, "God loves you, Pammy Sue."

I scratched my eyes, trying to shake off the nightmare and wipe away this vision. But Mom stayed by my side and took hold of my hand.

"Go away and leave me. I wanted my child, but you never wanted me, and I don't want you. It's all your fault. I should never have been born. Then none of this would be happening."

When I awoke, I felt empty. All I wanted to do was to leave the hospital but was too weak from losing quite a lot of blood, so they told me to rest and kept me sedated. Though I tried, it was impossible to remain calm. The recurring visions of my mother kept haunting me in my dream state, making it difficult for me to allow myself to sleep.

When I was free to go, there was only one problem. The hospital policy prevented patients from being discharged without someone to accompany them. I called the apartment every hour but couldn't reach Eugene.

I don't remember if I wore the staff down, or if, as Wild Bill's daughter, I had inherited the ability to convince people of what I wanted them to believe against impossible odds. Regardless, they bought into the story that my mother was on the train and would meet me at the station, allowing me to go.

As I walked toward the train station, the light, misty rain felt like angel tears and permitted me to mourn the loss of my baby; the baby who seemed so real on the Isle of Man left me with a heavy sadness I knew I would never recover. It cut too deeply for me to understand. Would my mother have had a better life if she'd never met Wild Bill and had five children in quick succession? Or did Wild Bill save her from enduring endless abuse from her father? Would I have been safer staying on the farm? I never dreamed I would one day ask myself this question, but at this moment, I would have endured a lifetime of abuse to save the life of the child I just lost.

On the train ride back to London, I gazed out the window at the blur of the countryside, trying in vain to make sense of the events leading up to where I now found myself. One day Eugene and I were philosophizing about life at the Old World; now, the relationship had deteriorated beyond repair, and I was on a train to Victoria Station, so far away from where I ever wanted to be. All I ever wanted in life was to feel safe and loved. Instead, I was alone and felt responsible for driving people who cared about me away, or maybe they just didn't love me enough to stay.

Arriving at Victoria weak and exhausted, I tried to phone the apartment again to see if I could reach Eugene. I listened to the phone ringing as if in a trance, only snapping out of it when I realized a woman with a young child was standing outside the call-box waiting her turn. I hung up the phone and opened the door, locking eyes with the child. I wanted to reach down and hug her, to smell her little head, and feel her soft cheek against mine. I smiled, and a pool of tears moistened my cheeks. I walked past the mother and child, catching the saltiness of the moment on my tongue.

When I reached the station at Hampstead and took the long ride in the lift up to Heath Street, I felt as though I would faint. With great care, I walked down the steep hill to our flat to find Eugene wasn't there, and I didn't have my key. Pounding on the door a few times before giving up, I slid down the doorway to come to rest on the doormat.

The neighbor across the hall heard my distress and looked through her peephole.

She opened her door and said, "My dear, what's wrong? Can I help you? Do you not have your key?"

"No, I don't have my key, Mrs. Wright."

"Well, let me help you up, and I'll make you a cuppa. You don't look well, dear. Have you been traveling?" She picked up the small case I had been carrying.

I wanted to burst into tears and tell her about the ordeal I had been through, but it was inappropriate. Though Mrs. Wright had been our neighbor for some months, we never exchanged more than pleasantries about the weather. I felt embarrassment and shame and knew by engaging in any conversation; a dialogue might ensue I would regret.

"I've been to see my family and my mum's not well," I said tentatively, my lips quivering to form the words.

The tea was just what I needed to calm my frayed nerves. Mrs. Wright's cat was purring and rubbing up against my leg as though she sensed my sadness. I felt comforted by the ticking of the grandfather clock and soothed by Mrs. Wright's chatting about the weather and local news. My eyes were feeling heavy, as it became difficult to keep them open, and I felt as though I might doze off.

As the sun began to slip away, a couple's laughter echoed up the stairwell. I recognized one voice as Eugene's and could tell he had been drinking the afternoon away.

As he attempted to insert the key into the keyhole, his companion giggled, "Give it to me, love. I can get it in the hole."

They both laughed like two teenagers.

I opened our neighbor's apartment door and stood there a moment before saying, "Would you like some help?"

The girl, who I recognized, stopped laughing. It was a model named Tiffany; we had shot a few months prior. I fought for Eugene to photograph Tiffany because he didn't think she was attractive enough. He complained she was too fat. I told him she reminded me of Carole with her dark hair and eyes and ample bosom, and he changed his mind.

When we were in the middle of the shoot, she got her period. I told Eugene I could see blood in her vagina through the camera lens, and perhaps we should stop filming, but he kept shooting. I left to run an errand. When I returned, I realized they'd had sex. There was a small trace of blood on Eugene's beard. The memory of this caused me to throw up right there on the landing.

"Sammy, what's wrong?" Eugene asked as though he was unaware of my condition. Mrs. Wright got up from her rocking chair and was standing behind me.

"I'm sorry Mrs. Wright, I will be out straight away to clean this up. Come with me, Sammy, my darling." He shuffled me across the landing and into the flat.

I could feel him giving Tiffany a look that she should leave. She didn't even try to excuse herself but scrambled down the stairs and disappeared toward High Street. I was embarrassed for Eugene in front of Mrs. Wright. I'm sure she never thought much of her bearded neighbor with the perpetual scowl before, and now, as she closed her door, I heard her mutter under her breath, "Poor dear."

I went straight to bed and fell asleep as soon as my head touched the pillow. I must have slept for several hours. When I awoke, I found Eugene passed out in front of the melted radio. I opened the door to the landing and cleaned up the now-hour-old vomit, reinforcing this wasn't a weird dream but a sad nightmare. As much as I loved London, I wanted to go home to Los Angeles. I didn't want to be anywhere with Eugene and vowed I would leave as soon as possible. The question was when, and how could I do it? What would I do once back in Los Angeles? I needed to think things through and come up with a plan.

It was a rainy morning about a few weeks later when Eugene announced we had to go to New York City. Though I was careful not to show it, I knew it wasn't an accident; I had been praying for this moment. If I got out of this situation, I would never let circumstances take me down the wrong path.

We left London about a week later, and I tried to take as many of my clothing items as possible without arousing Eugene's suspicion. Eugene now terrified me, and I never knew what to expect, so I was cautious and played things close to the vest.

When the plane took off at Heathrow, I kept my gaze out the window. We never spoke on the flight. Determined not to be his in-flight babysitter, I pretended to be asleep while Eugene ordered a vodka even though he also had a bottle stashed in his bag. By the time the plane landed, he was so drunk I almost had to carry him off the plane. I thought about leaving him right there and then at the gate, but we packed all my possessions, including my camera, in the same bag with his things.

By the time we checked into the Edison Hotel, Eugene had sobered up. After renting a safe deposit box in the hotel lobby where he stashed our valuables, money, and passports, we rode the lift eight floors to the depressing accommodations.

"I'm starving, Sammy," Eugene announced. "I'm going next door to the deli to order a corned beef sandwich and coffee. You want anything?"

The thought of eating anything from the greasy spoon next door, I found revolting. "No, thanks. I'm good."

I changed my mind realizing if he had to wait for two orders, it would take longer for him to return, so I had a few extra moments to be alone to think through my exit strategy.

"On second thought, can you grab me a toasted bagel and coffee?"

I knew getting away from Eugene would be difficult. He didn't love me, but he felt dependent on me and thought of me as his possession. He only requested one key for the safe, which he kept on him. I would have to come up with a plan to somehow steal it from him so I could grab my Nikon camera and enough cash to get back to LA. It was doubtful the hotel would give me a duplicate without his knowing. The only thing on my mind was getting as far away from this monster as possible.

Two days passed, and we were having lunch at Tavern on the Green with a Brit named Tony, who was good friends with Eugene and head of the prominent New York magazine, Club. The two men were throwing back vodka shots and were both becoming drunk and boisterous. As the sweat gathered on Eugene's brow, he removed his sport coat and hung it on the back of the chair. I could see the key to the hotel safe in the pocket of his jacket, and as I dropped my napkin, I reached inside and snatched the key with it on my way up. Adrenaline began coursing through my veins, but I managed to remain calm.

After a fresh round of drinks came to the table, the conversation shifted to revolve around Carole. The two men reminisced about her beauty and the tragedy of a life cut short. I felt alienated from the conversation but acted as interested as I could until they ordered another round of drinks.

"Eugene, would you and Tony mind terribly if I excused myself? I want to go back to the hotel and rest. I'm feeling a bit of jet lag."

In his inebriated state, he seemed oblivious to my presence at the table.

I got up to leave, kissing Eugene and Tony on both cheeks and said, "I'll see you guys later."

The moment had come. It was now or never. A brisk walk turned into a full-on gallop as I raced against time to get to the hotel, only turning around to hail a cab. When a taxi stopped, I was out of breath and shaking. "Edison Hotel, please."

"Hey, you, didn't just rob a bank, did you, little lady? You look like the heat is after you, or you saw a ghost," he said with a chuckle.

"I'm expecting a call is all. I'm running late and don't want to miss it. It's from my mum in England."

"Okay, well, let me take the shortcut," he said as he stepped on the gas.

I arrived at the hotel, and as though on automatic pilot, went to the safe. It took me a moment to locate the right one, and my hands were shaking as I inserted the key into the keyhole. I grabbed my camera, passport, and a small amount of cash. I considered darting up the eight flights of stairs to the room, but the lift doors opened, and by accident, I pushed the sixth floor before pushing the eighth. That made it two stops before mine, as another couple entered and was getting off on the third floor.

I began stuffing whatever essentials I could into my carry-on when Eugene burst into the room. He sized up the situation, realized I was attempting to leave, then walked over to the bed, picked up the case, and emptied it upside down, kicking the strewn garments and toiletries all over the hotel room. I snatched my camera to shove it under the bed as Eugene threw me across the room. I ran into the bathroom to lock the door, but he pushed it open and threw me against the bathtub, pounding my face against the faucet and shattering my front teeth. He kept punching me and throwing me against the wall. Within moments, my face was bruised beyond recognition, and one eye was so swollen I couldn't open it. All I could see was a pattern of swirling spirals.

The day I stood on top of Copy and Kissy's home in the fallen tree trunk and looked out over the slaughtered sheep's carnage, I knew there was nothing I could have done to save them. The wolves were too intent on getting what they needed to survive. Now I had come face to face with yet another wolf.

"Eugene, please stop. I'm begging you. I will stay. I don't know what I was thinking." I tried my best to mumble out the words but could barely speak through the pain. He continued to kick me before throwing me onto the bed and thrusting his entire weight on top of me. Then he wept.

"I'm sorry, Sammy. I'm so sorry," he wailed. "You can't leave me. Why do you want to leave me? Why does everyone leave me?"

I said, "It's okay, I'm sorry I upset you. I'm not leaving. I was just missing Los Angeles. Can you please go get me some ice?"

"I can't leave you. If I go get ice, you will leave me. I'm sorry, Sammy. I'm sorry, Sammy, I can't lose you, too," he kept saying over and over, sobbing.

Ice wouldn't help much, but it would be easier to breathe without the weight of his drunken body on top of me. I tried to calm him down as he sobbed over what he had done to me, grateful he stopped while I still had breath in me. I held his head on my chest and pushed his hair away from his face the way he liked, while my entire body throbbed in agony. I could feel my head swelling up like helium shot into a flaccid balloon.

The thought of jumping out the window of the eighth floor of the Edison Hotel had occurred to me, but now Eugene had passed out, I was relieved I hadn't. A surge of survival instinct welled up inside of me. I wouldn't let Eugene defeat me. It would take more than what just happened to consider splattering my body all over the street like an overripe watermelon at the grocery store, creating a mess for someone else to clean up. I summoned the strength and courage to acknowledge something I learned from a Sufi fable: *"This too shall pass."* I gathered my inner power to take care of my mess on my own.

The pain was excruciating. I ran my tongue over my front teeth, which now felt like tiny razor blades, one so sharp it cut my tongue. The taste of blood mixing with my salty tears quenched my thirst. When Eugene, at last, rolled off me, I lay as still as possible. I couldn't risk trying to leave in the middle of the night. I knew I would have to wait until morning.

The streets of New York City grew quieter, and I knew the morning was just on the other side of that stillness. Lying in the dark, I could feel my body starting to try to heal itself. Fluids were racing to the worst of my injuries as bruised areas continued to swell. My mind remained alert the entire night through the agonizing pain.

At daybreak, sunlight began streaming across Eugene's face through the one shade left a crack open. He woke up hungover and began shuffling around the room, searching for the hotel key in the mess he'd created the night before. Believing I was asleep, he closed the blind once he found the key and left the room to nurse his hangover with coffee from the greasy spoon. He was nothing if not a creature of habit.

Between the ride in the lift, the walk to the deli, and, if I was lucky, a short wait in line, I could do this. I could escape. The second I heard the door close behind Eugene, I jumped out of bed, pulled on my jeans and t-shirt and grabbed my purse and my camera from under the bed. I listened at the door for the "ding" from the lift. Inhaling a deep breath, I ran the hell down all eight floors into the alley in the opposite direction of the greasy spoon. When I reached the street, I hailed a cab, and I never looked back, leaving every stitch of clothing I owned behind.

15

HATCHING A PLAN

Oblivious to people staring at me, I bolted into JFK, knowing my life depended on it. At the ticket counter, I requested the next flight to LA. I could tell the airline personnel, and fellow passengers were looking at me sideways. My hair still had dried-up blood sticking to it, and the swelling was so bad in my left eye, I couldn't open it. The last thing I cared about was what people were thinking.

With the ticket clutched in my hand, I made my way to the gate. I would have to wait at least forty-five minutes before boarding the plane.

I slipped into the bathroom and, inside the handicapped-accessible stall, found a separate sink where I washed the dried blood from my hair. Swirls of red disappeared down the drain. I didn't dare look in the mirror, too terrified by what I might see.

Leaving the bathroom, I bought a soda and asked for extra ice, which I applied to my face. I sat on the floor across from the gate, maintaining an unobstructed view of the area in case Eugene showed up. My heart was pounding like a hunted animal.

When they called for boarding, at last, I continued to quake with fear until the plane left the tarmac. Once in the air, after downing several glasses of cheap wine, I settled in to rest my aching body. I kept my mouth shut, my eyes closed, and my body turned toward the window.

I needed the sleep because although it seemed as if we had just taken off, the flight attendant was announcing our final descent to Los Angeles. I felt my entire being relax. I was home. I took in the view—of millions of miniature cars, swimming pools, and houses that appeared as tiny dots connecting to form a

Lichtenstein-inspired painting, a welcome mat just for me.

I hopped into a cab, and the driver said, "Where to?"

"Can you recommend a hotel that isn't too expensive? I'm short on cash. I was in a bad car accident, and my parents are out of town. I don't have the key to their house. I need somewhere to hide out—I mean, hang out until they return."

"Okay, little lady. What a shame. You look like you got hurt bad. You look like you're lucky to be alive."

His words shook me to my core as I realized he was right. I was lucky to be alive. I rinsed out most of the dried blood from my hair, but I looked terrible as the bruises were by now in full bloom. There was no hiding in the bright Los Angeles sunlight.

When we stopped at a light at Crescent Heights and Sunset, I spotted the bohemian girl playing her recorder. I felt comforted seeing some things never change. But when she turned to the side, it was apparent she was pregnant. I remembered the first time I saw her and fantasized about choosing a simple life like hers. Now, I regretted I hadn't more than ever.

The cab driver took me to the 7000 blocks of Sunset Strip, a stretch of turf that was a far cry from Rodeo Drive, a string of sex shops, liquor stores, head shops, and Kentucky Fried Chicken. No matter what your vice, you could find it in the 7000 blocks of Sunset.

The hookers who turned rooms over every couple of hours were the only pedestrians to encounter out on the streets. The police patrol cars often pulled up alongside them but rarely arrested anyone because the prostitutes were part of the ecosystem.

When I checked into the Sunset Motel, the man at the front desk assumed I was a hooker who got beaten up, so he put me in a room next to the check-in desk where he could keep an eye on me. The walls were so thin he could hear everything going on inside my room, including when I went to the toilet, but I had no room left for modesty. It made me feel safe.

The hotel room became my hideout, a place without judgment where I could heal and figure out what to do next. Over the next two weeks, my wounds went from a dark purple to crimson to yellow, and before too long, I could cover them up with makeup, although my left eye still looked quite a mess.

I made a lot of new friends at the motel. Tommy ran the front desk during the day, and Big Ed, who took care of the night shift. A girl named Mandy, a regular on the Strip since she was sixteen years old but now pushing thirty, knocked on my door one day to ask if I needed anything. Mandy was the mother hen to all the girls who worked the Strip and one of the first women who showed me any kindness since I'd moved to Los Angeles. She was an African American with broad shoulders and a small waist, a body like a wrestler. Mandy knew everyone on the Strip, the good, the bad, the outsiders, and the insiders. After some initial chitchat, it was evident she was tiptoeing around the elephant in the room when she looked me straight in the eyes.

"Who did this to you?"

"It was my boyfriend."

"Your boyfriend did this? Well, that dumb ass isn't your boyfriend no more, right? And you know you don't have to stay holed up alone all day by yourself. You aren't the first girl we've seen beaten up by some asshole, but I wasn't expecting you to call him your boyfriend. Maybe your pimp, but not your boyfriend."

"Well, it's complicated. Eugene has... A temper."

"My Donny has a temper. This motherfucker has a problem! And we could make that problem worse. My Donny will kick his goddamn ass if you say the word."

"I appreciate your concern, I do. But nothing can change what Eugene did to me," I said, trying to keep it together.

"I need to get my teeth fixed now because I'm embarrassed for anyone to see me like this. I don't have any money, but I have this camera," I said, retrieving my Nikon from under the bed. "Big Ed told me about a pawn shop down the street. Do you think they would give me good money for it? I found a place in the phone book where I can get my teeth done, over on Western. I can't go out like this." My bottom lip trembled as I tried my best not to burst into tears.

Mandy held me close, and I wished she would never let go. It had been too long since I'd felt the safety of a warm embrace from someone wanting nothing in return.

"Don't worry. We'll get you there."

Mandy took out a bit of writing paper from the motel stationery and jotted down the make and model of the camera.

"Let me get the word out on the street about the camera. We'll find some fool willing to fork over enough money to get you right. A pawn shop's not going to give you what it's worth. But don't you worry. We'll find somebody. And we'll get you a ride over to the dentist on Western too. You just don't worry yourself about it now and get some rest."

The afternoon sun was dipping below the horizon, creating the most spectacular sunset, and I had become comfortable enough to open the window a crack. A thin breeze rippled through, making the blinds sound like wind chimes. I lay on the bed, staring at the ceiling, trying to shut down the chatter in my head. I imagined myself lying in the sun beside a pool, surrounded by a garden with fragrant flowers. If not for this image, I wouldn't have believed that I was living at Grayhall Mansion less than a year ago. So much had happened.

A few days later, I jumped when I heard a loud knock on the door. It was Mandy with news that one of the local pimps met a guy interested in the camera and would pay top dollar for it. And he was sitting in the lobby right now. I ran to the bathroom sink to splash some water on my face and run a brush through my hair. My stomach churned from hunger. But the excitement about the potential sale of the camera, and the end of my crooked smile distracted me. I slipped into flip-flops and emerged from the safety of my secret cocoon.

There, sitting in the lobby, was Ivan, Eugene's former accomplice. He offered a meek, "How are you, Sammy?"

Speechless, I stood there with my mouth agape. Mandy lunged at Ivan, grabbing his throat.

"Are you telling me you know this girl? Are you the fucker who did this to her? Big Ed, call T-Stripe and get him over here, now!"

"Mandy! Mandy! Calm down. Ivan isn't my boyfriend. But I want to know what he's doing here."

"Eugene is back in LA. He told me about what happened. I heard on the street about a young girl who got beat up and was trying to sell a Nikon camera, and I put two and two together and thought it might be you. I have eleven hundred dollars. I'll give it to you, and I won't tell Eugene a thing. But I want you to know Eugene feels terrible. He loves you, Sammy, he does. He's been looking for you. He wants to make things right. He's even stopped drinking."

Mandy had an expression on her face that said, *"Cue the violins."* She was pacing back and forth as I tried to take it all in, still stunned to see Ivan.

I felt an emptiness inside, hearing Eugene was looking for me. The idea someone was searching to find me was something new. Years had passed since I ran away from home, and no one seemed to give a damn. I could have been a statistic, a victim of the Hillside Strangler, and my family would never know. It broke my heart. Then it dawned on me; I *was* a victim of an evil person. That person was Eugene, and he was only looking for me out of guilt. He wanted to absolve himself of what he did to me. How dare he.

The weeks I spent healing offered a lot of time for self-reflection. I thought through how I would react to Eugene if our paths ever crossed again. His ego would not allow him to let go of me without his last say. But I was determined that if anyone were going to have the last word, it would be me.

I had very few resources available. Eugene owed me, so I accepted the cash from Ivan, making him promise not to tell Eugene he saw me.

"Okay, Sammy. Here is Eugene's phone number where you can reach him. He's back at the Crossroads," Ivan said, handing me a small slip of paper.

"Oh yeah, she'll be in touch, and we'll be right there behind her, ready to kick this sorry fool in the ass for what he did to her." Mandy couldn't hold back, and I loved her for it.

About six weeks later, I had a new set of teeth, and I felt confident enough to contact Eugene to meet for coffee. His eyes welled up with tears the second he saw me. I had changed. I had grown up. My teeth were straight, and I had lost a lot of weight. I tried to make a joke.

"Well, maybe Nina Blanchard will sign me now; I'm skinny, and my teeth are straight. All I need is a boob job, right?"

Eugene almost leaped across the table to hug me and tell me how sorry he was for what happened. I pulled away and made myself clear; I was not there to embrace the past. It was over between us, and I had no intention of reconciling with him—not ever.

"What we had together was a... Well, it was a *time*. But we both know that time is over. And I am sad about the unfortunate events that brought us to this moment. But here we are."

Unaccustomed to hearing me sound so in control, it was visible how uncomfortable Eugene felt as he shifted in his chair, sipping coffee. He tried his best to remain even-tempered, but I could see the rage burning behind his eyes. He didn't appreciate not being in control, and I had the upper hand.

"Look—if you want to make amends for what happened," I said, choosing my words with care, "I think there's a way to do so. Something that would benefit both of us."

I began unraveling the plan I came up with while recuperating the past weeks and could tell I captured Eugene's imagination. There were countries where he hadn't tried to sell his work in a long time, if ever, I noted. Wouldn't it be easier for me, a woman, to get pornographic photos from country to country? His stateless passport always made him a target to customs officials, but customs wouldn't hassle a blonde, blue-eyed girl. I would slip right past them as though I were a student traveling abroad. Also, wouldn't it be easier for me to flog his photos and accept criticism from the photo editors rather than for him to listen to critiques? Eugene had alienated several editors over the years because his ego wouldn't allow him to accept criticism.

"Have you ever been to Germany, Sammy?"

"No, but I'm keen to go."

Eugene grabbed a napkin and mapped out a plan for a trip I could take from London to Paris, on to Hamburg, crisscrossing back through Copenhagen and Stockholm, then back to London. Perhaps I could even fly to Japan.

We agreed to meet at his studio the following day to put together binders of photographs of all the different girls we shot during our time together, and a couple of new ones. Eugene needed money as much as I did, and agreed to split the profits.

As I looked at these young girls with fresh eyes, the realization that Eugene had slept with over half of them made me feel nothing. I wanted to spend as little time as possible breathing the same air as Eugene. It took a great deal of control to stay focused on the aim and not dwell on the past and what happened.

We curated a different book for each country, according to the taste of each magazine. We were meticulous as we made our selections, and I became an expert at viewing the photography and looking for little things that might make an editor reject a photo. Was it in focus? How was the composition? Did the girl look believable? There were many different nuances. By the second day, tiny paper cuts formed crisscross patterns on my fingers, but it was worth it because I felt driven to get these books together, get on a plane, make some money, and start my life over. Without Eugene.

He made a few meager attempts to rekindle some feelings between us as we worked late into the evening, attempting to spark a fond memory of something we had shared. But the memory of him banging my head against the faucet of the hotel bathtub remained prescient in my mind overshadowing everything else. I could still hear my broken teeth tinkling across the white porcelain, mixing with my blood before they swirled down the drain along with my self-esteem and the last bit of my innocence and dignity.

When we finished editing the photos, I checked out of the hotel and said goodbye to Mandy and all the friends who helped me recover. Mandy was still skeptical, but I assured her I had everything under control.

Eugene dropped me off at the airport, leaving me on the curb so he wouldn't have to pay to park. *"The white zone is for loading and unloading of passengers only. No parking."* Like music to my ears. I stepped onto the curb and felt my soul take flight. Eugene gave me a peck on each cheek and set the bags down.

"Good luck, Sammy."

He drove off, leaving me to wrangle two large suitcases and a carry-on. I hailed a skycap by waving a few bills in the air, and he took care of helping me with my luggage.

"Are you flying first-class, Miss?" the porter asked, noticing first-class tags from my previous life attached to one of my bags.

"Not this time."

The skycap looked at me with a twinkle in his eye and said, "Well, a beautiful girl like you should be. Let me see what I can do."

He took me right up to the first-class counter to check my bags in, and I got the upgrade. It was a sign I was on the right path, and my luck was changing. That first-class ticket would have cost more than the entire European itinerary. Once on the plane, I let my guard down for the first time in months. I could hear the shackles falling away as I clicked on the seat belt and put the headphones on. Janis Joplin's gravelly voice sang out "Me and Bobby McGee" as the plane took off. But I knew freedom was more than just another word. For the first time in my life, I felt less like I had nothing to lose and more like I had everything to gain—most of all, my freedom.

16

EUROPEAN TOUR

As the plane touched down at Heathrow, it felt, oddly, like I was returning home. I missed the English countryside, which reminded me of the rolling green hills of Pennsylvania. After checking into a hotel near the King's Road, with no time to waste, I scheduled an appointment to meet with the photo editor at Mayfair the next day. There was a ton of new work he hadn't seen, and I was sure he would pay top dollar as he had always been a fan of Eugene's.

After Carole's death, the Mayfair editor and Eugene had grown even closer. Everyone knew and loved Carole, and it was difficult not to empathize with Eugene after such a devastating loss.

Navigating the Underground with a bulky suitcase full of heavy binders required considerable effort. I felt vulnerable and somewhat of a target as I stood alone on the platform for the train to arrive. But I persevered. Though I left some binders and slides in my hotel room, I wanted to take as many pictures of as many girls as possible to this first meeting with the hope I would get lucky. Soon selling photographs of nude women who had sex with my ex-boyfriend would be a distant memory.

Mayfair magazine was in a timeworn building in a historic part of town next to a magnificent church. I remembered sitting alone in the church when I first came to London while Eugene went to a meeting at Mayfair. I had romantic thoughts of being married in this church wearing a lace-covered, white gown. Now, after everything that happened, I was only holding on to the hope of living a life where there would be no pain, no sorrow, only love. I was holding on to the belief the predicament I was in was only temporary. But the realization the dream of wearing a white wedding gown was no longer something I aspired to, was scorched across my heart.

Arriving over an hour early for my appointment, I sat on a park bench to gather my thoughts, breathe in the London air and be still with my memories. I tried to free my mind from the clutter and summon a positive image of the life I imagined I could have while appreciating the moment. I found remnants of a half-eaten croissant in the bottom of my purse and fed them to the pigeons that crowded around me, hoping for a morsel tossed in their direction.

The song "Feed the Birds" from Mary Poppins began playing in my head summoning memories of my mother taking me to the theater in downtown Pittsburgh for my birthday with my younger sister, and how special I felt. I could even picture the outfit she gave me for my birthday, which I wore to the theater. It was a navy corduroy dress covered in little bouquets, and it even smelled new.

Lost in nostalgia, I almost forgot about my meeting and scurried past the old church to the Mayfair offices, arriving right on time.

"Sammy, you're looking well. And how is Eugene?"

"Thank you. You are looking well, yourself." I paused before continuing. "Eugene is wonderful. He's been so busy shooting some commissioned work back in Los Angeles. I needed to come to London to get a few things sorted, so we thought it was a convenient time for me to connect with you and give you a first choice look at some of his new work."

The editor summoned his assistant to bring us tea and biscuits, over which we continued to make small talk.

"So, Sammy, I know how close you are with Eugene. Can you tell me, how is he getting on now, you know, in terms of the loss of Carole? I have often wondered if he would ever recover…"

Before I could think about how to respond, he continued.

"Have they determined the actual cause of her death? Was it Mandies and slimming pills...? Have they implicated Dr. Kells? It seems any rogue can maintain a Harley Street practice if they have enough money to pay the rent."

Eugene had never discussed the details surrounding Carole's death. Part of me wanted to poke the bear to find out more, like who was Dr. Kells? And what about the slimming pills? Carole was far from fat with a 24" waist. It wasn't difficult to guess; her insecurities stemmed from Eugene and his constant badgering. Lord knows I knew how that felt. No wonder it wracked him with guilt. My guess was he was the one who pushed her to see the Harley Street doctor. My mind was whirling with conspiracy theories, but I couldn't help but feel it was inappropriate and insensitive. The mere mention of Eugene's name made me sick, but I tried to maintain respect for Eugene's privacy over such personal information.

"As I already said, Eugene is well." I paused for a moment before continuing. "Let's take a look at some of his recent work, shall we?"

He shifted in his seat with a distressed look on his face as though he needed to pass gas. I proceeded to pull out about ten different spreads for the editor to peruse. As he mounted the sheets of slides to the light-box, examining each one under a loop, his body language told me he wasn't all that enthusiastic about the work.

"It's a pity, you know. Eugene was once a great artist, but it seems he has lost a bit of magic in his work."

Sitting back in his chair, he rocked back and forth for a moment before continuing.

"There's a new crop of photographers coming up who are, how shall I say this, more in touch with what our readers want to see."

Eugene took beautiful pictures of nude women. But even Mayfair, which was long considered a "tame" magazine, was looking for racier work. The new crop of photographers coming up was shooting for Cheri and Hustler. To compete against those magazines, everyone was abandoning the more tasteful nude photography for more explicit pornographic material. I desperately needed to make a sale. So, I decided there was no other recourse but to come toward this guy like only Wild Bill's daughter could.

"Perhaps you might like this girl?" I asked, pushing the slides labeled "Sammy" across his desk. It was a photographic spread of myself taken when at a sprawling estate in Topanga Canyon overlooking the ocean on one side and the city beyond. Eugene shot these photos before we left LA for England, and things were already rocky between us. I wore a cream-colored, diaphanous gauze dress—the picture of innocence. But scanning through the slides, the photos became naughtier and naughtier, revealing more than I cared to remember.

I didn't want to share such revealing pictures of myself with anyone, but I needed a sale, and I figured I had nothing to lose. Eugene shot these photographs when I was minor, so it wasn't legal to sell them. It's not as though anyone would ever come forward to sue the magazine or report it. I wasn't even using my legal name, and I hadn't signed a release. There was an intensity to the photos Eugene took of me. They were provocative and portrayed an intersection of love and hate, vulnerability, and strength, and it was combustible.

As the editor considered each slide beneath the loop, he lost his professional, stiff demeanor. He looked as if he was about to break into a sweat.

"Do you think these photos are more in line with what your readers might want to see?"

There was an uncomfortable pause before he answered.

"All right, then. I will take the Sammy set," he said, referring to the photos of me as though they were pictures of someone else.

"And I will take Abby. She's got quite a good story, and except for that California sunshine, it looks as though this spread took place in an English garden."

He let out a somewhat forced chuckle as he removed his glasses and rubbed his eyes.

"Care for another spot of tea, Sammy, while we get the paperwork done?"

"That would be grand."

I began packing up the rest of the slides into the suitcase.

"Please make the check to Eugene's studio. I can wait for it if that's okay with you."

We still had a bank account in England where I could cash the check by forging Eugene's signature. I had done it dozens of times when we lived in London, and the bank knew me.

"Of course, we will issue the check straight away."

He summoned his secretary back to his office to communicate the instructions. It could often take a month for Mayfair to pay, but I had so disarmed this man he was now under my spell. We had some tea, and I began relaying stories of adventures I'd had finding girls in Los Angeles, and how much fun I was having working there with Eugene. I spoke about the beautiful cliffhanger Eugene, and I shared, and the fabulous parties we threw to the delight of all our friends. I never let on for a moment the sale of these photographs was the only thing between my freedom from Eugene or spending the rest of my life looking over my shoulder because if I didn't escape his grasp, he would be my demise.

"You know, I almost forgot about another set I wanted to show you."

That got his attention, so I teased him further, asking, "Do you want to see it?"

"Oh, yes, please."

He sat forward in his chair with the unbridled eagerness of a teenager as I laid out four more spreads Eugene thought would be too racy for Mayfair, and he designated for Club.

By the time I left, I had sold six sets of photographs to the magazine and repaired Eugene's image in the Mayfair editor's eyes. The bulky case I had arrived with was lighter, as was my mood.

I skipped back to the hotel, thanking my lucky stars for being Wild Bill's daughter. I remembered when I thought my father would be my savior. What I never expected was for him to be my guardian angel. I had inherited so much more from my father than his thin lips and squinty eyes.

I decided the next stop should be Hamburg via Frankfurt, which was plagued by terrorist threats. Changing planes in Frankfurt, I was surprised by the formidable military presence of army tanks and armed soldiers patrolling the airport terminal. The long lines through the security checkpoint were moving as slow as molasses making me wish I had checked the awkward case of binders.

A male security guard said in German, "Next in line!" so I began to walk toward the checkpoint.

Within seconds, surrounded at gunpoint, I dropped my bags and threw my hands up. My carry-on sprung open as it hit the concrete floor, and slides of nude girls flew out of the binder rings, scattering the pictures in front of the soldiers. They were shouting in German, when I suddenly realized I had ventured to the wrong queue. All I could think to say was, "Parlez-vous, français?"

A guard picked up one of the sheets of slides, held it up to the fluorescent light, and began shouting something in German. Before I knew what was happening, they summoned a female security guard and two men to escort me to an interrogation room. The male guard grabbed my arm with aggression as he sat me down with force.

The interrogation room was claustrophobic and thick with cigarette smoke. I could feel my pulse quicken, and sweat trickled from my underarms as we waited for the rest of my luggage, which they pulled off the carts and brought into the room for inspection. *What would Wild Bill do? What would Wild Bill do? What would Wild Bill do?* I kept asking myself as I tried to summon my guardian hustler. They brought in all my checked luggage and ordered me to open the suitcases with the keys. Since Eugene and I had color-coded everything according to country, I took a gamble. I presented myself as a modeling agent who wasn't there to sell photos, only to represent models.

I had three binders of photos: hardcore porn, middle-of-the-road porn, and soft porn. I knew that it wasn't illegal to have soft-porn pictures in my possession. But some of the more hardcore images crossed the line in West Germany.

Summoning my gambler's instincts, with the skills I'd played to win at PIPS, I distributed the binders around to the officers. To see the photos as I intended, I handed the hardcore photos to the female security officer, the softer sets to the younger male, and the most innocent to the most mature male officer. I was gambling on the older officer not being offended by the less racy spreads, and therefore, swaying the other two officers to go along with his opinion.

The male officers looked at the images and studied them with care. Human nature, in its most primal form, has no language barriers. You could see the photos titillated the men. The female officer kept glancing up at me, somewhat bewildered, then looked over at the men and back at me as her face became beet red. When the men had their fill of sifting through the shots, they shoved the binders toward me.

The older man in charge who spoke the most fluent English said, "Well, I can say with honesty, I don't feel there is any crime in representing these beautiful women. The photos are artful and of high-quality photography. So, I don't see any reason to detain this young lady any further."

The younger male officer agreed and tried to lighten the mood by saying, "I can safely say I don't think she's a terrorist." The two men chuckled. The female officer closed the binder and pushed it toward me. I smiled at her, not too broadly, and said,

"Thank you."

Wild Bill was not much of a father, but his instincts for survival and flair for hustle were woven into my DNA.

Relieved and grateful to be on my way again, missing my flight was a mere inconvenience. There wasn't much to do at the airport, so I wrote a letter to Eugene to let him know about the sales in England. When I boarded the later flight to Hamburg from Frankfurt, I believe I was the only female on a plane full of businessmen.

As I sat down, the man next to me introduced himself as Marcus. After take-off, we struck up a casual conversation.

"Where are you from?"

"I'm from Los Angeles."

"What on earth brings a young girl like you all this way from Los Angeles by yourself to Hamburg? What are you going to do there?"

"I have some business... Can you recommend a good hotel?"

"What's your price range?"

"Something reasonable."

"Something reasonable? Let me think. I hope you won't take offense to my saying this, but I believe in Hamburg, you must be at least eighteen years old to check into a hotel unaccompanied by an adult."

"Well, it's a good thing I'm twenty-five."

"Twenty-five? That's unlikely."

"Why are you interrogating me like this?"

"Because you don't have the hands of a twenty-five-year-old. You have the hands of a young girl. I have my doubts you are even eighteen."

I looked down at my hands and realized I didn't have the energy to Wild Bill my way out of this one. I felt my cheeks get hot as I glanced over at him but looked away before we made eye contact.

An announcement came over the loudspeaker that we would land soon. Exhausted from the interrogation at the airport, I was cracking. The rigors of hoisting the suitcases around and trying to Wild Bill my way across Europe was taking a toll, and this was only the second stop. I almost blurted out, *"Okay, you're right! I'm not twenty-five. I've been on my own for so long now I don't even know how old I am or how I even got here."* But I bit my tongue and just looked away.

When the plane landed, I scurried along to the baggage claim trying to think on my feet of where I should stay. My original plan was to get to Hamburg much earlier in the day, so I could figure out where the magazine offices were and find a suitable place to stay nearby. Now that it was nighttime, my exhaustion caused a mild panic to ensue as thoughts of not being able to find a hotel clouded my judgment. Wracked with worry, I waited as the bags tumbled down on to the carousel. I could see Marcus out of the corner of my eye at a phone booth on the other side of the conveyor belt. The suitcase full of binders came out first, and I struggled to lift the bulky case.

"Let me help you with that luggage."

Surprised to see Marcus now standing next to me, I said, "I can manage."

"I'm sure you can manage just fine. But I am a gentleman, and I would like to offer you my help if you let me. I just spoke to my wife, Julia, who has prepared a wonderful meal, so I am asking you to join us for dinner if you'd like."

Somewhat dumbstruck, I was without words.

"We have a guest house. We'd like to offer it up to you to stay the night. You can leave in the morning when you feel refreshed. It's best not to be searching for a hotel at night. Especially for a young woman."

"I don't know what to say. That's very kind of you—and your wife. But I really couldn't impose on..."

Marcus cut me off.

"Come on; you've got nothing to lose. Staying with us is a much better idea than wandering the streets of Hamburg at night looking for a place to stay. You can find other lodgings in the morning."

He was right. I was hungry and exhausted, but what resonated for me was when he said I had nothing to lose. The phrase *"You have nothing to lose,"* had become my mantra.

We arrived in Blankenese about thirty minutes later and parked the car at the top of the hill, then walked down a winding pathway about a quarter of a mile to their home, which sat above the riverbank. The place reminded me of the Hollywood Hills because the houses were clustered together on the hillside. But Blankenese was along the Elbe River, and twinkling lights from the houses looked like tiny fairies dancing on the water.

When Marcus opened the front door, the welcoming party was Julia and the overpowering smell of the stew she had prepared with root vegetables served with thick slices of crusty bread slathered in fresh butter. Their home was cozy and warm. Photos of their family of two children age four and six graced a wall of the small dining room. The love and affection on display throughout their home reflected Marcus and Julia's deep connection and love. Their relationship was something I desired.

The next morning, embarrassed to have slept in past 10 a.m., I jumped out of bed and dressed, emerging from the guest house with my bags in tow. Julia saw me from the kitchen window and greeted me outside with a coffee.

"Oh, my gosh, I have to get into the city and get to work. My apologies for sleeping in so late. I guess I needed the sleep."

"If your business can wait, would you like to go shopping at the farmers' market with the kids and me? It's only a short walk, and the fresh air and exercise might do you some good."

I could think of nothing I would enjoy more than some female companionship. The fresh air and the vibrant market were just what I needed. Julia was easy to talk to—like a big sister would be. As we walked through the narrow walkways between stalls of fresh vegetables and handmade soaps, I opened up to her. I shared how I ran away from my family, and before I knew it, I was revealing to Julia some of my deepest secrets about things I had never discussed or admitted to anyone before. It felt cathartic to share my darkest sorrow and have permission to cry about something I had been holding inside for so long; I was almost in denial it ever happened.

"You've had a rough time. But your current predicament isn't your fault. You must remember that. Just don't allow yourself to get stuck in a rut of self-destructive behavior. You need to make some good decisions. Maybe you should try to reconnect with your family?"

She was right. I felt determined to grow beyond feeling sorry for myself and my lost childhood. But reuniting with my family didn't seem plausible even though I had never stopped missing my mom. In my dreams, I often pictured her face trying to remember every happy moment we'd shared. It was the little things Mom did that sprang to mind, like when she rubbed Vicks on my chest and put a cold rag on my forehead when I had the flu or let me sleep in her bed one time because I had a nightmare. Trips we made; the Sunday afternoon lunches with all the fixings. I tried to forgive my mother for turning a blind eye to the abuse and stay focused on trying to remember the good times. Maybe I could string enough good memories together like bread crumbs that would lead to a path of forgiveness—perhaps I could find my way home.

Julia and Marcus offered to let me stay in their guest house for as long as I wanted, but I left the next morning and checked into a small hotel in the city. The editors from Quick saw me the same day, and I sold several sets of photographs. The next day I met with Stern Magazine, where I sold more than I expected, all for top dollar.

I boarded a plane to leave Hamburg later that day, and there was a delay on the runway. So, I closed my eyes and tried to summon the most romantic memories I retained from my childhood.

Life on the farm in Western Pennsylvania meant blackbirds, peppering the sky in autumn, and picking berries in summer that stained our hands and lips. It was fragrant new-mown hay and ponies and wind-blown, tangled blonde hair. It was skinned knees and dirty sneakers, climbing trees and picking apples, filling our bellies until they ached. Every day was a veritable harvest of color, adventure, tire swings, and hayrides.

I woke up squished against the chilled window of an Air France jet, with drool sticking to my cheek, as the flight attendant announced preparations to land at Charles De Gaulle Airport. Paris awaited.

17

A STRANGE AFFAIR

Croissants and coffee go together like champagne and chocolates, and Paris had them all. I rolled down the window so I could take in every breath of Parisian air. With cash in my pocket, it was challenging to keep from asking the cab driver to abruptly stop at several places along the way so I could take in the local shops. I had reservations at the Hotel Le Littre on the Rue de Rennes in Montparnasse and was intent on staying focused. I had a big meeting the next morning at one of the most prestigious men's magazines in the world, so I booked the poshest place I could afford because I had to leave word where they could contact me for the meeting. I had an optimistic feeling about being in Paris for this meeting, so I wanted to settle in for the big day that was tomorrow and continued to keep the cabbie on course.

The Hotel Le Littre was like returning home to a place I lived for years as a peculiar feeling of déjà vu swept over me. The wallpaper in the well-appointed room, which coordinated with the heavy drapery and upholstered furniture, gave me the sense I had been there before.

The antique desk displayed the hotel stationery and pen with the same insignia. It taunted me to pen a short note to Eugene, letting him know I arrived in Paris. It was a task I felt obligated to get out of the way so I could pursue more gratifying activities involving museums, the Eiffel Tower, and the little café I'd spotted around the corner.

In the lobby, I slipped the envelope into the slot. Free, fearless, and unburdened, I stepped out of the hotel onto the lively streets of Paris. I didn't have to pretend to be someone I wasn't. In

Paris, it didn't matter if I was American or British. I knew enough French from two years of study in high school if I believed it to be so like my Gammy taught me.

I closed my eyes, and on the cool breeze, I could hear angel voices with French accents. All my senses were opening. After unburdening myself with Julia, I was ready to allow myself to enjoy the moment, believing I deserved happiness, and happiness would find me.

While enjoying a Croque Madame for breakfast the next morning at a cafe not far from my hotel, a young man approached me and asked in French if he could join me for an espresso. He had a gentle face, caramel skin, and dark eyes.

"Mais, oui," I said.

"So, you are not from here? Are you on holiday?" he asked, switching to English. His accent was a cross between British and Middle Eastern, as far as I could tell from the kids I had hung out with during my Royal College of Art days.

"Great to meet someone who speaks English. I was feeling a bit isolated though I've only been to Paris less than twenty-four hours. I'm here on business, but at this moment, it feels more like a holiday." We exchanged an easy laugh.

Then William launched into a lively conversation about his recent trip to India, and the thrill of a black diamond ski run in Switzerland before it became apparent that we had little in common. Not only had I never been to India or Switzerland, I had never skied. But despite our differences, neither of us realized we hadn't stopped talking until the morning slipped away to early afternoon, and the sun rose high in the sky, making me squint.

"By the way, my name is Samantha."

"My name is, well, it's too complicated to pronounce, so you can just call me William."

"Well, William, it's been delightful and interesting chatting with you; however, I must be on my way. There is a meeting I need to attend in about twenty minutes from now."

I got up from the table, and my napkin began to fall to the floor when I caught it mid-air, almost allowing one of the binders of nude girls tucked under my left arm to fall to the pavement. Though William fit the demographics of Lui's readership, I preferred to leave our chance encounter on the same mysterious note with which it began.

"My driver can take you there. Where do you need to go?"

"Thank you, but I prefer to walk. I need to gather my thoughts. It's not far."

"When can I see you again, Samantha? How about tonight for dinner?"

Realizing this man belonged to a different social pecking order, and was also self-absorbed and used to getting his way made me want to decline the dinner invitation. Another domineering man without my best interests at heart was not what I needed.

And anyway, what would I wear to a fancy restaurant? Everything I owned I left behind in England or left scattered about the Edison Hotel.

But before I said no to dinner because of my clothing, my stomach weighed in on the matter, and I gave in.

"Okay, it's settled then. My driver will collect you at 7:30 p.m., and where did you say you are staying?

"Oh, that would be nice!" I answered, not quite believing the words were coming out of my mouth. "I'm at Hotel Le Littre."

"Fantastic."

"Mais oui, à bientôt," I said as I turned away, glancing back, finding it impossible to contain my smile as I headed to the meeting with Lui. I felt relieved William didn't ask me about the two binders of photographs tucked beneath my arm.

At 7:30 p.m., a black Mercedes pulled up in front of my hotel and whisked me past the Champs-Elysées to drop me off in front of the Hotel George V, the eight-story landmark hotel built in

1928, as grand a hotel as I had ever seen. The driver rushed to the other side of the car to open the door for me. He extended his hand to assist as I stepped out of the limo wearing a gray tweed A-line skirt with a matching jacket, beneath which I wore a satin, pale-gray camisole and the matching knickers hidden beneath my skirt. A pair of red-patent leather kitten heels with bows on them coordinated with my bright red lipstick. It was the exact ensemble I had styled for a magazine spread Eugene shot with a storyline about a naughty female executive. I suddenly felt self-conscious, wondering how awkward it would be if someone had seen the photographs, before laughing at myself for allowing my imagination to run wild.

William greeted me with a warm hug in the lobby and led me to a secluded area where a bottle of Veuve Clicquot awaited us. Despite the attendant waitstaff, he broke the seal and popped the champagne cork himself. The aromatic bubbles overflowed. I unbuttoned my jacket enough to expose the sexy camisole beneath as William poured.

We gradually moved to a private dining room and feasted on a gourmet meal before William announced, "Let's go dancing!" He summoned his driver, and off we went, stopping to pick up a few people along the way.

Karl Lagerfeld, Helmut Newton, Paloma Picasso, and Loulou de la Falaise were all regular fixtures on the scene. At Le Sept Nightclub on Rue Saint Anne, everyone was loose, free, and ready to have fun. I shed my jacket and before long the rest of my suit and was dancing wearing only my camisole, knickers, and stockings held up by a garter belt with bows that matched my shoes. When we left the party, William put his jacket around me for modesty and drove me back to my hotel.

"May I walk you to your door, my sweet?" William asked.

I agreed, and as I placed the key in the lock and pushed the door open, I half expected him to throw me on the bed. But

William took my hand in his and raised it to his mouth and gave me a soft kiss.

"Bonne Nuit, ma douce, Samantha."

He turned on his well-polished shoes, disappearing down the hallway, leaving my head spinning from what had been one of the most fabulous nights of my life. William made me feel beautiful, and he had re-awoken a long-lost innocence; I thought I would never be in touch with again.

The next morning, with a swirling champagne hangover, I answered a knock at the door to discover a porter in the hallway who handed me a dozen long-stemmed roses with a note that read, "Bonjour, mon amour. William." I had but a moment to take in the aromatic bouquet when I realized I was late for my meeting at Lui with Daniel Filipacchi, a fashion photographer turned publisher. The day before, I had impressed the staff enough to score a meeting with Mr. Filipacchi himself.

Jeans, t-shirt, sweater, scarf, and I was out the door. I didn't have time to wash my face and reapply makeup, so I smudged the raccoon remnants of the previous night's maquillage, which looked as though I spent considerable effort to achieve such a magnetizing smoky eye. Satisfied it was working for me, I ran a brush through my hair and raced out the door. I couldn't be late.

I brought along the two binders of photos Eugene hoped would be perfect for Lui. He went to great lengths to emulate French photographer Francis Giacobetti, director of the softcore movie Emmanuelle, whom he idolized. He was sure these photos would fetch a high price. Though the girls in the photos were top quality, I didn't feel confident about impressing Mr. Fillipachi after looking around the lobby at all the beautiful cover photography.

One of the girls, Rowena, was from England but had a French mother and her French looks were unmistakable, down to the pouty lips covering her slight overbite. The other girl possessed an almost immoral beauty, with a look reminiscent of Eugene's model girlfriend, Carole. She had a full bosom and tiny waist and the same smoldering beauty, transcending innocence, evoking darker sexual fantasies. It wasn't the girls I was doubting. It was the photography itself. I thought Eugene had gone too far, trying to emulate his idol.

Daniel examined the photos under a loop, with his staff gathered around in the conference room. Though well-received, the consensus was they were nowhere near the benchmark of Lui's standards.

"Pity, but I don't like the lighting. You see here?" Daniel pointed to light, hitting the model's thigh. "The shafts of light are too harsh, which gives the design an overall hard-looking effect. We want the models to look soft, as though they are floating. Sweet and tempting. This set is lit too harshly."

Then one of the editors responded, "I do love the girls, though, and the styling is superb. It's a pity the photography isn't better." Everyone concurred. "The styling is French but with an American bent to it. It feels fresh."

It was the first time anyone ever singled out my talents. They were saying my styling was better than Eugene's photography. I could feel my confidence soar as a strong gust of wind lifted my wings, and I felt hopeful about my future. Someone thought I had talent.

"Who is the stylist?"

"Well... I did the styling."

"C'est bon! Do you have a book? I am happy to show your work to Monsieur Giacobetti. He sometimes shoots in Los Angeles, and I am sure he would be interested in working with you."

Another art director added, "Or we can set you up with our American partners at *Oui* magazine. Your attitude is perfect for *Oui*."

"Oh, that would be so wonderful! Thank you so much."

Up to this point, I never thought I was doing anything more than taking orders from Eugene to help him achieve the look he wanted. Putting up with his demands and being bossed around only to have him go to great lengths to criticize everything I did had beaten me down. But now I realized I had developed a signature style of my own. I was talented in set design and styling. I never dreamt cooking up outfits with hand-me-downs and shifting furniture around as a child would lead to such an esteemed compliment. I was ready to own it.

Walking back to my hotel, I stopped by an arts and crafts store and purchased a black photographer's book. I was eager to cherry-pick through the photos I'd styled for Eugene to select the best representations of the styling, locations, sets, and set dressing and create a book of my work.

When I returned to my hotel, there was a note from William inviting me to dinner that night. It was less of an invitation and more like a summons: "I will pick you up at 8:00 p.m. Wear something formal."

I didn't own a stitch of clothing that had a remote chance of passing as formal wear. I also couldn't afford to spend the money I had made so far.

I entertained the idea of turning the driver away to deliver a handwritten note to William, saying I was not feeling well. But the old refrain of 'nothing to lose' still rang true, despite my sincere attempts to change my internal narrative. And anyway, some champagne to celebrate my good news would be fun, not to mention a good meal.

I would have to get creative with the clothing options I'd brought along on the trip. Using my stylist's flair, I chose the see-through ivory dress I'd worn for the Topanga shoot I sold to Mayfair. Layering darker undergarments beneath to make it appear a deliberate look, it just might pass for formal wear, albeit with a flamboyant Los Angeles flair. I summoned the concierge to send a porter up to take my boots for a polish. They were high heeled with buttons up the side, resting just above the ankle. I wore them with sparkling stockings held up by black garters attached to a black, silk bodysuit with intricate lace gathered around at the bottom, forming a tiny skirt visible through the gauze dress. I tied my long, blonde hair into an up-do, which I complemented with black velvet bows removed from another pair of the Janet Reager lingerie I brought. I opted for minimalistic makeup, completing the effect with a sheer-pink shimmery gloss on my lips.

I looked in the mirror, and it occurred to me. I hadn't taken a moment to look at myself since Eugene beat me up in New York because I felt like damaged goods. But here I was, standing in front of a full-length mirror in the City of Lights, shining like a star, standing face to face with myself and feeling proud and fearless.

When the car came to collect me, William was in the back seat. His driver opened the door for him as he stepped out to greet me, extending his arm toward the interior and signaling for me to climb inside as he said, "You look stunning, Samantha."

Off we went to one of the most spectacular steak restaurants in the city (though I was a vegetarian.) It was tough to get reservations, but we waltzed right in as though William owned the place. Over our languid dinner, comprising at least ten courses, William asked more pointed questions about what I was doing in Paris.

As proud as I was about the day I had just experienced, my instincts told me William would not approve of my having anything to do with the skin trade.

I didn't want to lie to him, so I said, "I work with photographers as a stylist and set designer, and I'm here to sell the photographs we've been working on to a variety of magazines."

"How much payment do you need to accrue for these photos?" he asked. "Name the price, and I will pay you, so you needn't go about selling them any longer."

I almost choked on champagne.

"William, that's not possible," I said. "First, we're talking about hundreds of dollars for the photos themselves, not to mention the fact I have spent much of my time and talent creating them. I need to sell them to magazines to share my work with others. That's how I will get more work. It's my job."

"I don't want you to have to work anymore. A beautiful woman like you should not have to work."

"That's very flattering for you to say. May I have more champagne?" I felt flustered and at a loss for words.

"Certainly," he said, hesitating before continuing, "It appears I've upset you. That wasn't my intention. I only want you to know I want to take care of you. I want to keep you safe."

My mind was racing. "I want to keep you safe" were words I thought I would never hear from anyone. But what gave William the impression I wasn't already safe? Did I seem weak and vulnerable? I felt conflicted. I thought I was becoming more independent and more self-sufficient each day. I wasn't sure what his definition of safety entailed.

"But what if I enjoy the work I do?"

"There are many things I enjoy doing that I would be happy to give up to be with you, Samantha."

"Well, thank you. That's very sweet."

I wanted to get past this moment and change topics; it felt too heavy for me.

"William, did you know I'm a vegetarian? But here I am at this steakhouse, pretending to eat steak to make you happy. See? I would do just about anything for you, too."

We both laughed, and he held my hand across the table. Once we regained a lightness to the conversation, I couldn't help but acknowledge the feelings of attraction I had for William. He was intelligent, handsome, and debonair, but I could see red flags popping up and knew the last thing I needed was another doomed relationship. Maybe it was time to say goodbye to

William. I didn't want to, but I felt a strange pull that I must.

After dinner, we were driving along in the limousine when William handed me a small box. "Go on, open it," he said, egging me on, his sparkling eyes trained on mine with such intensity, all I could do was to accept the package.

I opened the delicate wrapping to uncover a small, red Cartier box. I lifted the lid to reveal a sparkling diamond tennis bracelet.

"Oh, William! It's magnificent. It's beautiful."

Flashing back to my embarrassment when I discovered the Cartier watch gifted to me was a fake, my cheeks became hot, and a fiery blush lit up my face. I was at a complete loss for words. I knew this was no fake, and there was no question William was sincere in wanting to light me up.

"A beautiful gift for an elegant woman named Samantha."

How could this be happening? I didn't even know this man's proper name, but what's in a name? I felt guilty for wanting to end things between us, while he felt otherwise.

We stopped off at a discotheque to dance. I was an eighteen-year-old Cinderella, an abused child, a teenage runaway who had squeaked through high school, and a battered woman. But I survived, and here I was, dancing in a Parisian discotheque like a princess wearing a Cartier bracelet with no less than fifty sparkling diamonds. Beneath the colored lights, with my heart pounding, we shared our first blissful, delicate kiss.

That night, Copy and Kissy haunted my dreams. I saw the sheep scattering as the wolves attacked, and woke up with a start. It was already 10:30 a.m., and the housekeeper was knocking on the door. I told her to come back in a bit and crawled back into bed to ponder my life.

With plans to see William again that night, against my better fiscal judgment, I went shopping. I bought an expensive outfit to wear—black slacks, a fitted, crisp white blouse, and a matching black jacket, with a pair of elegant, black velvet strappy heels to complete the ensemble. I looked refined and grown-up, and the sleek Cartier bracelet that adorned my wrist made me feel like royalty.

William sent his car to pick me up and whisk me off to the breathtaking penthouse where he had champagne and a spread of appetizers laid out on the terrace awaiting my arrival. He complimented my outfit as he pulled me close and teased, "Since the moment I saw you in the cafe, I knew we were a perfect match. And, tonight is the proof."

His black slacks and white shirt matched my outfit, and we looked handsome together. William was barefoot, as though he had no plans for going out. He put his arms around me from behind as we gazed out at the Parisian skyline.

I had a strange feeling come over me. I felt as though I was treading a thin line between the dark and the light. A thin line between a love song and a cry of anguish. A thin line between the devil and the angel.

William then asked me something no man had ever asked before.

"Samantha, are you a virgin?"

I felt I had no choice but to step on to the thin line and attempt to maintain my sense of balance. Like a tight-rope walker without a safety net, I replied, "If you are asking me if I would like to make love to you, the answer is yes."

Our bliss continued for three days, uninterrupted except by rounds of champagne, caviar, chocolates, coffees, and croissants delivered to our room.

It's a fine line between love and hate, saints and sinners, winners and losers.

On the third day, William emerged from the dressing area, showered, with a clean shave, and dressed as though he was going to attend an important business meeting.

"You must go now."

"Okay?" I said, wondering why I felt as though he was kicking me out. The stern look on his face frightened me.

"My mother has come to town."

"Well, I will shower and get ready. I'd love to meet your mother."

"You must be joking. I could never introduce my mother to you. I like you, Samantha. I like you a lot. I thought I might take you as a wife. But I will only introduce a virgin to my mother because I will only have a virgin as my wife."

His cruel statement bewildered me and punctured my heart. I felt used and betrayed. I had given myself to this man for the past three days, when all along, he knew how it would end. I pulled the sheet with me as I ran to the bathroom to wash and get dressed. When I turned on the bidet, I didn't know the upward faucet was in the "on" position, so water sprayed full blast into my face, soaking my hair. Shifting from humiliation and embarrassment to a fit of simmering anger, I dried off and got dressed.

There is a thin line between tenderness and a brutal beating, and William crossed it. Teetering on edge between laughing and crying, I refused to fall.

"You know, William… Whoever you are, I have expected this moment might happen. We're from two different worlds. You are trapped in your world. It owns who you are and what you do. But my world is just beginning to open up to new adventures and new possibilities. Because I have my freedom, and you don't. That's something you can't buy. Not for any price."

I caught William off guard as he convinced himself he had the upper hand. He thought he was in control of his emotions when suggesting I wasn't suitable enough for him; when, in reality, he wasn't right for me. I finished buckling my high heels and turned to leave.

"Don't forget to take your bracelet."

"Save it for your virgin. Goodbye, William." I pushed the call button to the penthouse to summon the lift and departed.

On my way out of the hotel, an entourage was entering with lots of expensive-looking suitcases. Amongst them was a woman wearing an elegant headscarf. I wondered if this could be William's mother. As our paths crossed, a chill traveled up my spine.

18

MAIS OUI!

The last words I exchanged with William resonated with me more than ever when I returned to London. I had my freedom. I could make plans, and I had options. I had the courage and desire to become an artist and rise above everything I experienced. That freedom was hard-earned and allowed me to become the best version of myself, not anyone else's version of me.

Eugene was stuck in the past, which sadly coincided with Carole's death. The skin trade had evolved since then, but he was unable to move forward.

I went to visit Vera in Chalk Farm to give her some cash as I had promised Eugene I would. I spent the day with her and her sister in the run-down council flat, sorting through shoeboxes filled with photos of her precious Carole.

The poor woman missed her daughter so much. It made me think of my mother. What if I had misjudged her, and she was going through shoeboxes of photos thinking about me? I stayed at Vera's that night and lay shivering on a tiny cot soiled with cat urine. The only way to generate heat was by inserting tokens into a meter above the doorway, which I continued to do until I fell into a frozen slumber.

Echoes of my mother's voice reverberated in my mind as I tossed and turned, fighting away the demons who taunted me. I chiseled away at memories made of stone and flesh and bone until I walked down a pathway alone.

I could picture sadness crawling beneath my mother's skin, though her eyes were without tears. Her hands rested in her lap with nothing to do because there were no shoeboxes of photographs to sort through, and no memories of me remained.

Thousands of black wings filled the sky until they covered it in darkness. Endless shadows serenaded the emptiness. Tears were the only currency I possessed, but they weren't for sale, so I couldn't "pay the piper."

My mother repeated this phrase a lot to me while growing up—meaning I had to accept the consequences of my actions. The only way she could justify knowing her father abused me was by convincing herself it was all my fault. I had to pay some imaginary piper for all my evil deeds and wrongdoings.

I woke up realizing it was time for me to let the piper know I owed him nothing. The piper owed me plenty, though, and I intended to collect.

I tossed another token into the meter as I gathered my things, including some items of my clothing Eugene had left with the sisters when he gave up the flat we shared. I departed before the sisters awoke and took the train to the airport.

On the plane to New York, I downed a Bloody Mary and fell into a dreamless sleep. When I awoke, I couldn't get Julia's words about reuniting with my family out of my head. In a spontaneous moment, I called my mother, surprised when the recording said the number had changed. I scribbled it down, wondering if, after all this time of building up to having the courage to call her, would I even be able to reach her?

"Hello, Mom? It's Pam."

"Well, hello."

"I'm passing through New York on my way back to Los Angeles, and I was wondering if I could, you know, fly down to see you in Pittsburgh? It's been a while," I said, trying to stifle a nervous laugh.

"Well, you know, we've moved. We live on Eichelberger Drive now," she said.

"Oh. So, you sold the farm?"

"Yes. Pap sold it, but he still lives with me. He has a room in the basement."

The deafening silence that followed made me embarrassed I called and made me want to hang up and pretend it never happened. Still, I missed the sound of my mother's voice. I had waited almost five long years to hear it again, and I wasn't about to hang up without her agreeing to see me.

"I would love to see your new house. If I can get there later today, would that be okay?"

"I suppose that would be fine," she said, sounding unsure.

Getting off the plane in Pittsburgh felt like reentering the Earth's atmosphere after being lost in space. The taxi driver dropped me off at 62 Eichelberger Drive. It was a modest suburban home with a well-manicured bed of flowers in a neat row in front of the house. There was no gravel driveway, no maple tree, no morning glories climbing wildly up the front porch and no smell of horses and the sweet scent of burning trash, its ashy embers floating in the sky above the garden like tiny black hearts. I rang the doorbell. To my surprise, an affable man answered the door.

"Hi, I'm Tommy. I'm, well, your mom and me, we are..."

My mother appeared behind Tommy and welcomed me inside. Tommy was Mom's new boyfriend. He had a slight build and wore his hair pushed back off his face, framing his glassy eyes. Tom looked as though he was in his mid-forties, like Mom. I learned they met at US Air, where he was a mechanic and worked on the tarmac.

A distinctive smell permeated the small living room, an unrelenting odor of alcohol lingering as though the stench might be creeping out of Tommy's pores. The unctuous film hung in the air like smog, attaching itself to the drapes, the furniture, and even to Mom, which was apparent when she hugged me. I had waited so long for that hug, but it felt cold and foreign. Tommy, I learned, was living with my mother.

Mom told me I could put my things in the room at the end of the hallway and said they already had dinner but asked if I was hungry.

I told her I ate already.

"I can't stay long. I need to get back to Los Angeles as I have important business to attend to," I said as we sat staring at each other across the living room.

"What kind of business?" my mother asked while Tommy popped open a can of beer.

I felt as though I had entered a parallel universe. There was never an ounce of alcohol present in our lives after we ran away from Wild Bill, save the port hidden in my grandfather's cabinet. My eyes darted around the room, looking for something that felt familiar, wondering how I could manage to eke out enough conversation to fill the emptiness.

Mom told me Pap sold the farm to a doctor who had promised to leave the old homestead intact and not sell off the land. It was a small consolation to know Copy and Kissy's former home would be preserved. I wondered what had become of Princess, but felt too emotional at the moment to ask. I tried to seem dispassionate about how profound it was for me to be sitting in my mother's new home with her new man, all the while knowing my grandfather was in the basement. It was hard not to address the elephant in the room. Or, in this instance, the monster in the basement. Just as he holed up in the barn the weeks before I ran away after my mother saw him raping me, maybe he knew better than to show his face.

It was a challenge to find common ground with two grown-ups staring across the room at me, one of whom had been my mother, but now felt like a stranger, as I'm sure I did to her. When I tried my best to strike up a conversation about my life in Los Angeles as a stylist and photo assistant, she and Tommy exchanged looks as though they didn't believe a word I was saying.

"I do wish I could stay longer, but I do need to be getting back to Los Angeles soon because I have an important producer to meet."

"So, Pammy, how is it that you have acquired a British

accent while living in Arizona, or is it Los Angeles now?" They both laughed out loud right in my face.

"I live in Los Angeles now. But I did live in London for a while, and I guess I'm a bit of a sponge when it comes to accents. I'm glad you both find it amusing, Tommy, how's a 'bout dat beer?" I said, trying to summon my best Pittsburgh inflection.

The next morning, I pretended to be asleep when they left together for work. The house was eerie and too quiet. I couldn't help myself but creep down to the basement. At the bottom of the stairs, I stood still. I could feel my grandfather's presence as I tiptoed closer to his room, which was off of the game room. I came within earshot of hearing him breathing before turning around and darting up the stairs.

Dressing in the same clothes I arrived, I called a cab and left, but not before scribbling a note to Mom letting her know I was needed back in Los Angeles on an urgent matter. The dream of reuniting with my mother had been a gut-wrenching eye-opener underscoring home, the place where I grew up, was as gone as gone could ever be. My mother had a new home and a new life. The images I carried in my mind of my sisters and I riding ponies and sled-riding were now consigned to memories, as they had all scattered like dandelion fluff on the breeze. My home was no longer out there somewhere waiting for me to return. It was now a place that lived inside of me to which I could return as often as I wanted. Home is where the heart is. Mine was beating inside my chest at an alarming rate, like a beacon signaling in the darkness.

The cab winded along Silver Lane, rolling to a stop at the intersection of Clever Road. Though less than ten miles from the farm, Mom now lived worlds away. I wanted to tell the cab driver to turn down Clever Road. I wanted to see the farm where I spent my childhood. I wanted to see my blind pony, Princess, but Mom told me Pap gave her away. I, too, now lived worlds away.

Back in LA, I rented a small car and found an affordable

apartment on Larrabee Street in West Hollywood just below the Sunset Strip. I arrived unannounced at Eugene's studio.

With little fanfare, I told Eugene, "Here is what I believe is your fair share of the money we made in Europe minus fifty pounds I gave to Vera."

Eugene looked pitiful in his dirty undershirt and boxers. He stood up and pushed his long blond hair off of his face, trying to catch up to the conversation as he pulled on a pair of gray sweatpants.

I placed the beat-up suitcase containing the last of the binders of photographs on the sofa.

"Here are the rest of the photos that didn't sell, minus the photos you took of me. I never signed a release for you to use them, and I was underage when you shot them. It could land you in jail if you sell them, so if you have others, I would recommend you destroy them."

Still trying to catch up with what was happening, Eugene asked was, "What did you get for the two sets we had for Lui?"

I wasn't surprised this was foremost on his mind because his ego made him believe his talent was on the level of Francois Giacobetti. I knew it would cut him to the core if I revealed they didn't sell because the photo editors thought they were inferior. Part of me wanted to deliver the news the way I had rehearsed it in my mind since leaving Paris. I could say they thought his photography was uninspired, and the only good thing about it was the styling. I might say they complimented the color palettes and finesse with which I tied the backgrounds into the shots. I could even say they thought I was talented enough to work with Giacobetti because this moment was mine to cut Eugene down to size. But I realized hurting him with words would not take away any of the pain he caused me, and Eugene wasn't worth the effort.

"They weren't buying anything. The photo editors had enough material for the moment. But they thought they were nice. I sold Anna to Club in London. They loved the set. They can't wait to see what you do next."

Eugene didn't react.

"Goodbye, Eugene," I said void of emotion. As I turned to leave, I could already hear him counting the crisp wads of bills.

As I closed the door on the past, it felt like opening the entrance to the future. I was free of Eugene. If it took flying around the world lugging an old suitcase filled with binders of naked women and having my heart stomped on in Paris to pay for that freedom, I was ready to own it.

My next move was to follow up on the tip I got from an editor at Lui about a photo editor's job at *Oui* magazine. I knew I could do the job because when putting Eugene's photos together and selling them, I realized I had a knack for storytelling. I knew how to edit the images into a sequence, so they'd make a compelling story and show off the girls in their best light. Because of Lui's recommendation, it was easy for me to get an interview with the chief editor at *Oui*.

Entering the Playboy building excited and confident, I rode the elevator up to the top floor, stepped into the lobby and told the receptionist I had an interview to see Mr. Cramer. The girl at the reception desk was beautiful, and I noticed her perfect manicure as she pressed on the intercom to announce my arrival.

"Please have a seat. Mr. Cramer will be right with you," she said, motioning to a sofa nearby.

Feeling self-conscious about the appearance of my less-than-manicured nails, I reached for a magazine to thumb through as one would in a doctor's office or the beauty parlor, but they were all Playboy or *Oui* magazines, which felt awkward. I curled my fingers around the leather portfolio, gripping the handle to hide my nails from sight.

"Miss Butter, Mr. Cramer, will see you now."

While Samantha Butter was a better name than Pam Butter,

the same moniker as a cooking spray, I realized at that moment that "Miss Butter" made me sound like a porn star. It seemed like a made-up name when spoken out loud.

Reminding myself it wasn't the time or place to obsess about my name, I walked as confidently as possible down the corridor to the office of the editor-in-chief. Mr. Cramer's position afforded him a corner office on the top floor, overlooking the Los Angeles skyline.

Mr. Cramer asked, "So what can I do for you, Miss Butter?" with a smile and a suppressed chuckle as he offered me a cigarette, which I declined.

He lit up the smoke and leaned back in his chair. He must have had a lot of practice with this maneuver as he seemed unconcerned his chair could tip over, landing him upside down. I couldn't quite shake the hope such a thing would happen as I already decided; I wasn't an immediate fan. He seemed cocky and full of himself. I guess a corner office can do that to a man.

I told myself; *You are here on a mission. To win this job and get your act together. Now is not the time to show rudeness towards this asshole. Now is the time to keep your emotions in check even if your name is Miss Butter.*

"I'm here to apply for the photo editor's job," I announced, trying to sound as direct and confident as I could while still obsessing over whether I should change my last name.

"The photo editor's job?" he asked, repeating the smile and the underlying chuckle.

"What makes you think you are qualified for that?"

"Here is my portfolio of work. I met with some of your colleagues at Lui magazine in Paris, and they recommended I get in touch with you when I returned. I just got back last week, so here I am. No time like the present, as they say."

Mr. Cramer continued to lean way back in his executive chair, scanning me up and down without as much as a gesture toward my portfolio. The awkward silence between us was palpable.

"I'm sure you are talented." He paused a bit before leaning forward in his executive chair and said, "I'd like to see some of those talents. You have a cute face, and small tits are in right now."

"But I'm not here to be a model, sir. I am a stylist and would like to become a photo editor."

I wondered what it would take for Mr. Cramer to open my portfolio. Should I straddle across his desk with my butt in the air? If I'd said I was here to give him a blowjob, his pants would have been off by now. But a simple request for him to leaf through my portfolio fell on deaf ears.

My face began heating up, and I thought I might morph into a cartoon character with steam shooting out of my ears.

"Well, since I'm not a model and you don't seem interested in the talents I'm offering, I won't waste any more of your time."

I rose from the chair, walked down the hall past the receptionist with the pretty nails, and pushed the button to summon the elevator. I got lucky as there was an immediate resounding "ding," and the metal doors parted, providing me with a swift getaway. I had pinned high hopes on this interview, and it had gone way off course. Now I had to endure an elevator ride of shame, starting at the top floor and stopping on almost every level to pick up another person who could size me up and down in my gray suit and red kitten heels, carrying my black portfolio. Never mind that no single person in the elevator had any clue of the rejection I had just experienced. I knew it, and the feeling I wasn't taken seriously hurt.

By the time the elevator reached the ground floor, I was over it. I owned the rejection and was ready to move on. I was just glad I had my parking ticket validated before the interview, so I wouldn't have to pay in cash for the humiliation.

No sooner had I arrived in the main lobby than the

receptionist called me over. "Are you Samantha Butter?"

"Yes."

"Mr. Cramer would like to speak with you," she said. "Please, can you go back up to his office?"

When I sat across from Mr. Cramer this time, he began by apologizing. "You are a poised young woman, but when you walked in, you didn't strike me as a candidate for the photo editor's job. I jumped to the wrong conclusion, thinking my colleagues from Lui were playing a prank on me."

I looked at him somewhat perplexed. "What kind of prank would that be?"

"Never mind. It doesn't matter. What matters is, while I don't think you're quite what we're looking for as a photo editor because we need someone with more experience, I understand you are a talented stylist. What would you think about coming on board on a 'perma-lance' basis to style for us? Lui's endorsement goes a long way, and after looking over your resume with spreads in Mayfair, Club Mondial, Quick, Stern. Some excellent work. I think we'd be lucky to have you. For an Australian, you certainly have the French aesthetic down."

Without a moment's hesitation, I swallowed my pride and said, "Thank you, Mr. Cramer. When do I start?"

Just like that, I got a job. And just like that, I was now Australian.

Freelancing as a stylist for *Oui* magazine began the next day. I got the job because I was talented but also because I believed in myself.

The editor had come up with an idea to open each issue with a teaser photo on a page dubbed "Openers," which detailed the content found in that issue of the magazine. He wanted the cute teaser photos to have a pay off with a more explicit or suggestive teaser image at the end of the magazine dubbed "Closers," which would give an overview and perhaps a sneak-peek of the next issue.

We'd sit around the conference table and collaborate on ideas for these vignettes. My concepts were stories inspired by events from my life, combined with my overactive imagination.

"What about getting a group of girls together to play cheerleaders?" I asked. "The models appear first in the Openers shot in cheerleader outfits with short skirts and pom-poms, ready to jump. In the payoff, Closers shot, jumping high enough to reveal we aren't wearing any panties. What do you think?"

"I love it," said George, the art director. "But you said 'we.' Are you suggesting you want to model in this spread?"

"You bet I do. I have cheerleader issues."

My comment made everyone around the table laugh. Little did anyone realize how true it was.

"Putting on a cheerleader's outfit and getting paid to do it? Are you kidding? Count me in."

Being able to laugh about some of my life's more heartbreaking moments was healing, helping me to mature out of feeling sorry for myself. There is no greater panacea than being able to laugh about oneself.

To fill out the squad, I called upon a few girls I recruited for Eugene over the time we worked together in LA. I impressed the management at Oui that I had such an extensive network of cute young girls willing to pose nude for the magazine.

During my time with Eugene, I had given up drugs. Since I wasn't into vodka, the most I ever imbibed was a glass of wine at dinner. But it didn't take long for me to convince myself I deserved to use whatever means necessary to forget the pain of everything that happened in my life, up to and including Eugene. I only wanted to feel good. If it meant getting high, I wanted to get higher.

My new desire for freedom from pain dovetailed with the times. In 1977, the decade seemed determined to end more decadent than the one before or the one to follow. There was no modesty. Why be modest when you are young and beautiful and high? Sharing one's sexuality was normal. It was all about free love.

I still had dreams of finding Mr. Right, settling down, getting married, and having a baby. But I was still grieving my unborn child, even though I may not have been willing to admit it to myself at the time. I didn't want to be someone's show pony, for fear my eye would get kicked out. I didn't want to wear a harness or be a blind pony.

I met a guy named Teddy at a farewell party he threw at the enormous house he had shared with his now ex-wife and kids. Teddy moved to an elegant bachelor's townhouse on Doheny Drive a few blocks from my apartment on Larrabee Street, and we began to hang out. He became my cocaine supplier and would give me a stash for making deliveries to his friends. Most of Teddy's friends were wealthy executives, directors or actors in the film industry, some of whom invited me to stay the night where I would, at least for the night, live in the lap of luxury, and drugs.

A few times, Teddy asked me to take a package to New York. As long as I wasn't busy with an assignment for Oui, any excuse to go to New York was a good excuse. I always flew first-class and mingled with the transcontinental crowd I'd meet in the upstairs piano bar. Ascending the narrow winding staircase covered in shag carpet with my book tucked under my arm, I acted as though I was organizing photos while enjoying a drink in one of the cozy swivel chairs. Before long, a man aproached me and asked, "Is this seat occupied?" His named was Malcolm Bricklin, and I soon discovered he was obsessed with talking about himself and his successful inventions. Among them was a car whose doors lifted upwards instead of sideways. While it was difficult for me to envision how it worked, he made sure that I knew everything there was to learn by the end of the flight, but the entire first-class passengers knew, too, as his enthusiasm quickly drew an audience.

Flying first-class was like attending a discotheque in the clouds inevitably kicking off, a party 30,000 feet in the sky, with people, crowded around the piano bar crooning along, drinking champagne, and snorting cocaine. Nothing in life compared with touching down at JFK and riding in a limo into the heart of Manhattan.

Studio 54 was a combustible ball of drug-addled energy. It was the ultimate sign of acceptance if you could waltz up to the club and gain admission while dozens of hopefuls craned their necks, unable to cross the velvet rope. A night in New York involving partying at Studio 54 made my heartbeat synchronize with the city's pulse. As soon as I stepped on to the dance floor, my spirit took flight and didn't touch down until the wee hours of the following morning.

One night there, I spotted Truman Capote. Two years before, I wouldn't have known who he was. Now I wanted to go up to him, introduce myself, and engage in a dialogue about the complex triple narrative of his book, In Cold Blood. An entourage of famous fans surrounded him, and I couldn't get close enough, but seeing him made me realize how much I had grown. I shared my thoughts on Capote with an attractive Wall Street guy called Party Marty.

We got wasted together, stumbling out of the club after 2 a.m. into a swirl of city lights before going our separate ways.

19

MEETING A DEVIL

My return ticket to LA was for later that morning, but I felt drawn to get to know Party Marty. Party Marty fancied himself the Bob Dylan of Wall Street. He was tall and wore tinted prescription glasses, giving him an air of mystery, as did his cowboy boots and gold jewelry. I thought Marty was a badass—a fast talker, charismatic, like someone you would cast in a movie to play the lovable bad guy. He had an air of living on the edge and reminded me a little of Wild Bill. He agreed to meet me at around 3:30 p.m. at a coffee shop.

"So, Sam, where are you staying?"

"Chelsea."

"That place is a shit show. How long are you here for?"

"Not sure, why?"

"I'm heading up to Woodstock tomorrow, so you're welcome to stay at my penthouse on Jane Street down in the village."

"Wow, Martin, thanks. That's cool of you. I appreciate it."

"Let's grab your stuff and head down there. I'll set you up."

We rode over to Jane Street snorting blow the whole way in the back of a taxi and then in the elevator on the way up to Marty's apartment.

When the doors opened, we spilled right into Party Marty's pad with a view from the penthouse that was magnificent. When shrouded in the LA smog, I felt protected. In New York City, I felt raw and exposed.

"So, Sam, don't worry about the cockroaches," Marty said as I stood mesmerized by the view. "They won't bite. My housekeeper went back to Guatemala, and the cocksuckers just took over the place. But let's have ourselves some Dom and head out on the town to Max's Kansas City, and then maybe we'll hit up CBGB's. Not sure who's playing tonight. I think it's the Ramones."

Creepy-crawly things were nothing new to me after having lived on the farm. My grandfather would disappear inside the springhouse with a baseball bat and emerge with eight or so rats hanging by their tails. They were after the watermelon kept there in a trough to stay cold. But nothing prepared me for the cockroaches in Party Marty's penthouse on Jane Street. They were everywhere. When I went to the toilet, two of the critters crawled across the seat just as I was about to sit down, which made me wet my pants a little.

I emerged from the loo, hoping Marty wouldn't notice the small wet spot between my thighs.

"Let's get the fuck out of here," he said, and I thought, *My sentiments exactly.*

On the crowded dance floor, I realized how different the scene was on the Bowery than 54 or the places where I hung out in Los Angeles. I was used to private clubs, wealthy men, and glamorous women. But this was the punk scene, and it pulsed through my veins like battery acid. It was loud, aggressive, and anti-establishment. I wanted to turn up the volume to drown out every negative thing I had ever been through and rebel against everything.

I leaned into the moment, which was all about visual art, literature, and individual freedom and expression. The name CBGB & OMFUG stood for "Country, Bluegrass, Blues and Other Music for Uplifting Gormandizers." A gormandizer is a ravenous eater of food, but what club impresario Hilly Kristal meant was "a voracious eater of music." I devoured it.

When we returned to the Jane Street apartment, my body was still pulsating, and punk music was a revelation.

As we lay in pitch-black darkness coming down from the coke, I reminded Marty, "I thought you were going up to Woodstock.

When are you leaving? Or do you not trust me here on my own?" I teased. "I mean, I'm not exactly alone. There are about a million cockroaches here to keep me company."

"I changed my mind about going."

"What made you change your mind?"

"You. You changed my mind. And as far as not trusting you? What's not to trust? You can have whatever I have that you want because you are possibly the most beautiful creature I have ever met."

I laughed it off as meaningless ramblings, but Martin was smitten and cuddled me close all night. We slept in the next morning and rolled out around lunchtime to get sushi. The fact that we were high on coke eighty percent of the time and the rest of the time we were sleeping or eating made me forget about everything.

"You like being my girlfriend?" Marty asked me one night.

"Your girlfriend? Is that what I am?"

His comment threw me because I considered us more like platonic buddies.

"Well, do you want to be my wife?"

I laughed hard as I snorted a few lines of coke before I realized he might be serious, which scared me. I liked Martin, but I was a far cry from being in love with him. He was nothing more than a temporary distraction. How could anyone even consider becoming Mrs. Party Marty? I hoped I wasn't leading him on. We shared a bed but never had sex. Hanging out with Marty was all just good fun for me. A lark. A chance to party in New York and forget about reality.

Then Martin laughed, and I laughed too, realizing Party Marty was teasing me. We were just pals, and this was all good fun. In another two days, I'd be on a plane back to LA. I had a styling job coming up at Oui, so I was going to enjoy this respite from work for all it was worth. Marty was tight with Kinky Friedman and the Texas Jewboys, so we ended up hanging out wherever they were playing. I didn't care where we went as long as there was a crowd of people, music, dancing, and cocaine. It was a world where I could be alone in my thoughts, but never be alone. It was a way of life that worked for me. We bopped around New York from one crazy scenario to another, every night another caravan of characters coming and going from clubs and private parties. Marty introduced me to music from bands like The Ramones, Blondie, and The Talking Heads.

On any night, a guy would show up and say, "Hey, hey, the doctor's here," and a small group would head into a separate room with the guy carrying a doctor's bag. People maintained they were getting shot up with vitamin B12 but were always secretive about it, and I suspected it was something else.

I'd say, "Well, hey, I want one of those B12 shots."

"No, you don't need one, you're too young," Marty said.

One night when we were getting ready to go out, Marty opened a vial and gave me a few hits off a little spoon he carried around his neck. My mini-skirt hiked up as I sank into the leather beanbag chair, and the coke brightened my senses. I could see between my parted bare thighs to the kitchen where Marty was tapping out several lines from a different vial.

The phone rang, and he disappeared into the bedroom to answer it. Crawling out of the beanbag chair, I went into the kitchen. A cockroach scurried across the mirror as I picked up a silver tooter and inhaled the mysterious-looking lines.

In an instant, I was aware this was something I had never experienced. Marty came back and saw the primo lines of heroin he laid out had disappeared.

"Hey, man, that wasn't coke. What are you doing?"

"I know what I'm putting up my nose."

"Samantha, you don't know. That was heroin."

"Well, now, I know. Anyway, you told me I could have anything of yours. So, there you go."

Within a few minutes, I knew I screwed up. I didn't want to do heroin. But I tried to play it cool and figured with all the drugs I had done in my life, what's one more? How different could it be from Quaaludes, LSD, mushrooms, cocaine, MDA...

I soon found out it was very different, as I slipped away into oblivion, melting down into the sad beanbag. Clouds separated in the sky, and my vision became as distant as a dream. Moonlight illuminated the room while I pondered deep thoughts and then watched them float away. I felt like a butterfly—a tremulous, fragile creature, short-lived, subsisting on little more than sweetness and light. My wings were beating so fast, but the layers of guilt, sorrow, and remorse weighed them down and made it impossible to take flight. I wanted to retreat to a cocoon, but the metamorphosis had taken place, and there was no going back.

Marty grabbed the keys, pulled me up, and said, "Let's roll."

Riding in the elevator from the penthouse, it felt as though we were rolling over peaks and valleys as it stopped on several floors before touching down in the lobby. It reminded me of a rollercoaster called the Jackrabbit at the amusement park from my childhood, Kennywood Park.

It was difficult remembering things that held meaning to me as a child. The abuse obliterated all of my happiest memories or pushed them to the furthest recesses of my mind. But now, I couldn't get my mother out of my head. I remembered the outfit she bought me to wear to Kennywood Park two summers before I ran away from home, making me sad and nostalgic. Though I experienced a range of emotions, I remained somewhat zombie-like, wearing a vapid expression. I felt numb. The vibrating traffic of cars and pedestrians in the East Village made me nauseous, and my skin was twitching. When we arrived at one of Party Marty's favorite haunts, a swanky restaurant called One-Fifth Avenue, we were now a group of about six. I sat down for only two minutes before I puked all over the table.

Our dinner companions erupted in laughter. The busboy seemed nonplussed as he casually cleaned up the mess as though it were nothing more than a spilled glass of milk. I felt better for it, downed a splash of cognac, and wished the night would never end.

The next morning, I slept in at Martin's. When I woke, I could hear him on the phone in the living room talking business.

"Let's pull the trigger on this deal and get it done," he said before hanging up. I wandered into the living room dressed in his shirt from the night before and nothing else.

"Well, look who's up. It's a real-life sleeping beauty. And you are a beauty. Come here and give me a kiss," Marty said, pulling me close.

Feeling shy, I pulled away.

"I want you to know, Marty, doing heroin last night was fun and all, but it was a one-time thing for me. It's not something I think I'll ever want to do again. Is that okay with you? I mean, I'm not judging you if you—"

"Shhhh," he said, grabbing me around the waist as he put his fingers over my mouth.

"It's no big deal. A client I made a big trade for passed that shit on to me as a gift. It was just a little bit, but lucky for us, he also gave me this." He pulled a massive bag of cocaine out of a box that sat beside the TV.

I ogled at the bag. "Wow. I've never seen that much coke before."

"The best part is, this is all for us. And this is primo shit. Let's get this party started right now," Party Marty said as he laid out some lines, living up to his name.

Martin and I stayed high on cocaine over the next few days, and we had a blast, club-hopping and rubbing elbows at parties with New York's most fashionable.

"I'll tell you, Sam. I've been working on a big idea. A prospectus I'm putting together that could make us millions," he said.

As high as I was, the phrase "make us millions" wasn't lost on me. It still seemed Marty was falling for me, which made me feel bad because I realized I liked the party more than I liked Marty.

"Okay, so what's the idea?" I asked.

"People are big into fitness these days, right? So, if you took all of those people in the gyms—pedaling like fools on the stationary bikes and jogging their asses off—and could channel that into electricity, you could create a new form of energy. That's why I am putting together a deal to build a gym—the most magnificent workout facility ever created—and call it 'GREEN.' I need a slogan for it."

"How about… Go GREEN, make the scene, and live clean?" I suggested.

"That's it! At last, someone who gets me and my big idea. We create gym memberships at facilities so large we have a monopoly on the gym industry. We put everyone else out of business. It's like going to 54 where you make the scene, and yet you are doing your part, you know, to create clean energy for the planet," he said, with so much sincerity it was hard not to climb aboard the Marty train and ride it wherever he wanted to go.

But in reality, I had an actual job—or at least a commitment to the work I was doing for *Oui*—and it was time to leave New York. Hanging with Martin opened my eyes to some new experiences, but I felt like an overripe piece of fruit that had passed its expiration date. It became difficult to connect the dots of how many days had passed and how much time I had spent being high. Living amongst cockroaches and howling through the city, dangling by a thread connected to reality, not my own, had grown tiresome.

When I returned to LA, I found my small mailbox overflowing with bills, junk mail, and a few checks from Oui, which I raced to cash. Party Marty kept calling me, but I let my answering machine run interference between us. I couldn't shake the creepy feeling of having tried heroin. It felt like inviting the devil to live inside my body.

Three or four weeks went by, and things were getting back to routine for me when there was an unexpected knock on my apartment door. I thought it was my buddy from downstairs since it was a security building. I swung the door open without hesitation or asking who it was, and to my amazement, Martin was standing on my doormat.

"Why haven't you been returning my calls?" he whined, like an abandoned puppy. "I've been calling you for days."

"I left a message for you on your answering machine. I'm styling a big shoot for Oui magazine at the Palm restaurant on Santa Monica Blvd. We're shutting down the entire restaurant and shooting most of the night with a lot of models and extras, so it's a ton of work for me. I need to stay focused, Marty. I can't play with you right now."

"Play with me? That's what you think this is? I'm in love with you, Sam," he said.

"Okay. . . Listen. I have to go. I have so much prep to do before tonight's shoot. You can crash here, and I'll see you later, okay?" I said, trying to dial things down enough for me to focus on the job. He sounded like a crazy person saying he was in love with me. I was sure it was the drugs talking, but it still seemed like a radical decision to hop on a plane to Los Angeles and show up at my door all because I wouldn't pick up my phone.

I don't think Marty believed me about the shoot until he pulled up in front of the Palm later that evening in a limousine. Murmurs of "Who's that in the limo?" reverberated through the crowd.

"Oh, it's this guy, a friend of mine who's in from New York," I said. But I was unamused by his impromptu appearance.

George, the art director, was over-the-moon as he yelled out to the photographer, "Shoot the limo, shoot the limo. It will give us more production value. Girls, go stand by the limo."

He turned to me and said, "Sam, what a great idea to get the limo here. Do you think your friend will let us get a few shots of the girls coming out of it?"

"I suppose we could get a few shots. But we didn't permit the sidewalk, and we're paying to shut down the Palm. They've used limos in spreads before. The Palm is an LA landmark."

But George acted the way a spoiled brat does when you won't let him play with certain toys. I had to cave in.

"Okay, a few shots, but be sure to get the Palm's signage, and then let's get the girls back inside."

I walked over to the limo.

"Marty, please leave. I'll meet you at Dan Tana's later. Okay? Please, be cool," I pleaded.

Martin got dropped off at Dan Tana's and sent the limo back to the Palm to wait and bring me there later to the delight of George, who thought it was such a brilliant addition to the shoot. George was so high on cocaine; he could have cared less about how stressed out Martin made me and continued to praise me up and down.

"Sam, you are a genius to get your friend to pay for the limo. What a cool prop."

I accepted the pat on the back and counted down the minutes until we wrapped.

When I got in the limo at the end of the shoot to go to Dan Tana's, I regret to say it was less about seeing Marty and more about wanting to have a drink, chill out, and get high because I earned it.

When I arrived at Dan Tana's, the maître d' escorted me back to Martin's table, where he held court with four other guys and a couple of cute girls.

"Hey everybody, this is my girl, Sam," Marty announced,

sounding a lot like Wild Bill.

In the booth, Marty handed me a vial of coke, saying, "Keep it. That's a little stash for my girl." I snorted a few lines with discretion at our table, and the crew of people expanded and contracted over the next couple of hours, with Marty picking up the tab. Wherever Marty went, the party seemed to follow and orbit around him. It was easy getting caught up in his world.

As we headed back to my apartment on Larrabee, the buzz from the coke made me want to keep partying, but Marty said he was too jet-lagged. After being on my feet all day and into the night, I gave in to also feeling spent. I smoked a joint and drank some cognac to come down off the coke. Marty stayed another day before returning to New York. I was glad once he left because it was hard to stay focused on my job when Party Marty was around.

The next day my modeling buddy, Rowena, and I walked around a track in Beverly Hills at the bottom of Coldwater Canyon Drive. I preferred to hike in the hills of Franklin Canyon Park, but Rowena was afraid of the trails because of the "beasties." Though I found it monotonous and uninspiring to circle the track fifty times or more, Rowena made up for it by telling me stories of her childhood in England. She was French but had grown up in England and had a lovely, lilting, upper-crust British accent. Her father was a Harley Street dentist, so her family was well-to-do. But she wanted to make it on her own and came to Los Angeles to pursue acting.

"My parents would kill me if they knew I modeled for a men's magazine," she confided.

"Then why do you it?"

"Because it's fun!" she giggled.

The "Openers and Closers" spreads were always the most entertaining as it was a great collaboration between the models, photographers, and magazine editors. I did everything I could to please George because I knew the happier he was with my work, I would keep getting calls for jobs.

There were times he seemed a little on edge around me, which began when he offered me some coke on set one day. I had no issue with him doing cocaine on set, but my instincts were to stay sharp around this guy, not do drugs with him, and not let him get too close. He became different towards the crew when he was high, barking out orders and asking models to get into poses that didn't seem to fit the Oui aesthetic. I knew there was an appetite for hotter and sexier spreads. But some of his requests and the way he asked I thought went too far. I would do my best to counterbalance his comments and coerce the girls into the poses while still helping them maintain their dignity by not exposing too much. It became a tricky balancing act.

When we broke for lunch, I asked George if it would be okay to run a quick errand. During my New York adventures with Party Marty, I had forgotten to pay a light bill and received a disconnect notice, so I needed to go in person to take care of it.

"Sure, Sam. Take as long as you need. Things are under control here."

When I returned, the shoot had resumed, but I didn't see George on set, so I went to look for him to make sure he knew I was back. I opened one of the location's bedroom doors and found George pulling up the zipper on jeans so tight; his flesh overlapped the waistband. Sprawled out on the bed, Rowena seemed out of it.

"What the hell, George? What's going on here?"

"This bitch is way too uptight. I couldn't get her to open her legs. She's useless. Get her out of here."

"Rowena? You okay?" I turned to George. "What's going on?"

I knew she wouldn't take any drugs. I scanned the room, noting a drink on the side table.

"Did you put something in her drink? Did you slip her a roofie? I know you've been giving the girls Black Beauties and coke. But this is low, even for you."

"I thought you were a smart girl, Sam. For a smart girl, you sure have a lot of questions. Don't you know smart girls don't ask questions?" he said, wiping a drip from his nose. "I think I need to find someone who knows how to get the job done without asking so many damn questions."

He took a hit from his gold spoon, slipping it under his paisley shirt, before wiping his nose and exiting the room as I sat there wondering what to do with Rowena. I hustled her out to my car, and when I got her strapped into the front seat, she threw up all over the dashboard with several forceful heaves. I got her to my apartment and applied cold rags to her head. I laid on the bed next to her to keep vigil, and by early evening, she roused.

"Sammy, what happened?"

"Oh, you just got sick. Don't worry; you will be okay. You didn't eat enough is all."

I tried to reassure Rowena everything was okay because I wanted to spare her heart from hardening as mine did when someone drugged and took advantage of me. Now, I trusted no one, and yet, I continued to put myself in harm's way. Why couldn't I see things for what they were? Was I as blind as Princess?

"Sam, I don't think I want to model anymore."

"I think that's a good idea. For both of us."

I put the kettle on and turned the record player up to listen to Van Morrison's "Bright Side of The Road." The next day, I got a call from the human resources department to inform me that I would receive my last check from Playboy Enterprises by mail.

20

A GIRL NAMED SAM

Oui was a dream job, and being fired gutted me. I needed to get out of LA, so when Teddy asked me to run an errand to New York, I jumped at the chance. Besides, there was $250 cash in it for me, and without a job, I needed money.

On a crisp fall day, I stood in front of One Beekman Place, sent to deliver an old man a package—some Quaaludes and cocaine. I knew this because I couldn't resist peeking inside in the confines of the first-class bathroom on the airplane. Most likely, the intended recipient of the parcel wouldn't miss one Quaalude, I thought, as I snatched it from the baggy, securing the wrapping.

One Beekman Place sported a handsome façade to its sixteen stories. Though opulent, a sadness permeated the building as though it had witnessed grander days, or perhaps the place was tired of appearing luxurious opting for a more bohemian aesthetic.

The owner of the home appeared in the dimly lit room. He was an heir to a massive grocery store fortune but presented himself more like a disheveled recluse. In a soft voice, he asked, "Do you have the package?"

"Yes. Here it is," I said, handing it over.

I asked, "Do you always walk around in your bathrobe at one-thirty in the afternoon? It's a rather lovely day outside. Are you ill or something? Is that why you've drawn all the curtains?"

I had to restrain myself from flinging open the curtains, which would have lit up dust particles like dancing fairies, perhaps even a few pesky moths would join the fun.

"Hey, I don't know you, I mean, this is the first time we're meeting and all, but would you like to go out for a walk or something? Sometimes it's nice to get out and trip around the city when you're doing 'ludes. You know what I mean?"

Realizing I let it slip I knew what was inside the package, I hoped he wouldn't take notice.

"How far is it from here to Central Park?" I asked, attempting to change topics. He didn't answer as he sat down in the wing-backed chair and examined the package, revealing the Quaaludes and cocaine inside.

"You know, if you wanted to consider tipping me with a Quaalude or two for delivering the package, I wouldn't mind it at all. I met this guy on the plane who offered me just about the best blow I've ever snorted and, well, I believe I had a tad too much. So, pardon me if I seem a little jumpy or too talkative. One lude would do me just fine, and I'll be on my way if you point me in the right direction to get to Central Park. I love it there. It is about my favorite place to go while here in the Big Apple. And, by the way, I loathe when people call New York City the Big Apple, and I don't know why I just said that. It just came out." I paused a moment before adding, "Sorry."

The man said nothing. Somehow, the less he said, the more it made me want to talk to him until I could get something—anything—out of him. He seemed sullen. His sunken demeanor somewhat frightened me, as if maybe he wanted these pills to off himself. But then I realized it was probably just me being paranoid again from too much coke.

"I love walking around Central Park and watching all the people. I love eating at Tavern on the Green, and I adore having picnic lunches there, too."

A single shaft of light entering the room through the drawn curtains made dust visible on the surface of a glass of water. The old man took a large gulp to wash the pill down his throat. Then, he offered me a tablet, which I snatched from his bony fingers as he said, "Central Park is about a mile from here. I could have a driver take you if you like."

The sound of his voice was deep and calming. His eyes were dark and glazed in sadness.

"May I?" I asked as I opened the Baccarat decanter, pouring myself a glass of cognac to wash down the Quaalude. "What is your name again? It's Huntington, right? I like your name. It's a cool name. A strong name. My name is just plain Sam."

No matter how hard I tried to calm myself down, I had ingested more cocaine than my 105-pound frame could process and had already taken half a lude. So, I kept talking to the old man as he sat there slumped in his chair, staring at me and looking annoyed.

"I have a song named after me. Well, not exactly named after me, but inspired by me. My dad, Wild Bill, he's good friends with Johnny Cash. He was always going on about telling Cash about his 'girl named Sam'—that's me—and Sue is my middle name, so Johnny just puts the two things together and comes up with the famous song 'A Boy Named Sue.' Oh, and my daddy is also the one who convinced Johnny to wear all black."

The Quaaludes were calming me down and lulling me into a relaxed state of euphoria. Still, I continued to ramble on about myself, telling him I was from England, lived in Australia for a while, and now called LA home, which is why I didn't have an identifiable accent. Huntington could have cared less about me or my backstory, but I discovered a real-life character who had sprung from my experiences. The stories I told were now a part of who I had become. Closing my eyes, I reflected on the past five years of my life since I ran away from the farm. What a journey it had been. Huntington didn't say a word. He just sat there looking somewhat bemused by the precocious young woman who had taken over his afternoon. Despite his wrinkled face, it was easy to tell Huntington had, at one time, possessed movie star looks. I was comfortable with him, and I thought he was with me. I felt my coming here on this day was no coincidence because he needed someone to comfort him. I began to believe the Universe was responsible for bringing us together.

"It's OK," I said when he didn't answer my questions. "I'm not one who likes to talk about myself, either," I said without the slightest bit of irony as I hadn't stopped talking about myself since my arrival.

"In fact, the less you know about me, the better because there are some things about me I don't like to talk about and some things I am not proud of that I have done. I mean, don't worry, I've never done anything bad to anyone, like hurt them or anything. I would never say, steal that crystal clock from your mantelpiece, although the thought crossed my mind I sure would like to have one like it someday. I love clocks. But I want to get these things for myself. It would just mean more to me that way."

I lay back on the soft chair and took in the surroundings as the Quaalude overcame my senses, making me feel I was having an out-of-body experience, as though I were flitting about the room like a firefly. Uncatchable. Lighting up every few moments just to remind the void, I was still there.

In a little while, my lucidity returned.

"So, where is your wife? Is she out for the day or away on a trip?"

Huntington didn't answer.

"And what about your kids?"

"How do you know I even have a wife or kids?" he snapped, scowling.

"Don't most heterosexual men have children by your age? I suppose you could be a homosexual, but I'm not getting that vibe from you. Half my friends are into men, so I should know. Maybe you just don't like kids."

His face seemed to contort, and I feared I might send the old man down the rabbit hole, so I tried to leave these personal matters for another time. I believed he enjoyed my presence even though he was a wee bit socially awkward.

"Well, this afternoon, you have me," I said, "because I'm not going to Central Park or anywhere else after you talked me into taking that lude. Today is a good day for me just to stay put right here, with your good company. You will keep me company, won't you?"

I curled up into a tighter little ball and pulled a coverlet over myself.

"I love being in New York because I like the feeling I can get around with public transportation. It's a respite for me from LA, and all the driving one must do out there. Do you know how much I hate to drive? It took me about five tries to pass my driver's license, but I still failed. Someday, I'll be getting a full-time chauffeur."

Huntington took another sip of water and looked at me as though he was only now acknowledging my presence in the room. I seized the attention.

"My needs are quite simple, except for the chauffeur business. Like I always say, as long as I have cognac, croissants, and clean sheets, I'm good. Oh, and sometimes I switch the croissants with chocolate, or champagne for the cognac, depending on my mood. But the clean sheets are non-negotiable."

"Well, that's more than I can say about myself." He paused a moment before continuing.

"So, you are the inspiration behind 'A Boy Named Sue?' Do you know the words? Can you sing it for me?"

"Ahh. . . Singing isn't my thing. First, I am tone-deaf. And second, well, if you want me to sing, I do know most of the words by heart."

Thanks to the cocaine, cognac, and Quaalude, I let go of my inhibitions, and without further ado, sucked in a deep breath and went for it. I sounded like a cross between a British schoolgirl, a drunken Australian cowboy, and a kid from McKees Rocks who had been hanging out with Valley girls in LA.

After rollicking through the first few lines, I caught my breath.

"I can't remember the whole song, but there are many funny lines. Something like—" I stopped to take a swig of the cognac, now on a roll.

But before I could continue, Huntington sighed and said, "I hate to burst your bubble, Girl Named Sam, but Cash didn't write the lyrics to that song. Shel Silverstein did. So, unless your daddy is good buddies with Shel Silverstein, too, I would venture to say that song has nothing to do with you."

As I took in this revelation, I wasn't sure how to react. My dad had relayed this to me for as long as I could remember. I had told and retold this story a million times, and no one ever questioned it. I flashed back to the first night I met my dad at Dave's Tavern when everyone hung on each detail of the story.

My cheeks flushed. Huntington must be right. I knew he was telling the truth because there was no reason for him to lie. I calmly stood up with the glass of cognac and perused the library wall, running my fingers over the leather spines. Books, ideas, stories, novels, collectors' editions, and poetry by Kipling and Tennyson burst from the shelves—I took it in, trying my best to compose myself.

When I felt ready, in a nonplussed manner, I said in my best British accent, "Of course, silly, I know that. It's just a funny story my father used to tell people over drinks at the pub. I thought it might amuse you."

With that, I slumped into the overstuffed chair and closed my eyes. Now, too high to make a run for it, I saw my younger self back at Dave's Tavern in Phoenix, meeting my dad at age fourteen. I relived Wild Bill, ordering me a rum and coke and retelling the Johnny Cash story. I saw the Estrada Brothers and the other bar cronies hanging on his every word only to erupt into laughter while "A Boy Named Sue" played on the old jukebox.

By the time I reopened my eyes, the afternoon sun was no

longer peeking through the cracks in the curtains. I was uncertain how much time had passed.

"Have you read these all books?" I asked, gathering myself.

"No," Huntington answered.

"Then why do you have so many? Do you think you'll ever read them?

"Probably not."

"Have you read *In Cold Blood?*"

"Why?"

"I admire Truman Capote's writing. In Cold Blood is a complex triple narrative, you know, and very engaging."

There was a long pause.

"Have you heard about the sleeping prophet, Edgar Cayce?" I continued. "If I could be anyone else, I would want to be Cayce. In fact, I have psychic powers like him. Can I tell you a secret?"

"Do I have a choice?"

"I love to sleep with books under my pillow because I think I might end up like Edgar Cayce and just know stuff—like everything that is in those books will go into my brain through osmosis."

"So, do you have any other interests, Girl Named Sam?" Huntington asked.

"I like to write poetry, but mostly for myself. I don't feel quite comfortable sharing it with anyone."

"Would you feel comfortable sharing something with me?"

"Well, I don't have a lot of it memorized, but it's all written down. Anyway, how about this one? Basalt eyes, balsam of my senses/What is the secret behind the clouds in your eyes? Basalt eyes, balsam of my senses./Are you the secret to the clouds in my eyes?"

"That's lovely," he said. "Who did you write it about?"

"No one. It's not about anyone. Or maybe it's about you," I said, giggling.

He chuckled.

"Basalt eyes . . ." His voice trailed off as he rose to answer the phone. I stared at the bag of drugs on the table and went for it, snatching another Quaalude while Huntington wasn't looking. I might need it to get through the night because suddenly, I felt a sense of paranoia and panic. It's not every day someone outs your father for being nothing but a two-bit con-man, making me nothing but his two-bit daughter named after his affair.

I could hear Huntington making some arrangements with someone. "Yes, that will be fine."

He hung up the phone and sauntered back to his chair. We both sat quietly, and before long, he dozed off.

When he opened his eyes, he said, "I'm glad we met."

The afternoon had slipped away to evening, flooding the room with a bluish cast.

"I have met and loved many beautiful women in my life. But with certainty, I can say I've met no one like you. And you aren't even a woman yet. God help the man who gets tangled up in your blonde hair."

In my current state, I wasn't sure if Huntington meant it as a compliment or a put-down. The drugs and alcohol had now taken full control of my senses. I felt as though my soul escaped my earthbound body and hovered about the room, exploring the textures of the fabrics and the smell of the leather and a musky scent reminding me of only the good memories of the farm.

"Don't think I didn't see you slip another Quaalude down that chatty box of yours," he said. "I think you should sleep here tonight lest the big apple takes a bite out of you. And don't worry, the sheets are clean."

Huntington led me through a hallway and down a few stairs to a comfortable four-poster bed. As I pulled the covers up around my neck, I drifted off to places I'd never been but hoped to revisit.

In this moment of comfort, I felt peace. Huntington had burst my bubble, but maybe it was time to face the truth: my daddy was a liar and a con-man. And I was just a girl named Sam.

21

WAKING UP IN WOODSTOCK

The next day, I slipped out in the early morning light as discreetly as possible. The pavement seemed to shift with each step I took as the autumn leaves crunched beneath my feet.

While I knew Dad made the story up, I tied so much of my identity to being 'a girl named Sam', who inspired one of Johnny Cash's biggest hits. The story had provided me with a sense of courage and importance. It made me believe I was somebody more special than Pammy Sue. How many times could my identity fall to pieces before I became like these leaves crunching beneath my feet— crumbled fragments once a part of something grander?

I knew I should rejoice Huntington saved me the humiliation of continuing to believe a story my dad made up. But the realization that there was nothing special about me left me feeling raw and exposed. There was only one thing I knew that could take this pain away.

I sat in Central Park, waiting until it was a reasonable hour to reach Martin. Time seemed to stand still as I waited for the sun to warm up the park and the streets to come alive. I knew there was no way Marty would be up before 11 a.m., but by 10:45, my palms were perspiring, and all I could think about was getting high and putting the past forty-eight hours behind me. I found a phone booth and dialed the number, preparing to launch into my Wild Bill persona.

Martin sounded groggy when he answered the phone.
"Hello?"
"Well, hello there, stranger. Guess who's in the city?"
"What? Sam? Is that you? Honey, where are you?"

"Uptown. But I'd rather be downtown if you know what I'm saying."

"I'm going up to Woodstock. If you want to come up, I'll send my driver. You wanna come up?"

"Can't wait to see you!" I said as I relayed the cross streets of where he'd find me before hanging up the payphone.

Martin said he would send a car, but I didn't know it would be a vintage 1958 James Young Body Rolls Royce Silver Wraith Touring Limo that would whisk me up to his place in Woodstock. When the car rolled by, heads turned—it was a jaw-dropper. I opened the vanity in the middle of the backseat with the curiosity of a child and, to my delight, discovered all the original lipsticks and powder compacts were still intact.

We picked up Martin at Jane Street, and he and I settled into the luxurious leather seats to take in the scenery. I forgot all about the fact I only called Martin to get high. The sounds of the city gave way to birds, and the aroma of conifers and sweet grassy fields turning color for the season replaced the urban smell of urine in the alleyways and trash turning sour.

It was about a two-hour ride to Woodstock, but worth every minute. Walking into Marty's cabin in the woods was a grounding experience. I hadn't felt so peaceful and such a sense of belonging in some time. At my core, I was a farm girl from Pennsylvania, and I hadn't realized how much I missed being in the woods. The tall pines bent over in prayer against the cold wind, and everything felt fresh and alive. The misty gray sky gave way to a spectacular sunset, and the air was dense with moisture.

Martin inherited the cabin from an old aunt, so the furnishings were lived in, cozy and comfortable. In Woodstock, I came to see a new side of Martin. We would start a fire and cuddle into the wee hours of the morning, talking until our throats grew tired. Old stories, new stories, poetry, and books—Marty's interest in getting to know the real me was endearing. I had become so accustomed to men disrobing me with their eyes if not their hands, but Marty preferred seeing me cozy, donning the oversized long johns he pulled from a drawer at his Woodstock house. We rarely connected physically beyond kissing, but our time together was more intimate than I had shared with any man in a long time.

Marty had a friend named Bobby, who owned a store in town called Hapiglop Bootery. They sold Frye boots, prairie-style hippie dresses, and vintage-style clothing. Martin took me shopping at Hapiglop, and I left with a new wardrobe of cowgirl boots and flowing maxi-dresses and a leather jacket with a detachable feather collar that I was obsessed with and wore almost every day.

We ate out nearly every night at the Bear Café, overlooking the Sawkill Creek. The vibe at the café was familial as everyone who went there seemed to be part of the Bearsville Woodstock music and arts scene, and most were on a first name basis with Marty. Bear Café was owned by the legendary manager, Albert Grossman, who also opened a new dining establishment in Bearsville called East-West Restaurant. Grossman invited local luminaries to a grand opening event. The crowd consisted of mostly musicians, who seemed happy to have Marty among them. When I took a seat at the long communal table, I heard someone hollering out, "Hey, Butter," and I jumped to attention, thinking they were calling my name only to find out they meant musician, Paul Butterfield. Marty got a big a chuckle out of telling everyone my last name was actually "Butter."

Even though Martin was thirty-eight, he exuded innocence and a playful, childlike demeanor. He had a way of making me feel I took life way too seriously. I suppose this stemmed from the fact that since I was fourteen, I was pretending to be older and more sophisticated than I was. Martin made me feel like I shouldn't have a care in the world. During the past few weeks in

Woodstock, I felt like I was making up for lost time from my girlhood as Martin chased me around the cabin, having pillow fights and playing hide and seek in the woods behind his house.

One day I overheard Martin throwing out financial jargon to someone on the telephone. I didn't pay much attention until he hung up the phone and announced, "I've got to run into the city, don't worry, not for long, just a quick business deal—in and out."

"I'll go with you. I can hang out at the Guggenheim while you have your meeting."

"No, you stay here. Enjoy Woodstock. I'll be back probably late tonight, so don't wait up for me."

Martin left early in the morning, and around lunchtime, I looked through the cupboards for something to eat. Little food, some stale cheerios, a few crusts of bread and some jam were all that were on the shelves. Martin never spent longer than a week at a time in the country, so he didn't stock the house with food, and we ate out most of the time since I arrived. I didn't have a car to drive to the market, and it was much too far and too cold to walk down the country road into town. Still, Martin would be home by morning, so I searched the dusty book cabinet shelves for something interesting to read and settled on *Surfacing* by Margaret Atwood. I might have thought twice about allowing myself to be pulled into the realm of the character's madness if I had known the depth of the book's plotline and how it touched on themes of identity and uncovering one's past. But at least, curled up in front of the fire, reading the book kept my hunger at bay.

Late in the afternoon, gigantic, graceful snowflakes, the kind I remembered from my childhood, ideal for making snowmen and sled riding began to fall from the sky. The white blanket transformed the trees and grounds into an early Christmas town. It was freezing in the house, and I couldn't get the furnace to kick in, so I added more wood to the fireplace and curled up to sleep.

The next morning when I awoke, it was still snowing. The

snow had risen so high, and I couldn't open the front door. Now, my stomach was growling for something to eat, and it dawned on me: I was in the middle of nowhere with no food, no car, and the roads were closed. The nearest neighbor was Todd Rundgren, but I didn't know which direction his house was, or if he'd even be home.

One of my teeth began to ache beyond reason, and my face swelled. I had been living with this toothache for a while but kept putting off dealing with it. I had developed a phobia of dentists from the first time my mother took me to one when I was thirteen, and he said, "I don't know where to begin. Your teeth are in the worst shape I've ever seen for someone your age." He turned to my mother and asked, "Why haven't you taken her to the dentist? She needs multiple fillings and may even need to have a few root canals from the look of these x-rays."

Angry, my mother said, "Come on, Pammy, let's go," as if it were the dentist's fault, my teeth were in such terrible condition. We never returned.

A bottle of gin I found tucked at the back of one of the upper cabinets was just what I needed to dull the ache. I must have blacked out from draining its contents on an empty stomach, but a scraping sound aroused me before I heard a loud banging on the door. When I peeked out the window, I saw it had stopped snowing. A man covered in powder had shoveled his way across the porch and was visible through the window. His mop of long, curly hair atop his head didn't quite seem to belong with his wrinkled face.

"Can I help you?" I asked through the window without unlocking the door.

"Hi there. Are you Sam?" he asked, raising his voice to be audible through the glass. Realizing he knew my name put me at ease enough to open the door.

"Yes. Who are you? Has something happened to Martin?"

"I'm Johanna Vigoda. A buddy of mine in the city told me

he ran into Marty, who said he left a young girl out in the woods before the snowstorm hit, so I thought I should come to check it out. The roads just got plowed enough so I could make it out here."

Johanna, I would come to learn, was a lawyer cum music producer who worked with artists like Stevie Wonder and Richie Havens.

"You don't look so great, kid. Your face looks swollen."

"I have a horrible toothache," I mumbled, feeling faint and hungover.

"Well, let's see if we can get you into town and to the dentist. Do you have a phone? I'll give my buddy a call."

"Yes, it's over there," I pointed.

Johanna picked up the phone and said, "Phone lines must be down out here. Can't get a dial tone. Come on, let's go into town and get this looked at."

The dentist was kind enough to open his shop for us and examined my tooth.

"That tooth has a bad abscess. I can't promise you I can save the tooth as it doesn't look good, and you have a severe infection. But it's best to try. You'll need root canal surgery, or you'll need to have the tooth extracted today. Either way, you need antibiotics. Do you have insurance?"

"No," I answered.

"Well, root canal surgery will cost you. Can you call your folks to see if they can send you some money?"

It choked me up the dentist thought I was the kind of girl who could call her parents. I always thought I presented myself as a competent and independent woman of the world who could take care of herself. I suppose my vulnerability was showing. I felt ashamed to admit I wasn't that kind of girl.

"I have the money. I'll pay for it," I said as I opened my purse and pulled out my wallet. "Here's $250. Will that cover it?"

The dentist looked at Johanna as though they were exchanging a silent consultation before delivering the news to the patient.

"I can pull the tooth, but it will cost considerably more to save it because all the roots of this tooth are bad, and you'd still need to have another dentist create a crown to cover it, which can be quite costly."

I felt defeated, as tears leaked out of the corners of my eyes. I hadn't spoken to my mom since I visited her on my way back from London. Our reunion hadn't gone as I had hoped, but maybe she would understand I really needed her now. Maybe I hadn't given her a chance to show me the motherly love I craved. Perhaps she would want me to call her. I wouldn't know unless I called. I didn't want to lose my tooth, and there could be a possibility Mom didn't want that for me either. Maybe this could be a moment between us where I would finally see how much she loved me.

"Is there a phone where I can call my mom?"

"Sure, right here in the office," the dentist said as he led me to a phone on his desk and quietly closed the door behind him.

After a few moments of chit chat, I said, "Mom, I am in a situation. One of my teeth is bad. It's infected, and I need a root canal surgery right away, or they'll have to pull it out."

"Oh, that's too bad."

"I don't have quite enough money, so I thought I would call to see if you could help me out. I can pay you back. I just don't have all the money right now."

At that moment, I cared less about whether she could help me with the money, and more about wanting to hear some tender words from my mom to ease my pain.

"I have no way of knowing if that's why you need the money. I'm sorry. I can't help you." That was it. That was all she said before saying goodbye.

I wished I hadn't made the call. The dull ache that began in the root in my jaw emanated through my entire being. I felt like an exposed nerve when I re-entered the room with the dentist and Johanna.

"I couldn't reach my mother, so let's just get this over with and pull it out."

Violent winds kicked up, bringing more snow, as the dentist shot my gums up with Novocain. The lights went out, but the dentist had a back-up generator. He discovered my teeth had hooks on the tips, making it extremely difficult to extract in one piece. He decided to sedate me because he couldn't operate as the back-up generator wasn't providing enough light.

I relived my entire childhood through the haze of the anesthesia. When I awoke, I was unsure whether any of it had happened. How could it have happened? It was all so surreal and twisted—a nightmare the likes of which Dante could only dream up. I had lived with the pain of my childhood for so long. Now, like the gaping hole where the tooth had been, it was gone.

Johanna stayed through my recovery, and afterward, we stopped at the market, and he bought me some groceries and firewood to take back to the house.

"We better hustle, Sam, I still have to make it back to my house, and there's no telling how bad this storm will get."

"Can you tell me again how you knew to come and find me?" I mumbled through the gauze packed in my cheek. Now that I wasn't reeling in pain as the Novocain hadn't worn off, I wanted to hear it again. Just to be sure I heard him correctly.

"You want the truth?" he asked.

"Yes. Please."

"Let's just say, Martin mentioned he left a young girl up in Woodstock and forgot about her. He was pretty high at the time, so my friend got concerned and suggested I check it out."

"I see."

"Listen, once this next storm passes, I need to head back into the city. If Martin isn't back, I am happy to give you a lift into Manhattan. You know so that you don't have to be out here alone in the woods. It's supposed to snow all day tomorrow. But they should have the roads cleared enough that we could leave the following day."

"Okay. Thank you so much for everything, Johanna."

We pulled into the driveway, and Johanna helped me with the groceries, then carried the wood to the porch.

"I'll see you in a couple of days. Okay? Rest easy, Sam."

I set the sack of groceries on the table and braved the cold again to fetch more firewood before the snow could bury it. It was coming down hard. I thought Martin couldn't get through because of the storms and the roads. I'd had visions of him stuck on the side of the road trying to get to me. Now, I knew the truth. He selfishly got high and simply forgot about me.

Once I got a fire going, I pulled a blanket around me and gazed into the flames. It was the same fireplace Martin, and I sat in front of for the past week, making such an intimate connection. I replayed our conversations in my head. Nothing seemed to make sense. I know Johanna said he was high, but how could that make a man forget about his girlfriend in a snowstorm, two hours away from Manhattan? Before he left, he had been the soberest I'd ever seen him. He said he was going there on business and coming right back.

I began rifling through his desk drawers looking for clues but only found past due notices from the phone company. I discovered the phone company turned the lines off months ago for nonpayment. Those important-sounding calls Martin had made about his Wall Street business were just a made-up excuse for him to go to the city to get high? Had Martin had been lying to me about his Wall Street business too? But why would he lie to me? I knew from experience people only lie when they are afraid to tell the truth. Or they're too embarrassed.

Johanna showed up a day after the storm, as promised. Martin had still not returned.

"Well, you're looking better, Sam. It seems the swelling's gone down. And I see you're already packed," he said, motioning to the bag by the door. "Ready to hit the road?"

Without making eye contact with Johanna, I nodded and picked up my suitcase.

"Okay, so where do we need to go?" he asked, assuming I was meeting Martin in the city.

"To the airport. JFK. That is if it's not too far out of your way."

"JFK, it is." Johanna didn't seem surprised I asked to go to the airport and turned on the radio, filling the quiet with music as I turned inside to reflect. I knew Martin wasn't right for me long before he left me in Woodstock to go to the city to get high. It suddenly all made sense. The reason Martin and I never had sex was that the heroin eliminated his sex drive. Though it stung to think he chose drugs over me, it was no different than when I decided to stay with Martin in New York for drugs over returning to LA. It was time for me to admit that none of this was Martin's doing alone. I was enabling myself.

22

COMING CLEAN

Once back in LA, my self-preservation instincts kicked in. I needed to get busy. I still had the card from Dave, the producer who had introduced me to PIPS, so I called and told him I had become a stylist and was looking for some work.

"Stylist? I do have something. It would be to work as the assistant stylist on a production called Superstunt 2. It's going to star Rock Hudson. You ever hear of the Superstunt series?"

"Oh, yes! That sounds great! I would love to." I had never heard of the Superstunt series, but I knew who Rock Hudson was, and my heart was beating faster than a hummingbird's wings.

"Okay, well, come over to the lot. You have the address?"

"Yes, yes, I do. And thanks, Dave."

Living in Los Angeles, one can become jaded to Hollywood movie stars. But not Rock Hudson. I attended every fitting of his dapper, blue cowboy outfit for the show, overcome with excitement every time I saw him emerge from the trailer. His smile was even more dazzling than the costume covered in sparkling rhinestones.

The day of the taping, Rock strode out of his trailer in that blue cowboy outfit, looking every bit as heroic as my childhood memories of Wild Bill riding up to me on the white stallion. It was a real Hollywood moment that also felt personal to me.

When an extra called in sick, Dave said, "Sam can do it. Don't worry, Sam, I know you told me you don't want to be an actress, but you just have to act like you are giving Rock a manicure. Go over to the wardrobe and see if you can get yourself dressed. We don't have time to find a replacement."

I put the pink manicurist's outfit on and encountered only one rather significant problem. I was a size double-AA, and she was a D cup. The older woman I was working alongside said, "Not a problem, sweetie. Come here," as she began stuffing my bra with padding.

Considering all I had to do was hold Rock Hudson's hand for almost an hour through multiple takes, I began rethinking this acting thing. It might not be such a bad deal getting paid a handsome sum because it was a national television show. And the money came just in time because without warning, I had another tooth emergency. My wisdom teeth were coming in impacted, causing another infection.

Right after I got my wisdom teeth pulled, and I was in too much pain to work, the phone rang. It was from Martin.

"Sam, how are you, honey? I miss you so much I can barely stand it. I have some wonderful news! I've sold my Jane Street apartment, and I'm at JFK right now on my way to be with you. I am moving to LA to be with you because I realize we belong together!"

"But. . . That's not what I want. I don't want to be with you, Martin. I've never wanted to be with you, and what's more? I never even want to see you again."

"Don't tell me you're still sore with me about the Woodstock business? I made a mistake. I thought I had stuff covered. My business just got complicated. But everything is okay now."

"Nothing is okay, Martin!" I said with as much conviction as possible with a mouth still stuffed full of cotton.

"Sam, why do you sound so strange? What's wrong, baby?" Martin cajoled.

"I just had my wisdom teeth pulled, and I'm in a lot of pain."

"I'll be in LA tonight, and I'll give you something for the pain, and we will talk it all through."

With that, he hung up the phone. I was just beginning to

feel like myself again. I hadn't been doing drugs at all since Huntington's. But I was just like any addict. Once you know you can dry out, the pull to get high again is stronger than ever because you believe you are in control. When Martin showed up at my door, within ten minutes, I was high on cocaine mixed with a bit of heroin, and he was rambling on about our future together.

The next day he went to sign the lease on a new apartment. I was still in too much pain to go, so he gave me some heroin.

He was so excited when he came back to tell me about the place. Hugging the hillside just above Sunset, shaped like a half-circle, the townhouse had a black-bottom swimming pool in the middle of the courtyard. Two gay couples jointly co-owned it, who, as far as landlords go, Martin said, were the coolest.

"They love me. I told the owners about you, and they said you could swim topless in the pool anytime you want, honey. Isn't that cool?"

I didn't know how he was so flush with cash, but the next day he went down to Robertson Boulevard and bought chic furniture to replace the furniture I had so proudly purchased on my own for the Larrabee apartment. I didn't have much—a couch, a lamp, a queen-sized bed—but they were so significant to me because they were mine. The peach-colored sofa I was still paying off ended up outside on the upstairs balcony to weather the elements, and Martin left my new mattress on the sidewalk in front of the Larrabee apartment. It disappeared within minutes.

Martin had me upgrade the small Honda I was leasing to a souped-up Camaro T-Top. By now, there was nothing left from my life as it was before Martin, and I had become dependent on him whether I wanted to believe it.

Martin had a way of making me trust him because he used a potent aphrodisiac—cocaine mixed with a little heroin. It numbed my fears, my good sense, and my reality.

With Martin, anything was possible again.

Once we settled into the new place, the bruises from the surgery faded. Martin had the Rolls Royce shipped out to LA. When the owners of the building saw it parked in the garage, they must have thought we were quite the sexy, successful tenants. Our mailbox included our names and the name of Martin's company, Darrington Equities.

While Party Marty had some business on Wall Street, times were changing, and I suspected his heroin habit was dictating what he needed to do for his livelihood. Because he played the drums, he kept saying he had some gigs playing, which I wanted to believe. And I did until he came back to town and had his drum kit with him. When the limo dropped him off, he made a stealth-like entrance through the back of the townhouse with five sizable drum cases emitting a powerful odor.

"What the hell?" I said. "Why does our entire house smell like marijuana?"

Hopped up on coke, Martin sounded paranoid as he blurted out in a loud whispered voice, "I made this deal," and then told me the drum kit contained thousands of dollars' worth of marijuana. It mortified me as Martin began frantically closing the blinds, telling me to keep quiet.

"Just stop, Sam," Martin commanded as he hit the stereo to drown our escalating voices. When Olivia Newton John's song, "Have You Never Been Mellow," began playing, I would have laughed out loud at the irony if I wasn't so blazing mad.

When Martin left town, I tried for a while to live a sober life, doing yoga, and working on myself. I rediscovered the recorder I bought inspired by the bohemian girl who played at the bottom of Laurel Canyon Boulevard. It was easy for me to pick it up from my former clarinet playing days. I learned several Beatles' songs.

While sitting on the massive four-poster bed raised high enough to view the Los Angeles skyline over the balcony wall, I played the small wooden instrument for hours on end, as the melodies parsed out feelings trapped inside. I could hear the lyrics to "Let It Be" in my mind while I played, wondering how my hour of darkness could become any bleaker. The lilting music conjured visions of my grandmother telling me to wake up to the sound of music and shine on because there will be a better tomorrow. How could I tell Gammy I believed tomorrow might never come?

The summer before I turned twenty years old, Marty, and I went on a heroin binge and got married in our apartment. We exchanged marriage vows sometime over the kaleidoscope of three days of debauchery. When I was lucid enough to realize we got married, I immediately wondered how hard it would be to get a divorce. I wasn't in love with Martin, and he wasn't in love with me. Martin was married to heroin, and for some reason, he was relentless in his determination for me to make the same vow.

I only snorted it, but it takes very little to get hooked. I didn't want to admit I was becoming an addict, but even when I wasn't doing heroin, I was thinking about doing it. I would try to get clean when Martin left for New York, but the second he hit LA, I demanded he gets me high as payment for leaving me alone for so long. The angrier I pretended to be at Martin for abandoning me, the more heroin he gave me.

The sad day came when Martin returned to Los Angeles unannounced after several weeks, and it broke my heart to realize he had become a full-blown addict. You could see it in his pinned and glazed over eyes, making him look as though he were blind. He obsessively scratched his body to the point he had marks covering him from head to toe. Heroin had overtaken him like an invasive weed.

Seeing Martin in dire shape, I wanted to help him stop using, but I had too many demons of my own. I couldn't resist being pulled into his addiction like a small car hitched up to a tractor-trailer. We would do heroin for a couple of days, and then he'd say, "You can't have anymore. You've got to clean yourself out."

Assuming I missed Australia, Martin had bought me a koala bear collection that consisted of about fifty to sixty little stuffed bears that looked down upon us from the built-in shelves surrounding the fireplace in our upstairs bedroom.

Martin took one of the koala bears, cut it open and hid a vial of heroin inside, then stitched the bear back up and packed it ready to send to his friend Bobby in Woodstock. When he took off to run some errands, he forgot the package and left it on the kitchen counter. I paced the room and jogged up and down the stairs to keep my mind off it, but I couldn't resist its contents. I peeled off each piece of tape, unfolding the wrapping without so much as a crease or a sound the way I used to do with Christmas presents on the farm. I knew Marty could bound through the door at any moment, but any fear I had of being caught was worth the treasure inside. I ripped open the koala bear, spilling out half the vial of heroin on to a mirror, then sewed it back together and wrapped it up again.

When his friend received the bear without the expected amount of heroin, he was furious, accusing Martin of cheating him. Martin never suspected I had tampered with the package and wrote it off as the addict's ramblings. But the lengths I went through to get high made me realize heroin was becoming a problematic lover to leave. I no longer just wanted it. I needed it, and I knew I was in trouble. I realized the only way to save myself was to get as far away from Martin as possible. But I justified staying with him by convincing myself I cared too much about Martin to abandon him when, in reality, I felt afraid to leave him because that would mean cutting myself off from the easy access to drugs. I was caught in a vicious circle spiraling downward.

I needed to fill up my tank and stopped at the station at Crescent Heights and Sunset. Shoving the gas pump into the

Camaro, I scurried to the bathroom to get high. A pregnant woman with long, greasy hair whose tan skin was like leather was hunched over the sink bathing a small boy with equally sun-parched skin. His curly blond locks were hanging over his eyes as he cast them downward with modesty. I went to wash my hands at the adjacent sink. When I glanced up, I saw her face, and I realized it was the bohemian girl who inspired me to play the recorder. She looked at me with swollen, sad eyes before asking if I had anything to get high, causing me to tremble inside. All this time, I thought she was happy and carefree, but she was an addict, and so was I.

    I decided right there I would do whatever it took to get Martin and I sober. I suggested we go away together and get clean. I didn't want to let him return to New York, where it was easier for him to get heroin, so when he insisted on going, I tagged along to try to run interference and coaxed him to go for methadone treatment. As we stood in line, pregnant clouds hung above us, and the image of the curly-haired bohemian girl haunted me. We waited in a queue of addicts for hours, and I watched him get wretchedly ill, shivering and throwing up.

    Just as the clouds were about to burst, he couldn't take it anymore, and he bolted to get a fix. We were crashing at a dingy four-story walk-up in the village. Sparsely furnished, it had a stench of dirty clothing and decaying food. Stacked dishes were overflowing in the sink. I couldn't believe Martin preferred this squatters' hovel over our romantic townhouse in the hills above Sunset because of heroin.

    I could hear Martin preparing to shoot up in the smelly bathroom. I never knew he was shooting the stuff until recently when he started mainlining, although he had been shooting it between his toes for some time. The door didn't close all the way, and I could see him sitting on the toilet, which wouldn't flush. It was a horrific sight to behold, but seeing his body respond to the drug's effects, making

Martin feel euphoric as his pain subsided was eerily enticing. I knew I could only stay healthy as long as my sobriety would last.

When he emerged, he said, "Sam, do you want a bump?"

"I'm good," I said, thinking how much easier it would be to give in. I hit rock bottom. Martin was on a suicide mission, and I was riding shotgun. Trying my best to pull myself together, I walked over and opened the window to breathe in the sweet smell of petrichor as the rain continued to wet the ground below. But the dirty sidewalk when wet smelled more like a sewer. I shut the window.

I believed, at his core, Martin wanted what his parents had—the stability of a loving marriage, maybe some kids. In his life, he was on that trajectory and was capable of making money through his investment firm beyond his wildest dreams. Unfortunately, heroin stole those dreams away, and he grew to love heroin more than anything.

I gathered up every ounce of self-preservation I had left and told Martin I was going back to Los Angeles on the next flight. Martin never even got up out of bed to say goodbye. He was too high.

On the way home, I realized I had to remove myself forever from the temptation and access to drugs. There was no going back. Worse, it now occurred to me I married this man. I would have to get a divorce.

Back in LA, I met up with Johanna Vigoda, who was in town and asked me to join him for dinner. He could tell I was in a bad place and suggested we go for a drive. We put the top down on his sporty convertible and drove out to Malibu to go up the coast for some sea air.

We were driving down the California Incline, heading for PCH just as the sun was dipping beyond the shimmering horizon. The ocean reflected the glowing orb like a mirror. Johanna said, "Ahh, the Pacific. What a spectacular sight, isn't it? The peaceful sea."

Just then, I spotted a dog a vehicle had hit that lay dying on the road. We almost ran over it. I screamed, "Stop, Johanna! Stop the car, please, please!"

He swerved to the shoulder of the narrow Incline—not an easy maneuver—and I jumped out and ran back. Johanna followed me. The animal was struggling for its last gasps of air, trying hard to cling to life.

"Sam, there's nothing we can do for this animal. It's hurt too badly to save."

I fell to my knees and put my face next to the dog and sobbed. I cried for the dog's pain. I cried for his soul and the soul of the driver who did this to him without even stopping. Then Johanna and I moved the dog off the road, placed stones around his body and wildflowers across his chest, which had taken its last breath. As the final sliver of light disappeared below the horizon, we continued to drive up the coast, riding in silence for miles before turning back. Johanna dropped me off at the townhouse I had shared with Martin.

"If you need anything, just call me. I'll be there for you. No judgment."

I fell asleep sobbing but woke up refreshed because my sleep had been untroubled by nightmares or memories of the farm, which hadn't been the case for a long time. It felt as though that dying dog took the demons burdening me and carried them off to heaven.

I slipped into a robe and went down to the black-bottom pool for a skinny dip at 5 a.m. There was a calm in the early morning. The entire city seemed to be asleep. I swam across the deepest surface of the pool, holding my breath so as not to alarm the stillness.

23

SAMANTHA SONG

"You have a collect call from Sam Butter. Will you accept the charge?"

The receptionist at the Estrada brothers law firm put the operator on hold for what seemed like an eternity as I anxiously twisted the phone cord. My heart pounded as I tried to gather up what to say to Lionel when he answered. Lionel knew I had been on the outs with my dad ever since Wild Bill put sugar in the gas tank of my car, but that would not be enough of a reason he wouldn't take my call.

A memory surfaced of one of Gammy's soap opera storylines saying if the marriage had not been consummated, it could be annulled. I remembered the look on Gammy's face when I asked her what it meant. As always, she knew just what to say. "I hope you never need to know the answer to that question, Pammy."

"Sam, is that you? Long-time."

"Lionel, thank you for taking my call. I need some help. Some legal help. I'm in a lot of trouble." I thought about telling Lionel our marriage had never been consummated, but for that to be believable, I would have had to reveal the extent to which I had become dependent on drugs. I knew I was a drug addict, but I didn't want to put that stigma out into the Universe or risk I'd have to enter a rehab facility. Nothing frightened me more than being caged.

"What's wrong, Sam? What happened?"

I explained the whole mess to Lionel, leaving out how deeply I had gotten into drugs.

". . . And so, before I knew it, I married the guy. I need to get away from him. I'm scared," I said, bursting into tears.

"Since you married recently, and it's only been a short time, if you come back and live in Arizona for a while, you'll be able to get the marriage annulled quickly, because of the way Arizona's divorce laws work."

I contacted Angie to see if I could stay with her for a few months.

"Sure, you can, Sam. I moved into a two-bedroom apartment with a roommate, but she left town. So, I have plenty of room."

"Thank you, Angie. I'm so grateful to you. But please, don't tell Wild Bill. I don't want him to know I'm in town. I don't want to see him right now."

"Okay. But you'll tell me what's going on, right?"

"Sure. I'll tell you."

I packed up as many belongings as I could fit in the Camaro T-top and drove to Arizona to dry out and stay long enough to get a speedy divorce.

Away from Los Angeles and the party scene, in the desert stillness of Arizona, I realized how chaotic my life had become. I had dived headfirst into the depths of sadness and madness. I had been higher than the skies and every level in between. My life felt out-of-control, and it all seemed meaningless.

But I finally realized—every scary situation I allowed myself to fall into, every time I chose the path more broken, had accomplished one thing. It delivered me from evil. It made me forget—at least for a while—about Jeremiah Davis Deemer. So, it was worth it. It was worth all of it.

Not doing any drugs or alcohol of any kind seemed impossible the first week. The hot Arizona sun helped, and by the second week, I began to feel better.

I was twenty years old and getting a divorce from a heroin addict whom I never loved and I barely remembered marrying. Allowing myself to become addicted to heroin was another in a long series of mistakes I made while still trying to run from my past. It was as though I set my life on a repeat button—like one of my dad's old Nat King Cole records—just skipping back to the same refrain. And I was too messed up to move the needle. Pain equated with the only feelings of love I had known since I was a little girl. But I was discovering my inner strength. Even though my grandfather seemed hell-bent on destroying my soul, he couldn't. If pain controlled me, I would use love and self-acceptance to control the pain.

When the day arrived for my court case, I felt so much sorrow over the entire ordeal. But the emotional turmoil was an unnecessary waste of energy. The judge granted my petition for divorce as if it was nothing more than changing the channels on the car stereo. Martin never showed up at court, and I never saw him again.

The Estradas invited me to Dave's Tavern to celebrate. I felt too emotionally fragile to see my father and felt determined to stay sober, even avoiding alcohol—a near-impossible feat when out with Wild Bill. I promised I would call to let him know where I landed once I got settled back in LA. Lionel told me Wild Bill would be going to Hollywood Park soon, and maybe it would be a good idea to see him and put the past behind us.

As much as I wanted to see Wild Bill, I was afraid that if my father saw me, he would recognize the pain behind my eyes. He would know I hadn't been truthful about the extent of the ordeal I had been through, and I didn't want him to judge me. He didn't have that right.

Once back in LA, a photographer friend named Jonny told me I could stay at his studio for a few months if I watched his cat as he had to go to Europe. He was having a going away party that night, so I should come by early, and he'd show me around before people got there. I had to return the Camaro Martin leased for me as the payments were in arrears. I dropped it off and hitched a ride over to the studio across the street from the Old World

Restaurant, where I first met Eugene.

Traffic was bumper to bumper on Santa Monica Boulevard, so I arrived later than expected. When I entered the studio, a man with brown, curly hair and big, brown, soulful eyes appeared hunched over on a stool, playing guitar and singing his songs to an enthusiastic audience of eclectic people—friends of Jonny's. His clothes were thrift store finds with a disheveled but purposeful aesthetic. But it was the clogs and curls sticking out on the sides of a black beret that conjured the memory of the bearded man with the long fingers, writing in the black journal spotted during my first encounter with Eugene.

He smiled at me while he sang, and I smiled back. After he finished his set, he put his guitar down as music piped into the room from the stereo. People were milling around talking and laughing and drinking wine. The guitar player approached me, saying, "Pardon me; I think we've met before. But I can't place it. You ever been up to Woodstock? Because I think we might have met there."

"I've been to Woodstock," I said, hoping he would not bring up Party Marty, which I already decided I would deny.

My eyes darted around the room nervously. A couple who wanted to speak to the guitarist about his music interrupted our conversation, so I took the opportunity to slink away to mingle with some other guests.

A while later, he approached me again and said, "It was at Albert Grossman's East-West Restaurant in Woodstock. Bearsville. That's how I remember you. I was with Paul Butterfield, and we laughed because your last name is 'Butter,' right? And it was funny because, you know, everyone always calls Paul 'Butter'—so we just thought it was funny to meet someone whose actual last name was Butter."

"My name has been the bane of my existence. But I'm glad to hear it gave you a laugh." I shuffled through my memory bank, before recalling the encounter.

"Then Levon Helm ate the swirled butter on the table saying, 'This is the best Brussel sprout I ever tasted!' So more butter jokes ensued. Ha. How could you forget that?" he chided me.

We laughed in unison, the first time I heard myself laugh in a long while. It felt good—like I was breaking out of a crusty shell that had formed around me—like a cocoon.

"Well, nice to meet you again. I'm Sam, and you already know my last name, so we'll skip that formality."

"I'm Hirth. Hirth Martinez. I live next door, below my publisher's office in a studio."

"That's an interesting name. I've never heard it before."

"It's Basque. My mother is Basque."

"Well, Hirth, I guess we will be neighbors. I'm watching Jonny's studio while he's gone. So, I guess I'll see you around."

"Okay, Sam. I'll see you around." With that, Hirth tipped his beret and disappeared onto the big, bright street.

It was then I realized he was the same guy I saw writing in the journal over two years ago. I couldn't recall meeting him in Woodstock, but it was unmistakably the same guy. It overwhelmed me thinking about how much I had gone through since then. I felt like I might collapse from the weight of the memories.

The next night, I went for a walk down to Barney's Beanery on Santa Monica to shoot some pool and get a bite to eat. I hadn't shot pool in a long time, not since hanging out at Dave's Tavern, and it made me sad I didn't reach out to Wild Bill before leaving town.

When I returned to the studio, feeling lonely, I laid my body to rest on the mattress on the floor. The cat curled up next to me, purring, and I realized Jonny forgot to tell me her name. It was a beautiful, late summer night, so I opened the industrial windows that pushed outward and were held up by a metal bar. A while later, the most beautiful guitar music began streaming through the open window.

It was Hirth softly playing his guitar and singing, launching into song after song as I sat still by the window listening—straining to make out the words. His words and masterful guitar playing was healing and hopeful. I drifted off to sleep more peacefully than I thought possible, purring in unison with the cat.

I awoke to the cat curling its tail across my face, begging me to open a tin of food. I could hardly blame her; it was almost noon. I pulled on my jeans and headed over to Old World Restaurant, partially for convenience, but also somewhat curious if I would run into Hirth. He was there, writing in his black journal. I walked over to his table.

"I heard you playing guitar and singing last night."

"I was hoping you did because I was playing for you. You looked like you needed to hear some good music."

"I did, indeed. I've been traveling in Europe for the past few months, and I think the jet lag finally caught up to me. I feel much better now."

"Oh, so it was jet lag. Well, take a load off. Have a seat."

Over coffee, I learned Hirth had been a child prodigy, playing guitar with the likes of Ray Charles and BB King. He'd also met Bob Dylan, who heard some of his songs and told Robbie Robertson of the Band about him, leading to the eventual release of two albums on Warner Bros. Records—the first produced by Robbie called Hirth from Earth and the second by John Simon called Big Bright Street. He was biding his time until his next big break came along.

I began spending time with Hirth in his humble cellar flat, more accurately, a crash pad, courtesy of David Rosner, Hirth's publisher. He also managed Neil Diamond's catalog, among a few other artists.

Hirth's cellar refuge gave him a peaceful place to sleep between two blankets on the cement floor. Between playing guitar, writing songs, and reading books ranging from Genet to Rimbaud to Celine, he was content. Wondering what to do next in terms of work had become all-consuming since leaving Martin. But Hirth helped me to step away from the tangled mess my life had become, and find joy in simplicity. He turned me on to his favorite poets, Charles Bukowski, Allen Ginsberg, and Kenneth Patchen. Hirth encouraged me to express myself in words on paper, then wrote melodies to them. They were quite naïve by comparison to his artful style of songwriting. But it was cathartic for me.

Hirth loved to hear me sing, though I could scarcely carry a tune and could barely stay in pitch. I had a breathy little voice, heavily influenced by Stevie Nicks, while Hirth drew comparisons to Bob Dylan, Tom Waits, Dr. John, and Warren Zevon. I accompanied him to dive clubs where he performed, and he encouraged me to sing on stage with him and the other musicians. We played gigs at the Comeback Inn in Venice or did poetry readings and sang songs at Beyond Baroque hosted by the poet Dennis Cooper.

When I attempted to write songs, they didn't reflect the depth of what I had experienced. I couldn't open up. Even though I was sick of lying about myself, I found it challenging to know when and how to stop, so I kept the disguise that I was Australian. I knew the photographer would return soon, and I would move on to the next chapter of my life, which I decided wouldn't include being from Australia. It was time to let that go. I felt good about myself again, and I knew I was going to be okay. I felt deeply indebted to Hirth.

Hirth was hoping our relationship would blossom into something, but I made it clear from the beginning that I preferred to stay good friends. He was much too innocent a man for a girl like me. With all my heart, I felt the weight I carried inside would be too heavy a burden for an artist whose head deserved to stay in the clouds.

It was the last week of my stay on Holloway Drive as the photographer was due back to Los Angeles by the end of the week. I was bounding down the steps for one of our regular sessions in his cellar-dwelling when I heard the most beautiful song floating up the stairwell. I stopped to listen just outside the massive studio door as Hirth sang. By the second verse, I realized he was singing a song he had written about me. Now, there really was a song inspired by me—it was about me. A song Hirth named Samantha.

24

THE MYSTIC BUMS

Hirth Martinez stole my heart with a song.
"What do you want to do today?"
"How about we go for a walk?"
"Where do you want to go?"
"Let's just start walking and see where we end up."

We dubbed ourselves "the higher order of the mystic bums," as we slept in until around noon, drank copious amounts of coffee, wrote songs, sang or talked, and walked. We didn't own a car, so anytime we wanted to go somewhere, it was on foot. Sometimes we would be out walking for eight hours or more. We would walk on foot from the cellar flat in West Hollywood to Los Feliz thrift stores to rummage through the used clothing and bric-a-brac with no intention of buying anything because we didn't have any money. Then we'd saunter back to our cellar abode, sometimes arriving after dark.

By the time the photographer returned from Europe, Hirth and I were lovers, and I moved into the cellar below his publisher's office. Hirth was a poet who cared less about the trappings of wealth or material possessions and more about everyday experiences we could share together. We lingered in an intimate bookstore called Book Soup, perusing art books, and reading poetry. We spent every day learning, observing, absorbing art, and the world.

He reminded me of my imaginary friends, Copy and Kissy. He loved me and believed in me, and being in our secret cellar hangout below the strip, reminded me of the haven I discovered in the old tree trunk.

In the street above, buses shifted gears, horns honked, sirens and bells sounded, and cars screeched as they came to a jarring stop for pedestrians, who yelled out obscenities. Laughter brightened the air. Good news and bad circled the city blocks. Garbage collectors and building inspectors, mopeds, quarrels, misfits, and rejects added to the mayhem. Construction workers and their machines tore down a block of boutiques and sleazy bars up the street, demolishing brick walls that had stood for decades on the Sunset Strip, making way for a hi-rise.

I loved hearing about Hirth's favorite books and poetry, and his theories about UFOs and government conspiracies to cover up the truth. Hirth wasn't political, but he didn't like Republicans.

"I never thought I'd see the day when an actor would try to become president," he complained about Ronald Reagan, in whom he found no redeeming qualities. "He'll never get elected."

Politics aside, very little ever seemed to bother Hirth. He was the most relaxed person I had ever been around. Life seemed simpler with Hirth, and I became a lot calmer. I was no longer worried about what I needed to do to pay the bills because there weren't any bills. I lived inside my journal, where I wrote poetry and drew pictures. I never thought about what the future held after discovering happiness living in the present. I tucked away the past to make room for my heart's desire to enjoy every moment with Hirth.

Our life together was light and breezy until one day, the payphone installed on the studio wall rang, and I answered it.

"Is Hirth there? I need to speak to him now!" an angry woman demanded.

I peeked around the corner with the cord stretched as far as it could go while keeping my hand over the receiver, motioning for Hirth to take his phone call. He shook his head to let me know I should say he wasn't there. I assumed it was a jealous old girlfriend, so I covered for him.

"He's not here," I said.

"Oh, come on! I know he's there and who are you? Where's the Frenchie? Last week he was in love with a French woman. English, French whatever. I know he's there. Tell him I need money for groceries for his kid."

She slammed the phone down, and it reverberated in my ear. Did this woman just say *his kid?*

I hung up the phone and walked around the corner.

"You need to get groceries for your child." A lump grew in my throat.

"I'm going for a walk, cool?"

"Sam, wait. It's not what it seems. Let me explain."

Hirth followed me out into the chilly evening air. The sunset was so spectacular, that it might have seduced me into hearing Hirth out and believing whatever excuse he was able to conjure and coerce me into believing.

"Not what it seems? Do you or do you not have a child?"

"I was going to tell you. I was waiting for the right time. Since my ex-wife and I split up, I've had a lot of the tough breaks. All she cares about is money. I give her what I can. I try to see my daughter when I can, but it's kind of hard without a car or a place to live. It's not like I can bring her here."

"Then you need to figure it out. Because I don't think I can be with a man who has no place in his life for his child. I'm sorry. I'm going for a walk. I need to be alone."

Hirth's omission of the fact he had a child reminded me of my dad, and the fact Dad had no room in his life for me. The familiar feelings of abandonment returned like re-runs from my childhood playing out in my mind. Dad stretched out drunk on the couch listening to Nat King Cole, fighting with my mother, disappearing from our lives for weeks at a time. Then as our relationship grew, it became less about being abandoned and more about being victimized. He lied about Johnny Cash, got me fired for stealing broken poinsettias, and put sugar in my gas tank.

Being Wild Bill's daughter was something I knew I could never come to terms with unless he wanted to show up as a real person. I wanted to change and gain control over the feelings of abandonment I had from both of my parents, and I didn't want to be witness to seeing it happen to someone else. Maybe this newfound reality I was waking up to would make me feel secure enough to want to make it work with Hirth. I was, after all, not exactly true to Hirth. I lied about my name, my past, my upbringing, my family, my schooling, and my drug addiction. Just because I had it tough, did that entitle me to be so untruthful about myself? Maybe I was at a turning point? Perhaps I should try to see things through his perspective? Was it time to stop running?

When I returned to the cellar flat, Hirth was there waiting for me.

"I'm sorry, Hirth. My instinct is to run away. It always has been. I've been running away my whole life, but I'm tired of running. I want to stay and make a place where you can have your daughter come and stay with us."

"Like I said, it's not like she can stay in the cellar with us, Samantha."

"Well, what about this place next door?"

A door with a boarded-up window next to the studio piqued my curiosity for some time. Hirth pulled back a loose board that hinged on a rusty nail, and I peered through a tiny crack. We could see a large room which lit up my imagination. We got busy and removed the boards, allowing me to climb in through the window. Once inside, I found a large room with a smaller room made of glass, which had, at one time, been a sound booth. A sink and a toilet were in the back with another tiny room behind them. We decided we would turn this rundown, abandoned former studio into a place where Hirth could bring his daughter.

Together we used elbow grease and my eclectic decorating

skills to fix the place and, within a week, transformed it into a somewhat comfortable apartment. Now, the glass sound booth with makeshift curtains would serve as a cozy room for his daughter. We rigged a hose from the sink to the outside so that we could shower. The backroom by the sink became a small kitchen. We found an old frying pan and a hot plate in the trash, and with some of Hirth's gig money, we purchased a small portable fridge. At the kitchen table in the back of the new cellar-dwelling, I began committing Hirth's rambling prose and musings to typewritten documents, determined to find him a publisher.

Though I hadn't met them, Hirth's parents called him daily on the payphone that hung on the studio wall next door.

"I told my parents about our new place, and my dad offered to build a fence to block off the entryway, so we'll have more privacy and security. Isn't that great?"

Hirth's dad arrived a day later to install the fence. His name was Sam, and he was as brown as a sun-kissed berry, which contrasted with his snowy white beard. A crop of white hair protruded from beneath a tweed cap. Hirth looked a lot like his father except for his skin color, his being pale by comparison. When Sam finished putting the fence up, he suggested we ride back with him to East LA for a home-cooked meal.

"You go on, Hirth. I'm not hungry."

But Hirth and his father insisted. "It will upset Nana if you don't come," Hirth said, referring to Helen, his mother. I thought it was weird Hirth called his mother and father Nana and Papa, but those were the names given to them by his daughter.

I caved and found myself in the backseat of Hirth's father's car, cruising 65 mph on the freeway, heading toward a home-cooked meal in East LA.

Hirth drove, and his dad rode shotgun. It was alienating to see Hirth behind the wheel, checking his rearview mirror, switching lanes, and flicking on and off the turn signal. Until now, Hirth and I existed together in an imaginary place and time, like Copy and Kissy in the fallen tree trunk. Seeing Hirth interacting with his father and driving a car had somehow made him human. It was the beginning of the end of the Mystic Bums.

When we arrived, Hirth leaped out of the driver's seat and ran over to open the gate to enter the driveway. The smell of homemade cheese enchiladas and chili rellenos drifted out of the small, open kitchen window, where I could see two women hustling about the tiny room. A bell rang out as Hirth opened the gate. The sound triggered a vivid memory.

At sixteen, I wanted to mark the milestone I achieved by graduating from high school by returning to Pennsylvania to visit my mother. I hoped she would see me in a new light, but more than that, I wanted to tell Mom how much I missed her.

It took most of the money I saved to purchase a red-eye ticket to Pittsburgh. But when I arrived, I realized I hadn't precisely thought the visit through. It wasn't as though I could simply walk up the garden path and say, "Hey, there! I'm home." I was terrified of what my grandfather might do if he saw me. I knew Mom wouldn't be home from work until evening, so I checked into a Howard Johnson motel and waited for the sun to set so I could go to the farm, under cover of darkness. That way, I could sneak up beside the tomato garden undetected and get a glimpse of her through the kitchen window. Even if I didn't get the chance to talk to her, I felt a deep need to see my mother's face.

As dusk was approaching, I ventured out of my hotel room and stuck out my thumb. It took me two rides to get within walking distance of the farm. I made my way up over the familiar hillside to the open field just beyond the barn, then crept closer and closer. I didn't count on the dogs barking. Someone clanged the bell to scare off any potential intruder, and I crouched behind a tree, squinting my eyes to see if it was Mom, but it was my grandfather. Even seeing him at a safe distance away, made me weak in the knees. I took off running and never looked back, leaving the next day without seeing Mom.

"Samantha, come in and meet my mom and my sister," Hirth said, snapping me back to reality.

When I stepped inside the small house, the smell of tortillas, chili, and cinnamon blended into one distinctive aroma, overtaking my senses.

Helen, the matriarch of the family, had black hair flecked with grays, and her skin was pale, like Hirth's, reflecting their Basque ethnicity. She wore an embroidered apron that reminded me of Gammy.

Dinner was ready, so we crowded around the small table to dig in. Before Helen's cooking, I had never eaten authentic Mexican cuisine. The flavor of the sauces she had spent hours simmering on the stove played together so well it tasted like jazz.

After the meal, Papa took Hirth outside for a quiet father/son exchange. Papa lifted the heavy garage door, and Hirth's mother and sister followed a safe distance behind with me bringing up the rear. As the garage door opened, it revealed an old white VW station wagon sparkling like a new car.

Hirth's old VW had broken down at least a year prior, and Papa paid to have it towed away, Hirth thought, to a junkyard to sell for used parts. The past year, his father spent his time and money to restore the old clunker to as good as new. He now presented it to Hirth. It was such a loving gesture; this kind of parental love was foreign to me. While I teared up, Hirth seemed to take it in stride as though he expected it.

"We know how much you miss your daughter, son. Now you can drive here to visit her whenever you want or even pick her up from school," Helen exclaimed.

Hirth's father took him to the gas station to fill up the car, so we could have enough in the tank to make the drive home leaving me in the company of his mother and sister.

Helen asked me, "So, what has Sammy been up to?"

I thought it odd she was calling me by a name no one, but Eugene had ever called me by, I and it threw me off. "Well, I've been..."

She cut me off with a chuckle and said, "I don't mean you, Samantha, I mean, Sammy, my son. I'm sorry. I just can't seem to allow myself to call my son Hirth. I can only call him by his God-given name, Samuel, or Sammy. Or the nickname he's had since he was a boy, Red."

His sister chimed in, "Mom, it's not like it's a new thing. Hirth Martinez has been his name for the past ten years. I don't know how he came up with the name Hirth. Before he was Hirth Martinez, he went by Robert Hirth."

The revelation "Hirth" wasn't a Basque name as he had told me and was a made-up name surprised me, though I tried not to show he hadn't shared this detail about himself with me.

"Well, you know, Red, or Sammy, has been writing and working on new songs. He's so talented."

Helen continued heaping praise on her special son filling the awkward moments until the white VW puttered back into the driveway.

As we were leaving, she offered, "Samantha, anytime you want to do laundry, come down and use our machines. It will be a lot easier than lugging clothes to the laundromat. God bless you, dear.'

"Thank you, Mrs. Martinez." I headed for Hirth's shiny new VW, now overflowing with groceries. It seemed out of character for the Mystic Bums to have a car with a full tank of gas and a trunk filled with groceries. I felt conflicted; my pride bristled at accepting a handout. But this was family. I realized I hadn't been around a real family in a long time. I was a feral cat. I didn't like the feeling someone was taming me or making me domesticated. Survival was all I knew and trusted. Feelings of running away welled up inside of me.

On the way home, I asked Hirth, "Do you think your parents like me?"

"They love you. Who wouldn't? But they don't approve of our living together before we get married. So, if we are going to keep this thing together, we'll have to get married."

"That was a joke, right?"

"No, unfortunately not. That's my parents. They are old-fashioned."

Getting married was the furthest thing from my mind, let alone becoming a step-mother. I couldn't take care of myself.

A few weeks later, Hirth picked his daughter up after she got home from school for her first sleepover at the new cellar flat. She was six years old but so tiny; she appeared even younger. She also seemed sad, which I sensed as soon as we met. That night, Hirth had a gig in La Puente, over an hour away, which meant he had to leave at five o'clock, allowing little time for him to spend with his daughter. I felt responsible for trying to entertain her, challenging without a television, so we colored, and talked.

"You know, my Nana doesn't like you. Nana said she thinks you aren't good enough for my daddy."

"Oh?"

"Yeah, she thinks you are stuck up and not very smart. I was excited to meet you, though."

She looked at me sideways, waiting to see how I would react. I could tell she wanted her words to sting. I sensed she wanted a rise out of me, but her revelation had a different effect. I cared less about what Hirth's mother thought of me, and more about his daughter's trying to elicit a conflict. I could tell she was in pain, and it was complicated. I couldn't help but feel she was becoming a version of me—someone with a hole in their heart, leaving an emptiness inside. Her way of dealing with her internal pain was to try to make me feel as bad as she did. If I could raise us out of our circumstances and provide some stability for Hirth's daughter, I could help make a difference in her life, making me determined to get a job.

I put her to bed in the makeshift bedroom long before Hirth rolled in late after the gig. The next morning, we quietly got dressed, and I took her out for pancakes before driving her home. When I returned, Hirth was awake having coffee. I had so many things bottled up inside that I wanted to tell Hirth about the first evening I spent with his six-year-old daughter. But he never asked a word about it. I was hoping he would wake up and realize that we needed to improve our circumstances in part for his daughter's sake. But Hirth refused to acknowledge we lacked anything. Sometimes what's missing in your life are the things you can't see, like the pain hidden in his daughter's eyes.

Up and down the strip, everyone knew Hirth as a quasi-celebrity and the pet poet of many. Glenn Goldman, who owned Book Soup, was a fan of Hirth's. One day when we were browsing through books, I asked Glenn if he would consider paying Hirth a stipend to play guitar for patrons.

"Are you kidding me?" Glenn exclaimed. "It would thrill me to have Hirth play any night of the week."

At first, Hirth enjoyed playing at Book Soup. A few of the regulars seemed to know he was the famous "Hirth from Earth," the title of his first record. Hirth put a small jar out for tips, and Glenn either paid him in books or a small stipend based on sales.

One night, without warning, Hirth decided he hated playing at the bookstore and walked out saying, it was a waste of his talents. He was holding out for that big break.

When Edward James Olmos of *Zoot Suit* fame called Hirth to work on a theme song for a film project he was working on called *The Ballad of Gregorio Cortez,* we thought his big break had arrived. Eddie and Hirth grew up blocks from each other in East LA, so it was only natural they would collaborate on a project together. We hoped the money from this assignment would be enough to spring us out of the cellar and into a lovely apartment with a real shower.

Hirth devoted all of his time to working on the theme song. Despite all the passion he put into it, Eddie ended up not going with Hirth as the writer, but hired him to play guitar on the soundtrack. I felt so bad for Hirth having his dream dashed that way and tried to buoy him up as best I could.

"I was hoping this would be the big break I had been waiting on to ask you to marry me. But I don't want to wait anymore. Will you still marry me?"

Dreaming of becoming Hirth's wife was a fantasy but not one I ever expected to come true. Though becoming closer with his family made him more real, somehow, I still preferred the image of Hirth as my imaginary friend. I didn't want to make another mistake, and our relationship happened so fast. I knew I had to be honest about my past before I could move forward in a real relationship, but how could I tell Hirth the truth? Would he still love me by another name, another history?

On the morning of March 7, 1981, I put on my favorite navy-blue dress adorned with a pattern of flying books with white wings to marry Hirth. Papa had been in on the surprise, and he fashioned a wedding ring for me out a nickel creating a circle on my left ring finger that resembled a tattoo for the next ten years of my life.

On the way to the home of the man who was to officiate, I asked Hirth, "Is Hirth your real name?"

"Of course, it is. Why?"

"Well, why does your mother call you, Sammy?"

"I went by that name for a while. I was Sammy Phillip on my first record. Then I was Robert Hirth."

"Oh," I replied, realizing he hadn't answered the question.

I remembered when we met, Hirth told me it was a Basque name and came from his mother's side. Realizing he told me a lie, I sat motionless, looking out the car window at the scenery in West Hollywood until I was about to burst.

"Hirth, I need to tell you something. Please pull over."

Hirth pulled the VW over to the curb.

"Okay, what?"

"I'm not from Australia. I'm from Pennsylvania, and my real name is Pamela Sue Butter. But my dad called me Sam, and so I just kind of went with that."

"That's cool. Whatever." Hirth lit up a cigarette.

I couldn't believe how nonchalant Hirth was about the revelation I lied to him about my name.

"Well, I don't want to be dishonest about who I am. You've let me become a part of your family, and now you want to marry me. I think we should tell your family the truth about me. I am not Australian either. I pretended to be British to forge a new identity, and then someone thought I sounded more Australian, so I went with that, and it's gone on for years now. I've been running from my past since I was fourteen years old." I felt nauseous before adding, "And, I've been married before."

"Don't sweat it, Sam. My folks dig that you're an Aussie, and it's no big deal! You don't even look like a Pam, so who would ever find out? Why does it matter anyway? You're Samantha. What's the big deal?" he asked, offering me a cigarette.

"And besides, I was married before too. We just won't tell my folks you were married before, okay? Now you will be Samantha Martinez. Sounds good to me."

He pulled the VW back onto the road.

We drove up in front of a small house in Hollywood with dried grass in the tiny front yard and went inside. An Indian man officiated the ceremony, which was over in less than five minutes. I realized this ceremony meant more to Hirth's parents than it did to Hirth or me, so I justified getting married as though we were paying them back for all they had done for us. I didn't understand what marriage meant, even though I had jumped through hoops to get divorced less than a year before. I questioned my sanity.

Forging a future built on lies about the past, I worried doomed our relationship. But for the moment, Hirth and I were happy. So, I followed Hirth's lead to live in the present and stop worrying about the future. And forget about the past.

In April, the month after we got married, Hirth got a gig at McCabe's' Guitar Shop, a live music venue on Pico Boulevard in Santa Monica. It was prestigious to play at the intimate venue; full capacity was a mere 150 people lucky enough to secure tickets in the backroom dedicated to concerts.

The billing featured Hirth Martinez and Garth Hudson from The Band, and they packed the show. Garth's wife, Maude, who also sang background vocals on Hirth's albums, joined them on stage. Maude was a fantastic vocalist with a big voice and presence—a stark contrast to my wispy soprano and diminutive stature. I didn't want to perform, but Hirth insisted.

Before we went on, Maude encouraged me not to be nervous and offered me some arnica to calm my stage fright. The funny thing was I never got stage fright, but thanks to the power of suggestion, when I looked out at the sea of faces packed into the small room, I became panic-stricken. What if I forgot the words? I suddenly felt as though I had come down with lockjaw.

I had never heard of arnica, but Maude said, "Put seven of these pellets under your tongue and let them melt."

I became dizzy. I thought it must be the arnica.

The next day, the local papers, including The LA Weekly and The Reader, reviewed the concert, and one review singled me out. It read, "Maude Hudson's powerful voice strongly overshadows Samantha's singing. We'd like to hear more of Samantha's angelic voice."

I could only assume I captivated the critic with my Stevie Nicks-style attire, so much so, he failed to notice they turned off my mic because I was out of pitch. Far from being a singer, I was Hirth's muse. In exchange, Hirth had been my healer; being with him was therapeutic.

The precise path of Hirth's destiny served as a constant reminder of how my life meandered along with no rhyme or reason. As a little girl, I loved pushing furniture around, designing things. I loved history and art. But rather than foster my interests, my curious nature often got me into trouble or drew punishment.

Since I had been on my own, I worked as a waitress, sold waterbeds, became a champion backgammon player, and a photographer's stylist.

Now I was Hirth's muse. I wondered if I could have been any random lost girl who stumbled into the party the night we met. He was lonely, and I filled an emptiness in him. But even though my life lacked direction, I was curious about where life could take me. But as Hirth's muse, he preferred all roads led back to him.

I grew restless, and I was yearning for my independence. So, I began looking for work to make a fresh start. I knew I didn't want to style nude photoshoots anymore, but I wasn't sure what to do next, so I threw myself out there to find any job.

I applied for and got a job at a small boutique on the Sunset Strip called Pourelle. Most of the people who patronized the store were cross-dressers looking for a safe place to be male, trying on women's clothing. I was the perfect employee for Pourelle because I created a "no-judgment-zone," and news of my styling expertise spread through the West Hollywood community. Soon I had increased the sales, and the owner was happy with my work. Hirth hated it. He berated me about working at such a dumbass job and thought I was putting myself on display at the store every day, even referring to me as a cheap mannequin. His harassment over my job became untenable.

To keep the peace between us, I applied for a job at *The New Zoo Review* as a receptionist. It was a kids' TV show that had gone into syndication, and the owner, a woman named Barbara, was a real ball-buster and became an inspirational role model for me. She never took "no" for an answer.

The only issue I had with the job was Barbara expected me to have a car to run errands. One such regular chore was to go to the Beverly Hills post office. It was about a mile away, a very short distance if you are traveling by car and not so far to walk unless you are wearing heels. I was much too proud to admit I didn't have a car and feared I'd lose the job if she found out the truth because she made it a prerequisite when she hired me. So, when asked to run to the post office, that's what I did. I took off my heels and ran as fast as I could barefoot. It was quite a good exercise, but somewhat hard on my feet, so I started carrying a larger purse to bring my trainers.

When winter rains came, I could have borrowed Hirth's car. He never used it to go anywhere. But Hirth would instead, pick me up and run Barbara's errands with me, all the while complaining. I know Hirth wanted to feel I needed him. I did. But I needed him to be the artist he was when we fell in love. I wanted him to work on his music. I didn't want him to be my chauffeur. He wasn't happy, and I was miserable.

When I agreed to be the Hippo character from *The New Zoo Review* in the Macy's Day Parade, to get a free trip to New York, Hirth demanded I quit the job.

"How could you think it was a good idea to be a hippo in a parade?" he asked. "That's just humiliating. I won't stand for it."

"I thought it would be fun to go to New York. I don't see why my dressing up like a hippo would humiliate you. You wouldn't even be there."

"If you go to New York and wear a hippo costume, it's an image I won't be able to un-see ever, even if I'm not there," he said as he grabbed his jacket and took off in his car.

Hirth was also angry I'd quit smoking, and this was an excuse to vent and run off to have a smoke since he became self-conscious smoking around me.

A short time later, I quit the job, which made Hirth very happy. He began taking me with him when he had gigs with the Polo Four, a band comprised of childhood friends from East LA. They played standards for weddings or corporate events. It impressed me Hirth took these jobs even though I knew he hated it. He'd make fifty to one hundred dollars per gig, and it was great to have the extra household money.

The jobs were a considerable distance away—as much as two hours or more—in towns that fanned out from East LA like Montebello and Rancho Cucamonga. Hirth had a friend named Jimmy, who played bass at these gigs, who was into Scientology and was always talking about being audited and getting clear. I had enough of Scientologists when I first moved to Hollywood, so I was wary of Jimmy, but he adored Hirth. Sometimes Jimmy would pick Hirth up and drive him to the gigs to save Hirth the gas money.

If Jimmy couldn't pick up Hirth, it was better if I rode with him because I could keep him awake on the long drive back to the cellar flat.

I tagged along to a wedding celebration for a seventy-year-old couple. For the couple's first dance, the Polo Four played John Lennon's "(Just Like) Starting Over." A man named Mark David Chapman gunned Lennon down in front of the Dakota in New York City six months before. Hirth and I were walking down Holloway Drive to Barney's Beanery when someone yelled out their car window, "Lennon's been shot." We were still the Mystic Bums when Lennon died. Remembering that night made me realize how much had changed between us.

The couple's senior friends joined them under the lights. They all looked so graceful as I imprinted their faces on my mind. Someday, when I grew old, I wanted to remember how it felt being young, watching all of those older people waltzing on the dance floor. I tried to picture myself being old and dancing with Hirth. Turning the clock forward allows you to see a fantasy. But turning it back, there is only harsh reality staring you in the face. A sad feeling came over me; I knew that night, I would never grow old with Hirth.

25

PURPOSE, PRIORITIES AND PERFUME

Though Hirth was furious when he found out I applied and got a new job as a receptionist at a design firm, he agreed to drive me to and from the office each day in the old VW.

I arrived on the first day wearing my red patent leather kitten heels with bows. What seemed so chic in Paris partying next to a billionaire now looked awkward and out of place. I wanted to fit in, but it was apparent from the moment I applied that I lacked a formal education, which set me apart from everyone around me.

A few times, they asked me to take notes during their creative design meetings. Ideas would come to me, and I felt eager to contribute. One time, I raised my hand to say something as if I were in a classroom, which gave everyone a good laugh.

"You're here to take notes. So please don't raise your hand unless it's for permission to go potty."

It was clear it an innocent joke, but it was at my expense. I never felt more like an outsider.

The exception to my feelings of alienation was when I got to be in the company of the owner, Rod Dyer, a South African man who took a shining to me. Sometimes he'd walk past my desk and show me some designs and ask my opinion about them, always intrigued by my answers. He was impressed with my knowledge of the world from having traveled throughout Europe. His words of encouragement gave me hope that eventually, through hard work and determination, I might learn design despite my lack of formal training.

Wild Bill used to say, "You can only play the cards the dealer gives you. The trick is to play them close to the vest." Now, I understood what this bit of wisdom meant. Every day, I brought my lunch and went for a walk, finding a corridor or stoop between buildings to sit alone. I tried to be as professional as possible and say as little as possible. I needed this job and not just for the money. I wanted a career, and everything about the atmosphere at Rod Dyer Design inspired my creativity and made me want to explore and learn how to express myself. I could be good at this.

When Hirth arrived to pick me up after work in the old VW one day, I overheard one of my co-workers say, "Look, her Daddy's here to pick her up!"

I turned and quipped, "He's my friend, not my daddy. I learned how to drive on the left side of the road in England, which has made it challenging to pass my driving exam. I'm lucky to have such a kind friend." I shot them both a sour look.

When I got into the car, I slammed the door.

"What was that about?" Hirth asked.

"Oh, nothing..."

"Well, good because I have some exciting news to share. Linda—you know, the receptionist at Bicycle Music—gave her notice to quit today, and Rita asked me if I thought you could handle the job."

"What did you say?" I asked.

"I said, 'Of course you can!' Now I won't have to drive you anywhere since we live downstairs. And we can hang out all day when you're not busy."

Finally, a job Hirth could be happy about so he'd stop making my life a living hell with his constant complaining. It didn't matter if I thought I could do the job or not or that I was happy working at the design firm and thought it might be a real career starter for me. What mattered was Hirth didn't think being a receptionist at Bicycle Music was a stupid job, and he'd no longer have to drive me.

David Rosner, Hirth's publisher, out of an abundance of kindness, gave me a shot. Besides having a soft spot for Hirth, Kenny Rogers was interested in doing a cover of Hirth's song "Winter Again," making it easier to overlook the fact I was underqualified. For one, the job required taking down a lot of dictation and then transposing it into impeccable typewritten documents. Because it was tinted a pale shade of tan, even one typo on the Bicycle letterhead necessitated retyping the entire text. David would not allow White-Out. Ever.

Shorthand was something I never took in school, and my typing skills were only about forty wpm when the job required ninety. But Hirth's happiness seemed to make up, at least partially, for my lack of skills.

That's not to say I didn't try very hard to please my new boss. The dictation was the tricky part for me, especially the first few months. On at least one occasion, I left David's office and returned to my desk only to realize I couldn't decipher my scrawl. It looked like complete gibberish on the page. It was humbling and embarrassing to admit I couldn't make out a single word, and he would have to dictate the entire correspondence over. I was lucky he didn't fire me on the spot, but before long, I could almost expect what he would say next, as he had a distinctive way of crafting correspondence. I made up a form of shorthand I could understand, consisting of symbols and abbreviations.

When the job wasn't busy, I tried to secure bookings for Hirth at local music venues like the Comeback Inn, The Roxy, McCabe's, and poetry readings in Venice.

Now that I was working full time at Bicycle Music, it began to feel awkward living in the cellar below. I suggested to Hirth that he play the "Samantha" song for David. I thought it could be a hit for Julio Iglesias or maybe Ray Charles. David loved the song and, in exchange for the rights to it, agreed to advance Hirth enough money for the deposit to rent an apartment. It was only about $1000, but it meant we could get out of the cellar, have a real shower, and cook on an actual stove. Between that and the stipend Hirth ended up earning from his guitar session work on *"The Ballad Of Gregorio Cortez,"* we moved to a cute one-bedroom apartment at 366 South Cochran in the Mid-Wilshire district.

To me, an apartment with an actual shower was luxury well worth $425 a month. For Hirth, it meant more stress and more driving. I was making $800 a month at Bicycle Music, which was enough to cover our living expenses, leaving little room for anything else.

We started arguing all the time and stopped being intimate. Hirth was the king of put-downs that stung like bullets every time he was drunk on wine, which became more and more frequent.

"You would have made a fool of yourself in a pink hippo costume if I hadn't talked you out of it! The only reason you have a good job is because of me! Without me, you would have nothing."

Defensive about his inability to provide a consistent income, he refused to stoop to any level that lessened his stature as an artist. But that set him up to be kicked in the gut twice as hard when it didn't pan out for every promising call that came in like the call to work on Julio Iglesias' album.

Had I known renting an apartment would cause our relationship so much stress, I would have left well enough alone and stayed in the cellar. Now, Hirth was back to driving me to and from work each day and complaining about it. When we went to East LA, and Hirth left with his father to "gas up" his car, I felt like we were back to looking for handouts again. I began to loathe taking piles of laundry down to his parents while he sat around eating his mother's home-cooked meals like a king. I started going to the local laundromat in the evenings after work to maintain what little independence I had left. I preferred keeping our dirty laundry to ourselves.

When I could talk Hirth out of going to his parents on the weekend, we managed to have some good times. I loved it when he took me to Parmahansa Yogananda's Lake Shrine, where we meditated and walked, leaving with incense or a small carved buddha for our apartment.

He sometimes took me to Village Recorders, where he had spent his glory days recording his album with Robbie Robertson. Hirth's association with Robertson made him somewhat of a star to Dick LaPalm, who operated The Village. LaPalm was an exciting and colorful guy who believed in Hirth's talents and enjoyed having him around to reminisce about the good old days. The Village was home to the Allman Brothers, Beach Boys, Lennon, BB King, and Tom Jones, and LaPalm could recall countless stories.

The Village was in a building built in the 1920s as a Masonic Temple. In the 1960s, Maharishi Mahesh Yogi converted it to his Los Angeles Center for Transcendental Meditation. Many of the unique Masonic characteristics remained from the original structure, including the stained-glass windows that gave the place a hallowed feel. When you walked in, the walls reverberated with the musical genius of albums recorded there —Aja by Steely Dan, Joe's Garage by Frank Zappa, and Planet Waves by Bob Dylan. Hanging out there seemed to give Hirth a renewed hope he would one day be recording again. He believed in the power of positive thinking. So, he never felt he had to work toward a goal. He thought he could manifest things by thinking it would be so.

I asked Dick one day, "Do you think you could put the word out Hirth is looking to do some session work?" It was something Hirth, and I had spoken about, so I thought it was appropriate to bring it up.

"I didn't know you were up for doing session work, Hirth, but sure, I'll—"

"Right now, I'm focusing on writing. I'm not playing guitar

much these days. Come on, Sam. Let's head out."

Once in the car, Hirth went off on me. I listened but was aware it was his fear of failure talking. Fear of failure stopped him from putting himself out there as anything but the mysterious singer-songwriter Hirth Martinez. If Hirth couldn't be a famous recording artist, he found contentment retreating to the safety of his parents' house in East LA to wait for something to happen, buoyed up by his parents' belief it would indeed come to pass.

Though I respected how much Hirth's parents loved him, I couldn't understand how, having worked hard their entire lives, they gave so much to their adult son. I felt that giving to him so freely prevented him from seeking out his success. Hirth was thirty-eight years old. It was time for him to grow up.

One Sunday morning, I refused to go along with Hirth to East LA. That ignited a considerable fight, which made me realize how much tension was building up between us. I'd grown up relying upon my grit. The contrast between us was forging a great divide. All hope depended on Hirth's big break. Everything I accomplished was to be of service to him until it happened. I believed in Hirth's talents, but what if his time never arrived? What then? I had expectations for myself, and paramount among those expectations was having a partner with whom I could become a woman. I didn't want to be his little girl, though that's how he treated me. He obsessively made drawings of me as a pre-pubescent girl who never aged. Maybe it was because he didn't want me to grow up. Because if I grew up, he would also have to grow up.

I went along with Hirth to East LA to keep the peace, though it was becoming increasingly challenging to accept how much his parents spoiled him. After packing up our clean laundry and overeating heavy Mexican food, I fell asleep on the hour-long car ride home, feeling empty and depleted at the end of the long day.

I felt invisible. I began thinking about my Uncle Jim because I craved a familial connection. I needed to talk to someone who knew the real me.

So, when Hirth was picked up by Jimmy for a gig with the Polo Four, I reached out to Uncle Jim, to see if we could meet me for coffee. I knew I wouldn't have enough time to make it to Long Beach without Hirth knowing I borrowed his car, so Uncle Jim met me halfway at a Denny's coffee shop.

I hadn't seen my uncle since the backpacking trip in the High Sierras when I was twelve. He didn't even know I was in Los Angeles, and I surprised him when I called, and he agreed to meet me right away. So much happened, I didn't know where to begin. I bottled things up inside for so long; I was about to explode. Over coffee, I opened up about the strange trajectory my life had taken since I ran away. Uncle Jim listened, allowing me the opportunity to get things off my chest without judgment. I confided in him about how much I had suffered at my grandfather's hands and how the pain from that experience had scarred me and made me feel worthless, leading me down a dark path for the past five years.

We began meeting often, and I found these secret meetings with my uncle therapeutic and healing. He counseled me to let go of the anger I was feeling to find a path to forgiveness—especially of myself. He knew it was best for my young heart to learn forgiveness, to discover the redemptive power of prayer, and letting go of the past.

When JD Deemer came for a visit to Long Beach, Uncle Jim brokered a lunch between us. I finally told Hirth about my aunt and uncle in Long Beach, and he drove me down to meet my grandfather. Upon seeing Pap after all the years that had passed, he looked so much frailer—he seemed incapable of doing the things he had done to me.

I almost felt sorry for him. It seemed pointless to bring up the past now. He was so old that I no longer needed to fear him.

We went to lunch at a Mexican place. Hirth and my grandfather seemed to hit it off well.

Because I never told Hirth about my grandfather's abuse, I waited until he got up to use the restroom to ask Pap the question I had been wondering my entire life, "Why did you give me the blind pony?"

It was the first time I ever saw my grandfather cry. It was as if that one question I posed in the Mexican restaurant opened a floodgate of emotion.

I didn't have to engage in any other dialogue with my grandfather. That one question and his response told me what I knew all along. He gave me the blind pony to control me by making me feel I wasn't good enough for a more worthy horse. He took Misty away from me just to exert even further control over me.

For the first time, I believe he showed remorse for what he had done to me. He stole my youth. He'd set me on a path of self-destruction that only by my will I survived, and it felt liberating to tell him so if only with the tears streaming down my face.

I could never choose a religion, but I believe in the profound power of love and forgiveness. At that moment, it happened. The scars that had grown so thick over my heart to the point I could no longer feel it beating in my chest began to untangle, and fresh blood circulated within me. Uncle Jim was right—forgiveness is possible. I forgave myself for all of the hate I felt toward JD Deemer and the abusive spiral of shame and guilt he caused me. But that didn't change anything about the way I felt about him. I knew there was nothing he could say or do that would allow me to forgive him.

When Hirth returned to the table, he teared up at the sight of my grandfather and me holding hands as we both cried, but I never shared the reason. I admired Hirth's family too much to share the painful memories of my family. Hirth may have relied on his parents too much, but it was hard to deny I wished someone cared about me half as much as they cared about their son.

At lunch, Hirth mentioned I was looking to buy a new car because it was hard to share the old VW. Two weeks later, I received a check from my grandfather as a down payment on a vehicle. The only way I could cash that check was to consider it a down payment on my freedom. No amount of financial compensation could pay for what he did to me.

The independence of having a car did make things less tense between Hirth and me, and I became less resistant about our weekend sojourns to his parents' house.

When Princess Di and Prince Charles got married in July of 1981, it was a global event broadcast on television. We got up at the crack of dawn to drive to East LA to watch with Helen and Sam. Helen made a festive breakfast for us, and we gathered around the TV to hang on every moment. I felt like I was part of a real family, and I mattered to them. Seeing pictures of London made me reminisce about the time I fantasized about having an entire family there who wished me well and shared the Christmas holidays with me, making fig pudding. But the reality was, the only time I spent living there, was with Eugene, and that almost killed me. There was no way for me to express to the Martinez' my gratitude for being part of their family.

Early on Monday morning at work, a curious woman named Charlotte Hart called the office from Houston, Texas. She idolized Neil Diamond and wanted to see if it might be possible to get tickets to his upcoming show that was sold out. By the sound of her voice inflected with an indiscernible accent, I got the impression she was most likely in her early 70s. She told me she owned a gallery called Hart Gallery, but her son was now managing it, and she was lonely. I felt sorry for her but also admired her tenacity, so I did everything I could to score those tickets. I not only found tickets but also secured a backstage pass for her to meet Neil.

To show her appreciation, Charlotte sent me a bottle of expensive Giorgio perfume from the Beverly Hills store of the same name. It had been some time since I received a gift of any kind, so I was grateful, and although I didn't like the perfume, the bottle looked fancy on my small, thrift-store dresser.

Charlotte continued to call me after the concert, just to talk, often venting about her son. I learned her beloved second husband, Samuel Hart, built their business, Hart Galleries, before passing away in 1975. She felt her son was attempting to make her appear crazy so he could steal the business from her. The gallery meant everything to her, and it made her furious he shut her out.

"My son's not even a real Hart," she said. "He took Samuel's name, now he's taking his legacy and running it into the ground with that tart of a wife, Wynonne."

"Can't you take your gallery back from them?"

"It's too late. I trusted Jerry. He's my son, but he's not a good person, and his wife is toxic. All she does is try to copy me. From my hairstyle to my perfume. She has no class."

About six months had passed since I'd scored the Neil Diamond tickets, and I ran out of people to whom I could re-gift the Giorgio perfume that she continued to send me every couple of weeks.

"About the perfume, thank you, I received it. But, Charlotte, really, I have enough now."

"A woman can never have too much perfume, dear!"

"Well, maybe we could switch it up?"

I didn't want to tell Charlotte how much I hated the smell of Giorgio, but it seemed like an egregious waste of money.

"Of course, dear. What would you like?"

"How about Chloe?"

Chloe was the first thing that popped into my head because I saw an ad for it that I liked. If Charlotte wasn't going to stop sending me perfume, I figured I should at least get something I might consider using. Within a matter of a day or two, a bottle of Chloe arrived from Neiman Marcus. When I opened the package, I burst into tears. It may sound silly, but it meant something that Charlotte listened to me, and we could have honest dialogues about everything under the sun. With all her eccentricities and quirks, over the next two years, this odd woman became more like a mother than my own. Charlotte called me just to say, "hi." She could tell when I was down and always knew what to say to cheer me up. She became as vital to me as though she were my mother. Charlotte was the only one I confided in, and she in me.

It thrilled me when she called and said, "I'm coming to Los Angeles next week and will be staying at the Beverly Wilshire. I'm not planning to stay long, so let's have drinks and food in my room. Bring Hirth, and tell him to bring his guitar. Maybe he can play a concert for us."

Hirth and I drove around Beverly Hills, trying to find street parking, then gave up and drove the old VW into the hotel's porte-cochere, and the valet handed Hirth a ticket. Grumbling about having to pay to park the car, Hirth took his guitar out of the boot and slung it over his shoulder.

Entering the gilded hotel made Hirth uncomfortable, but it gave me a feeling of happiness that had been missing in my life. I knew my way around the place by memory. Some things don't change. Dialing Charlotte's room number from the lobby phone to let her know we had arrived, and she summoned us to her suite.

In the elevator on the way up to Charlotte's room, Hirth appeared hopelessly uncomfortable. I wondered if bringing him into this environment was a mistake that I would end up regretting. With his guitar hanging over his shoulder, he looked like he was on his way to a gig, which was the only way he could justify being part of this scenario. He convinced himself the experience would provide fodder for the novel he wanted to write, and it would be a bestseller.

Charlotte flung open the door and wrapped her arms around me in a tight embrace. Once she let go, we settled onto a sofa. Charlotte opened a bottle of Veuve Clicquot champagne on ice, causing me to reflect on the past several years.

Champagne flute in hand, I floated over to take in the sights from the impressive window overlooking the city street below. Taking a moment to process it all—the opulent suite, the view out to Rodeo Drive—I realized how much I had been through the past two decades of my life. I had been an abused child, a teenage runaway. I'd been Backgammon Girl, rubbed elbows with debutantes and celebrities, and wallowed in a cesspool of drugs and despair only to find emotional stability in the humblest cellar-dwelling with a gypsy poet. Then I became his wife and a stepmother to his child. But something about the moment made me realize I still had a long way to go.

Hirth and Charlotte exchanged awkward pleasantries as strangers do.

"I forgot you two, don't know each other!" I said, turning away from the view and the past to join Charlotte on the couch in the present.

Though this was the first time we met face to face, I felt I had known Charlotte my entire life. As the champagne flowed, Hirth sat looking uncomfortable on a wing-backed chair while Charlotte and I talked up a storm.

Charlotte turned to him and said, "I'm so glad you brought your guitar. I am hoping to hear you play."

That was all Hirth needed to hear as he launched into his playlist of gig songs. At first, he played old standards he performed with the Polo Four, providing lovely background music to our endless chatter. As the evening progressed, and Charlotte and I were on our second bottle of Veuve, enjoying delicious caviar, Hirth decided to draw the attention back to himself. He began serenading us with the greatest hits of his Warner Bros. albums, competing for our attention. What made Hirth's music so unique was it demanded you listen to it. It wasn't music meant to play in the background, and Hirth didn't like being a background player. He wanted to take center stage because I think he wanted to impress Charlotte.

"Oh, my! He has quite a gravelly voice, my dear. He's not a real singer, now, is he?" Charlotte quipped.

Hirth's sophisticated chord changes and jazz stylings, and his voice, weren't Charlotte's cup of tea. She was aware of how much effort I put into booking Hirth's concerts and working on documenting his copious volumes of poetry. But she confided in me that night all of the energy I had been making might be a waste of my time. She had no point of reference for the caliber of talent Hirth possessed. I realized through our hours of phone conversations; I painted a picture of Hirth as the singer-songwriter discovered by Bob Dylan, the misunderstood artist to whom, one day, the world would awaken. Perhaps, a mere mortal could not live up to the picture I painted.

"I don't understand his songs. He sounds like he's talking gibberish," Charlotte whispered to me under her breath while Hirth was in the middle of a rousing rendition of his classic song "Coming 'Round The Moon." It wasn't quite the time or place for Hirth to be trying to dominate the moment or sucking all of the breathable air from the room. Charlotte was ready to jump out of her skin from the onslaught of words tumbling from his mouth, while he played guitar licks that sounded like pelting rain, or were they bullets?

Then Charlotte said the unthinkable to Hirth. "Darling, could you stop singing and just play for us while we talk? Do you know any Neil Diamond songs? Just play the melodies for us.

Don't sing."

I thought Hirth might blow a gasket.

By this time, we were well into our third bottle of champagne, and I was feeling a bit nauseous, so I quickly stood up and announced, "I almost forgot I have a big meeting tomorrow. Unfortunately, we have to leave now, or I won't be in shape for the meeting. I wish you were in town longer so I could see you again."

I hugged her, kissing her on both cheeks.

"Perhaps you will come to visit me in Houston."

"I would love to, Charlotte. You are so amazing, and I am so happy we finally met in person though I feel like we've known each other my whole life."

"Likewise, dear," as she shot Hirth a look, he was unaccustomed to having never had to deal with an unapproving parent.

Hirth packed up and made a swift beeline for the door, exiting without saying goodbye. Charlotte and I continued our extended farewell out into the hallway, hugging and telling one another how much we loved each other. Hirth had already summoned the elevator. He was pushing the button over and over as though that would make it arrive faster—his pent-up anger from the evening on full display.

Though I could relate to how Hirth was feeling, once the elevator doors closed, I wanted to say something about how socially awkward his behavior had been. But the last thing I wanted there to be was a scene, and I could tell Hirth was walking on tacks. When we presented our ticket to the valet, to add insult to injury, we didn't have enough money to cover it. I had to call Charlotte from the valet's booth and ask if it was okay to charge it to her room.

"Twelve bucks to park a car," Hirth mumbled as he turned the key in the ignition. We drove home in silence.

"I feel nauseous," I said.

"Well, you shouldn't have drunk so much champagne with that crazy lady," he said. "I hope you're happy you finally met the great Charlotte *Fart.*"

His response was less than mature and enough for me to know I best keep my feelings to myself.

Nine days later, I discovered my nausea wasn't from the champagne. On June 17, 1983, I found out I was pregnant.

26

VIGNETTE NOELLE

Becoming pregnant was the Universe telling me my life had meaning. This child, this baby I was carrying would grow inside my womb and enter the world likewise—with purpose, with intent.

I could picture my unborn child's face as though I were looking at a photograph, and I sensed her soul within my soul.

The first person I shared the news with was Charlotte Hart, who sent me another bottle of Chloe perfume to celebrate, which I added to my now massive collection.

"Samantha, this is such wonderful news! You know I will be there for you if you need anything," she assured me before offering her prediction. "I think it's a girl. Maybe you will call her Chloe!"

We laughed as she continued to share stories of what childbirth had been like for her, imparting words of wisdom, even though it was apparent her disappointment with her son, Jerry, had grown deeper since when we first met. I think her troubles with her son and daughter-in-law, and my alienation from my mother were part of what bonded us together.

"So, when are you going to tell Hirth?" Charlotte asked.

"I don't know. Maybe tonight. I just don't want to send him into a downward spiral.

He's been doing good."

"And what does 'doing good' mean? Is he working or even trying to find work, or is he still just leeching off his parents? You need to confront him, Samantha, and tell him it's time for him to give up this notion that lightning will strike for him. It must rain before lightning happens. He's a grown man. It's time he grew up to take some responsibility for his actions. It takes two to get pregnant. He is in this with you."

Charlotte's counsel resonated with me as I repeated the words to myself: *We're having a baby. We're pregnant.*

The thought Hirth might not want this baby never once crossed my mind. For a while, things had been rocky between us, and I wondered if we had gotten married without thinking things through. The good times with Hirth were great, but the dark times were awful when he got moody. Now that I was pregnant, I had a responsibility to our child to make it work. All that mattered was the life we were bringing into the world.

That evening, we ate dinner and sat down in the living room to listen to music. I had gathered up the courage to tell Hirth about our baby when the phone rang. It was his ex-wife sounding upset. Their golden retriever was hit by a car and lay dying on the side of the road. Hirth's daughter was inconsolable. I could only imagine how devastated and helpless she felt. Hirth tried to calm her down, but I could hear her through the phone line across the room.

"Daddy, he's dying, he's dying. Please come! Oh, Daddy, Daddy!!!"

"I would come over now, baby, but I have a gig," he said, lying through his teeth.

I got up from the chair and walked back to the bedroom, re-entering the living room as he was hanging up the phone. I was only about eight weeks pregnant, but I already felt a bond with our child, like nothing I had ever felt before. She was strengthening me.

"Hirth, I have never questioned why you lie to your ex-wife and child that you have a gig when you don't. I have never pushed you to do anything you don't want to do. But now that I am going to be a mother, I don't see how I can turn a blind eye to your behavior towards your flesh and blood."

Hirth looked at me with a blank stare.

"Here, see for yourself," I said, as I handed him the pregnancy test with the visible pink plus sign showing the test was positive.

He stared at it, and the color in his face drained. Becoming a father again and losing me as his "little girl" made Hirth feel he wasn't in control. I was his muse and his child-like bride. Having a baby wasn't part of the plan.

"I suggest you go to your daughter now and don't come back until she feels safe."

When Hirth left to take care of his daughter, I cried myself to sleep. I knew in my heart things were about to become very challenging. Getting pregnant wasn't something I had planned, but in my heart, it felt right.

In the months that followed, I became synonymous with everything Hirth tried to avoid, fatherhood, and adulthood. He put up a barrier between us to keep me at a distance and withdrew his affection.

I didn't care if he blamed me. Our child was already a part of my world. So, if it took Hirth Martinez to get here, I was okay with that. I tried to tell him everything was going to be okay, but I could tell he was nervous about telling his parents. How would they react to his becoming a father again when he couldn't take care of the child he already had?

I overheard Hirth's conversation with his parents on the telephone a few days later. It was a gorgeous Los Angeles day, and the forecast was calling for an even more pleasant weekend, so Hirth suggested we all get together in our neck of the woods.

"Can you guys meet us at the Farmer's Market tomorrow for lunch? We have some big news we want to share."

As soon as we saw Nana and Papa crossing the parking lot, their broad smiles led me to believe they already knew what news was coming.

We only sat down long enough to order coffee when Hirth blurted out, "We're pregnant."

Without hesitation, Helen gushed, "We are so proud of you, son. A new grandchild is the best news ever."

Hirth beamed with pride but I knew it was less about his unborn child than it was about pleasing his parents. A new grandchild would ensure free canned goods and gas for Hirth for the rest of his parents' natural life.

Then Papa turned to hug me, and his acknowledgment I was part of this exciting news made me optimistic. Maybe we could become a stable family. Despite the considerable challenges we faced ahead, the most pressing for me initially was maintaining a healthy relationship between Hirth and his daughter, my step-daughter.

I could already see the damaging effects an absentee father had on his young daughter's life. I was trying my best to love her and provide her with the attention she deserved, but with a new life growing inside me, I could tell she was slipping further away each day. A baby would only draw a deeper wedge between Hirth and his daughter. But he was too selfish to understand the dynamic and the sadness that was growing in his daughter's heart as my belly expanded. I vowed to keep our family together, so my daughter wouldn't feel the pain of not having two loving parents.

When a woman becomes pregnant, each day that passes feels unique. As your body changes, you can feel the connection with the life growing inside, and you can see the changes on the outside. These changes are so apparent for the mother, less so for the father.

But, those feelings of creating a family unit never clicked in for Hirth. His dream of having another shot at becoming a prominent recording artist never gave way for any new goals to enter. He played guitar all day and fought his writer's block when the words wouldn't flow.

We continued to drive down to East LA to do our laundry and have his dad gas him up. I stopped complaining about it and decided it was best to save every nickel we could for our child.

When I was about eight months pregnant, all I could think about was my baby, but Hirth's daughter was turning ten years old. I wanted to do something special for her because I didn't want her to feel like our daughter's imminent birth took precedence over her birthday. I bought her a two-wheel bicycle that Hirth and I took down to East LA for Papa to help me put it together. I turned the whole event into a scavenger hunt, hiding notes around the property with clues until the last one was a riddle to open the garage. I'll never forget the pure joy on her face when she saw the bike with streamers coming out of the handlebars.

Helen made a delicious lunch, and I brought a birthday cake. After cake, the family went outside to the patio to relax with a coffee. I felt overwhelmed by the volume of dishes to wash, so I called for Hirth to come inside to help.

We were talking about what a great surprise the bicycle was for his daughter when all of a sudden, Helen stormed into the kitchen, saying, "My son does not do dishes in my house!"

Maybe it was my raging hormones, but her comment reduced me to tears. Papa was in the backyard under a tree with Hirth's daughter, and I ran out of the house crying and into his arms. Hirth followed behind me.

"I don't understand her. I don't understand why it's her place to say her son doesn't do dishes in her house. He is my husband. The father of our child. He's thirty-nine years old, and a grown-up now, with two children."

Papa comforted me by holding me for a moment. Then, with the saddest eyes, he released me, knowing he couldn't take sides.

"Hirth, I need to leave. I can't bear to stay another minute. Take me home, or I will walk back," I demanded.

We left in a sea of sorrow. A veil of silence separated us until we were halfway home, and I asked, "Why couldn't you just stand up for me? Say, 'Hey, Mom. I want to help my pregnant wife. The mother of my child.' Why did you let her speak to me that way?"

He mumbled through the veil, "That's just how she is."

The truth was apparent. Helen had Hirth tethered to her apron strings, and he was too insecure in his manhood to let go.

On February 16, 1984, our beautiful daughter, Vignette Noelle, was born. Our little seven-pound, twelve-ounce bundle of love was everything to me. She looked just as I envisioned her in my dreams: dark eyes, curly dark hair, refined features. I remember going over every square inch of her body, scanning for any little resemblance to myself. But she was her daddy's girl in every way.

Almost every picture of Vignette's homecoming is of Hirth with Vignette, or Hirth, Vignette, and his family, or Vignette with his family. There are only two pictures of Vignette and me. None exist of the next-generation Martinez family—Hirth, Samantha, and Vignette.

A month later, there was a Martinez family picnic lunch outside. They poured a fresh bit of concrete on their patio to add the new family member's name alongside those etched into the family's history. The names already cemented included Hirth's ex-wife and first child, and every name Hirth had ever gone by including "Red" and "Sammy," etc., and the rest of the Martinez clan. Hirth scrawled a bit of a song he wrote for Vignette into the cement.

That day, I felt awkward no one suggested writing my name in the cement. Maybe I could have picked up the stick myself and carved my name. But something held back from doing so. It was the feeling that I had been having ever since we stopped being the Mystic Bums. Hirth and I didn't belong together, and I didn't want to memorialize our mistake next to his ex-wife's name.

But having a child made me realize I wanted an extended family for my daughter, so I was delighted to have Uncle Jim and his wife, Marian, become surrogate grandparents to Vignette. Just as my uncle had encouraged me to see my grandfather several years ago, he suggested I invite my mother to attend Vignette's naming ceremony.

"Sam, you have already done the most difficult thing you needed to do to move on with your life. You forgave your grandfather. Now that you are a mother, it's time to heal the wounds between you and your mother. It can happen. You'll see," he assured me.

So, I called my mother and told her I would be having a naming ceremony for Vignette, and invited her and Tommy, to attend.

"I'll speak to Tommy about it. What exactly is a 'naming ceremony'?"

"It will be like a baptism. Uncle Jim is officiating, and Aunt Marian is helping me put it together. It'll be at their house in Long Beach. I'd like you to be there."

I don't think she'd realized how close I had become with my uncle and aunt in the past few years. My uncle was the only person in my immediate circle I had told about being abused by my grandfather. When I got pregnant, I made a solemn vow the cycle would end with me. My child would want for nothing. I would always care for her and keep her safe from harm's way.

The invitations went out, and my mother and Tommy RSVP'd.

From the time I first reached out to my uncle for counsel to this moment had been a long journey toward healing. I expressed to Uncle Jim; I wanted this celebration to close the circle of abuse that had haunted my family for decades. He agreed it was time for all of us to celebrate with forgiveness.

The ceremony would include a Kahlil Gibran quote about love, a quote from Rumi, and a few traditional Christian passages. Uncle Jim would anoint Vignette's forehead with a drop of water, applied by a rosebud from their garden. Aunt Marian ordered a beautiful cake that read, "God Bless You, Vignette." She had no grandchildren of her own yet, and Vignette was everything to her, as they were everything to me.

When the big day arrived, everyone showed up at my aunt and uncle's home in Long Beach. Hirth's family knew I was at odds with my family, but they were excited to meet everyone, including my aunt and uncle, who adored Hirth. Helen was in an elegant navy dress, Papa, in his best suit.

My mother arrived reeking of the Giorgio perfume I re-gifted to her as a peace offering. It had been ten years since we felt a mother-daughter connection. Mom's hair was stiff with too much hairspray, and it was clear she and Tommy were hung-over. The Martinez family seemed baffled and somewhat bewildered. Why didn't they have "Australian" accents like Samantha?

It was more like a surprise party than a christening. And the surprise guest was "Pammy." Who was this Pammy to which my mother and Tommy kept referring? My aunt and uncle knew I changed my name to Samantha. And they understood and respected the reasons why. My mother knew about it, but she and Tommy refused to accept I no longer wanted to carry around the name of my father's affair. Instead of respecting my wishes on this momentous day, they seemed hell-bent on repeating "Pammy" every five minutes. The event was supposed to be a naming ceremony for Vignette, not an outing of my birth name.

"So, Pammy," my mother chimed in, "how much weight did you gain with your pregnancy? I gained twenty pounds with each of my five kids—well, except for, Pammy," she chuckled, addressing Helen. "When I got pregnant with Pammy Sue, I ate everything in sight. I must have gained forty pounds."

I held my breath, hoping she wouldn't launch into the story about why she named me Pammy Sue, and I felt grateful she spared me that humiliation. Helen raised a quizzical eyebrow at Hirth as if to say, "Who are these people? And why do they keep calling Samantha, Pammy?"

The ceremony was beautiful, despite the confused faces.

When I look at the pictures of three generations that day— my mother, my baby girl, and me—we look like any typical loving family, and I feel proud to have these memories. As alienating as it was to fake some normalcy semblance, the pictures tell only the story of a devoted family frozen for all time in a photograph. A photograph to erase the years of pain like it never happened. It's a photo I can show to my granddaughters, and they can attest to their granddaughters of the three generations of love that came before them.

Hirth's family found the situation perplexing but didn't ask questions. As embarrassed as I felt over the ordeal, I was angry that Hirth never allowed me to be myself in front of his family. I realized we had built a life on lies. I should have been truthful to the Martinez family.

Despite how crazy things seemed, I remained as graceful as I could and kept the event focused on our precious daughter.

Tommy and my mother met Hirth and me back home at our apartment on Cochran Avenue, and Hirth broke out a bottle of wine to celebrate. Tom and Mom were already tipsy as I know they snuck off to the bathroom at the ceremony to sip vodka from those tiny bottles you get on the plane. I could smell it on them despite the Giorgio perfume overwhelming the room. Mom applied more each time she went to the bathroom for a nip. When she left her purse open, I saw a few empty bottles inside and snapped it shut when no one was looking.

When I got Vignette to bed, I entered the living room and poured myself a glass of wine. My mother was retelling the story of how I came to be named Pamela Sue. Hirth checked out, orbiting in space and trying to find a landing spot. My mother bewildered him.

I remembered how asking the simple question, "Why did you give me the blind pony?" cut through years of pain with my grandfather. I tried to compose a question that might resonate in the same way for my mother; I wanted some kind of emotional breakthrough to happen. It was time I told her I deserved her respect. I became an adult despite her parental abandonment. I didn't want to dwell on the past, but she kept bringing up the genesis of my name. If I could let go of the past, she would need to do so too if we were to have any meaningful relationship in the future. So, I found the courage to confront her.

"I get why you may have wanted to name me after my father's affair. You were young and immature, and he hurt you beyond reason. But why do you seem to relish telling people the story of how I got my name? Why do you still want to rub it in you named me after Dad's affair after all of these years?"

Perhaps I should have chosen a time when she wasn't intoxicated since I think the moment might have played out better if she was sober. But since I seemed to have gotten her attention, I continued.

"First, I haven't gone by that name for more than ten years. Why can't you understand it isn't funny or interesting or anything but hurtful you named me after my father's affair? I'm sorry he cheated on you. I am. But I don't understand how telling people will help to ease your pain. And what I can't understand is how you don't see how much pain it has caused me. Why can't you just get over it? I am Sam now."

My mother stood up like she wanted to leave.

"Is that why you allowed your father to molest me? Because you never wanted me?"

"I don't have to listen to this. Come on, Tommy. We're leaving."

She slammed the door behind her, waking Vignette. I picked my daughter up and held her close as I poured myself another glass of wine. My mother didn't realize I became numb to her walking out on me over the years, so the drama was a waste of precious time we could have spent healing our relationship. If she didn't want a relationship with me, I knew I would survive. I loved her, but it's hard to keep loving someone who doesn't love you back.

Several weeks later, I received a phone call.

The voice on the line said, "You been to Powder River? It's a mile wide, an inch deep, it's too thick to drink and too thin to chew."

"Hi, Dad."

Wild Bill came into town to play the ponies at Hollywood Park, and I agreed to meet him at the track because I felt a need to reconnect. I hadn't seen him since he put sugar in my gas tank, and so much had happened since then. The biggest thing, of course, was the birth of Vignette.

Dad enjoyed telling tall tales, but only on rare occasions spoke about anything emotional. Despite this, I couldn't help going on to him about the explosive night between my mother, her new husband, and me.

"Can you believe after all this time she can't just accept I go by Sam now? I don't want her to call me Pammy Sue."

"Damn, we had seven to two odds on that race. That jockey didn't have his head in the race," he groused. "Let's go get a drink at the Turf Club, Sam."

Wild Bill wasn't paying attention to anything I said.

But when he ordered our drinks, he said, "You know, my buddy Johnny Cash used to say, 'You build on your failure. You use it as a stepping-stone. Close the door on the past. You don't try to forget the mistakes, but you don't dwell on them. You don't let them have any of your energy, or any of your time, or any of your space.'"

There was a long pause. "You know, your mom never even drank a beer with me. It made me want to drink more. Go figure; she ended up with a drunk anyway."

I never told Dad I knew Johnny Cash didn't write "A Boy

Named Sue" because I realized it didn't matter. Cash may not have written the song, but the song reminded Dad of me and was the only proof I had that he thought about me and remembered me all those years we were apart. It proved he never forgot he had a girl named Sam.

I hugged Wild Bill as though I wouldn't let go with my newborn daughter, sandwiched between us as we said our goodbyes. He peeled off a few C-notes—my share of the day's winnings.

"Gimme a kiss. Butter girls got no lips. Take care of my grandbaby. She is a winner, like her mama. I'm bettin' on you, Sam."

He slipped a few bucks to the valet guy and cigarette dangling from the corner of his mouth, he nodded in my direction to acknowledge he was paying for me, too.

When the valet brought my car around, I strapped Vignette into the car seat. Elton John's "Little Jeannie" was playing on the radio, the lyrics oddly underscoring the moment's emotion.

I couldn't shake the feeling this might have been our last trip to Powder River.

27

THE HART FAMILY

Four weeks after giving birth, I returned to my full-time position at Bicycle Music. It took every ounce of will I could muster to walk back through the double doors of the office and leave my baby behind with Hirth. But I did it.

It also took every bit of nerve I could summon— with two swollen, lactating breasts—to ask for a raise. But I did it. I didn't get the increase, but I was proud I asked. We were desperate for cash. The only thing helping me keep it together was the sage advice from a woman pregnant with her second child at the same time I was pregnant with Vignette.

She said, "Don't worry. Babies feed themselves."

So, I shouldn't worry that my shoes had holes in the soles, and I couldn't afford new ones? The money would materialize when it was time to buy diapers and other essentials for my daughter? I still believed in magic, but I stopped relying on Hirth to create it for us. The thing about magic, I discovered is, magic comes to you when you believe in yourself.

Bicycle Music moved to Third Street, a stone's throw away from Farmer's Market, and ironically only a few blocks from our new apartment on Cochran and Third. After the convenience of living in the cellar flat below Bicycle Music, who could have predicted we would again live within walking distance?

Now I could walk to work, and Hirth could stroll down to the Farmer's Market every day with Vignette for lunch so I could nurse her in the old VW while he made the rounds with his cronies. He thrived on the fuss the Market regulars made over Vignette, and he never tired of hearing how much our little cherub resembled him.

Hirth sounded convincing when he told me while I was nursing Vignette in the back seat of the VW that he was networking with the Market regulars, most of whom were old musicians to get good-paying gigs. I had a realization one day while sweating profusely in the un-air-conditioned car with Vignette at my breast. Hirth sounded like Wild Bill did when he left the house in those crisp white shirts that mom ironed each day. I kept believing in Hirth because I wanted Vignette to have a father.

Even though I had such a sporadic and unstable relationship with my father, I always let Dad off the hook by saying, "He was my father, and that was enough." While that may work for a father/daughter dynamic, it doesn't translate to a husband and wife—a father and mother. Hirth lived in denial that everything would be okay, and we would somehow survive as a family without his making any effort to work. With my back to the wall, I knew I needed to find a better paying job because I couldn't trust Hirth just like my mother couldn't trust Wild Bill.

Responding to an ad for a job that would pay me a mere twenty dollars more per week, underscores how desperate we were for money. I was willing to give up a job where I was comfortable and throw myself into an unknown experience for the sake of our child. Our marriage was beginning to buckle under the weight of parenthood, and the only thing I could do was try to make more money for our family to survive.

I could finally relate to how Mom felt with five little girls and a husband looking to leave his troubles on the bottom of a whiskey glass, waiting on a lucky streak that never came.

I told David Rosner I had a doctor's appointment and found myself seated across two attorneys in a high- rise building at Sunset and Doheny Road across from Hamburger Hamlet.

"Can you type?" they asked.

"Yes. . . I'm fast."

"Can you take dictation?"

"Yes."

The interview process comprised only a few more questions with one-word answers because the two men seemed interested in only one thing. Make that two things. My lactating breasts were the size of cantaloupes. I doubt they would have been so enthralled with my breasts had they known I gave birth six weeks prior, and my breast enhancement was due to being flooded with milk.

It was a paralegal position for which I was under-qualified. But I always had faith I could learn whatever I needed to and could at least fake it until I figured it out. The first week on the job wasn't challenging. I had to keep the office open, answer the phones, take dictation, file legal documents, and restock the refrigerator with drinks from John & Pete's.

Jerry, the head honcho was away in New York, and his LA partner, Peter, was in court all week, so I brought Vignette into the office with me, stowing her little carrier seat under my desk while I typed away. I even got some critical Xeroxing done—of Vignette's feet and her tiny hands.

I had to be careful because I didn't want anyone to see her. If I left my desk to go back to the file room, I locked the door to prevent someone from coming in and snatching my baby. After the mail carrier had come and gone, I deadbolted the door because I wasn't expecting anyone for the rest of the day. At that point, I decided my work could wait until Monday, and we would just play together. We went into Jerry's expansive office and stood in front of the large, open window looking out at the city below. It was a sweet moment for us as I explained to Vignette all the fantastic things that she would one day accomplish.

Vignette fell asleep after nursing, and I put her back into her little carrier to get at least a little work done when a banging on the door startled me. I ran to open it, and Jerry came storming in like a whirling dervish. His sudden return to Los Angeles on business was unannounced.

"Why the hell is the door closed?" he asked.

"There have been some robberies in the area, and I was in the file room and by myself, so—"

"Okay," Jerry snapped. "Come, take dictation."

Vignette didn't wake up through all the commotion because she was in a milk coma. After Jerry disappeared into his office, I ran back to deadbolt the door again.

I breathed a sigh of relief when Jerry left to meet a client without discovering my little stow-away under the desk. The next day, I came clean to him about my daughter, my failing marriage, and the fact I was in over my head. He assured me I could keep working until I found another job. I was realizing being myself, and being honest was the best way forward. The days of pretending to be someone else would not work for me anymore.

Through my colleague, Rita, from Bicycle Music, I got an interview at Chappell Music, and was hired. The position was challenging, and I came home exhausted at the end of the day to find my now nearly one-year-old wide awake because Hirth let her sleep all day. Spending time with Vignette was the best part of my day, but most nights, I didn't get to bed until two or three in the morning. I had to leave for the office at eight o'clock. Lack of sleep was catching up with me, and I felt I might be on the verge of a nervous breakdown.

My boss was demanding, causing me to walk on eggshells and bite my tongue. Under normal circumstances, I might have thought this prima donna's behavior was amusing, but it increasingly made me feel as though I was coming unglued. Changing jobs in quick succession added to my stress, but it was the post-partum depression that caused me to cry on the way to and from work and stop eating. I already wasn't sleeping because I was up all night with Vignette. As depressed as I was, holding my baby was the only thing that stopped the madness and made me feel calm because I knew she needed me to take care of her.

Exercise always made me feel better, so my doctor suggested I try to get back to a physical routine, which would help with the post-partum. But the fact I chose Jane Fonda's tapes to work out to drove Hirth insane. He returned from a walk one day while I was working out and went berserk, yanking the plug to the VCR out of the wall.

"I hate this godforsaken music. Why on earth do you insist on playing Michael Jackson music in front of our child? Do you want to ruin her for life? I'm an artist. How do you expect me to create when I come home to you jumping around to this horrid music in that ridiculous purple get up?"

Vignette began crying, so I lifted her out of the walker and into my arms. I tripped on one of the toys, landing on my tailbone with our daughter still clutched in my arms. Vignette was all right, but my tailbone hurt, and I knew for sure my heart broke when Hirth walked right past me without trying to help us up.

Raised voices and slamming doors made our once loving home a war zone, and it wasn't a healthy place to raise Vignette. I never stopped believing in Hirth, but I realized he didn't believe in me. He questioned every choice I made, including something as petty as the color of my workout outfits.

I heard about a position at Windham Hill Records advertised as an A&R (artist & repertoire) and production assistant job. It sounded creative and similar to what I had been doing at Chappell. I had enough of my current boss, so I applied and got the job. The woman who hired me quit on my first day of the job. The company took the A&R part away from the position, and it became a hardcore production job—meaning the physical manufacturing of the cassettes and records. I was unqualified for a job so technical, but I couldn't risk losing it and questioned my sanity for giving up the position at Chappell. I couldn't believe I thrust myself into another vulnerable position.

A&M Records handled Windham Hill's distribution, so it

was there I attended my first production meeting. Aubrey Moore, the head of the production department, bellowed out to the newcomer across a massive conference room table, "Windham Hill, did you ship the parts yet?" All eyes around the conference table were on me, and the only thing with "parts" that came to mind was chicken parts.

I glanced around the room wide-eyed before responding, "The wing or the thigh?"

After a moment's pause, a few people stifled a chuckle. When Aubrey Moore said, "Are you going to fry it, or shake and bake it?"

The entire room erupted into laughter, but it wasn't to make fun of me. It was a show of appreciation I wasn't trying to pretend I had any clue. My lack of pretense endeared me to my colleagues at A&M.

Aubrey turned to Janice, a woman who worked in production under him, and said, "Janice, spend the day with this kid and help her get up to speed so we can get some records pressed for Windham Hill."

Within three months, I could have told you anything you would ever want to know about album mastering, manufacturing, printing, and press checking. Janice was a fantastic mentor and took great pride in her protégé. The first press check I went on was a big success. Within a year, Geffen Records recruited me to be the liaison for Geffen's production through Warner Bros. It was a prestigious move and came with a sizable pay increase.

Hirth got his first steady job since we met -- a job on a cruise ship for several weeks, so I put three-year-old Vignette into a Montessori preschool.

With Hirth gone, I had time to reflect. I missed his presence, but I realized the quality of my life with Vignette was better without Hirth there to pick a fight. There was no screaming or slamming doors. Vignette loved going to preschool and made friends with ease and became her teacher's favorite student. She stopped sleeping all day, which made the evenings a lot more enjoyable and allowed me to get some sleep. I felt my sanity returning. And I enjoyed getting back to my Jane Fonda workouts, purple tights and all.

Why couldn't Hirth be a part of this reality? The three of us, being a family together, enjoying what we wanted, living the way we wanted to live?

One night while Hirth was away, I pulled a book off the shelf to read, and a bookmark with a drawing of me slipped out. It was one of the thousands of pictures he drew depicting me as a pre-pubescent girl with long, blonde hair and small breasts. Hirth drew them of me before I became the mother of his child when I was still his muse, and we were The Mystic Bums, I knew he loved Vignette, but he was no longer attracted to me, and he resented something I had no control over. I matured. I grew up, and my aura was that of a woman.

Through a series of heartfelt calls with Charlotte Hart leading to more perfume, I decided I would confront Hirth when he returned about our relationship. Was it something we could work out? Was he willing to make a go of having a real-life together?

When he returned with an STD, there was nothing left to talk about, and I asked him to move out. I think he already resolved to go but seemed relieved when I was the one to ask, making it "not his fault" our marriage fell apart.

Falling in love with Hirth Martinez was easy. Breaking up with him was painful, and one of the most challenging things I've ever done. In my heart, I still loved the artist, Hirth. The father of my child was the person I was holding in contempt.

In an attempt to end our relationship as amicably as possible, I agreed to pay for Hirth's car payments on a new set of wheels I bought for him, as well as his insurance with one condition. He had to pick Vignette up from school at least a few days a week. He commuted into town almost every day to hang out at the Farmers Market on Fairfax, a thirty-five-minute drive. Despite my paying his car expenses, he was never available to pick up our daughter at Page School on Robertson, a fifteen-minute drive from the Market. Waiting for his lucky break occupied all of his time.

All those years, he tried to convince me how stupid I was to take the temp jobs. Now, I was flourishing in my career as the head of the graphic arts department at Geffen Records, and he remained in the same place, stuck, waiting on his next record deal.

After everything I had been through in my life, the one thing I knew was my daughter's well-being, and security was paramount. If Hirth felt caring for his daughter infringed on his behaving like the artist he was destined to be, then I would give up the fantasy of there being a possibility of our reuniting, and I would stop relying on him for anything. I filed for divorce and began mapping out what it would take over the next two decades of my life to launch Vignette into adulthood. Protecting her and shielding her from harm was my heart's mission.

We moved to the hills above Sunset to share a house with another single mom whose son went to the same school, which made it easy for us to split the costs of a nanny. This situation also worked out well because we could carpool to and from school, and I was closer to my office at Geffen Records. It was ironic because David Geffen was aware of Hirth's talent for years. At times, I thought it should have been Hirth checking in at 9130 Sunset Blvd. But it was me.

Vignette thrived at her private school, where everyone loved her for her creative spirit and friendly nature. She was everybody's best friend, and quite possibly every teacher's favorite student.

"We live in Beverly Hills. Does that mean we're rich, Mommy?"

"We would be rich no matter where we live, because of who we are, Vignette."

"Who are we? Are we Mexicans?"

"What do you mean? Why do you ask?"

"Our last name is Mexican."

"Well, yes, we have a Mexican last name."

"Why do we have the same last name as Dad? You aren't with him, and neither am I. And why do you have blonde hair and blue eyes, and I don't?"

"A lot of people from the same family have different eye color and hair color. It's not that unusual. I have three sisters with blue eyes like mine and two sisters with brown eyes like yours."

"Oh, okay. Goodnight, Mommy."

"Goodnight, Vignette."

A few weeks later, Vignette's first-grade teacher sent a private note home asking if I got remarried because Vignette was signing her name Vignette "H."

"Vignette, why are you signing your name 'Vignette H.'?" I asked. "Your teacher called me about it."

"Because I want to change my last name to Hart like Aunt Charlotte."

"Why do you want to change your last name?"

"Because I like it. And because Daddy never wants to see me, so I don't want the same name as him. Charlotte is our real family, Mommy."

I was at a loss for words as I tucked her into bed. I wasn't sure if I should insist that she keep the name Martinez. Charlotte came into our lives when I needed a mother figure, and Vignette needed a grandmother. I came to depend on her for moral support and advice. She sent Vignette her first tutu. It was Charlotte who never forgot a birthday or was there to celebrate a milestone. I must have underestimated how much her daily calls meant to Vignette.

The court date was pending for the divorce, and my attorney petitioned the court for me to resume my last name—Butter. Did

I want to assume that handle again? It took me years to erase the painful memories of being named after an affair, of growing up in an abusive home and running from my past. I felt conflicted about whether I should drop the last name, Martinez. The phone rang. It was Charlotte calling me long distance from Houston after her prerequisite glass of sherry, in need of some company.

"Charlotte, do you know how important you've become in our lives? Vignette wants to change her last name to Hart. I think she thinks you are her real grandma."

Charlotte responded, "Samantha Hart has a nice ring to it."

By the end of our phone call, the Hart family was born.

28

JUDGMENT DAY

I never dreamt what began as a fairy-tale relationship with Hirth would deteriorate as it did. When I first met him and realized he didn't take care of his daughter, I should have run the other way. But I wanted a family, and though things didn't turn out the way I hoped, I had Vignette, and I couldn't imagine my life without her.

Reflecting on this made me realize that maybe I should have more empathy for my mother and how hard it must have been for her with five little girls and a deadbeat husband. I found myself regretting I had, once again, lost all connection with Mom. With Hirth's parents' loss in Vignette's life, it became more important to me than ever to mend the fence between us. It might never evolve into a typical mother/daughter relationship, but I wanted to try for the sake of Vignette. I wanted my daughter to know the loving experience of having a grandmother. Charlotte was more like a fairy godmother, and I knew the difference between blood and sherry.

After my grandfather passed away, my mother and Tommy retired to Florida. When Great Aunt Martha died, my mother told me she had a few things she wanted to give me from my aunt's estate and suggested I fly down for a visit with Vignette. Despite all the conflicts we had experienced, I knew my mother loved me as I loved her. I suspected there would always be unresolved feelings between us and baggage too heavy to bear. But the life I had lived these past years made me feel as though I could carry the world's weight on my shoulders. So, Vignette and I booked a flight to see her grandma and grandpa.

My divorce lawyer suggested I take along affidavits regarding changing my name to Samantha for my mother to witness. The documents stated that since I was born, my father called me "Sam," which evolved to Samantha, and rather than return to my maiden name, Butter, we'd be changing both Vignette's and my last name to Hart.

When the cab dropped us off at Mom's house, I felt as though I was entering a funhouse at an amusement park. My stepfather, Tommy, lit off his rocker, welcomed me with a Mai Tai. They had a pool enclosed by a dome-like screened porch so the nasty Florida bugs couldn't get in. And they had a fridge outside to keep the drinks handy and flowing. It was like a tropical paradise one might stumble upon if one were a Smurf. Everything was slightly cartoonish, with garden gnomes and fake plants and animals. Crickets and the trickling sound of waterfalls accompanied the luau music. My mother was wearing her bathing suit with a Hawaiian-type skirt wrapped about her, and she presented Vignette and me with similar gets ups to put on.

Over Mai Tais, I asked Mom if she would sign the affidavits to the court regarding the genesis of my name. She seemed tired of telling the story of how she decided to name me Pammy Sue and signed the affidavit. It was a lot less stressful than I thought it would be. I think she understood how difficult it was to divorce Hirth, and she seemed to want to make things easier for me, which I appreciated. Once the paperwork was out of the way, I tried to relax and enjoy my visit.

Later that evening, Mom presented me with an antique bowl with a floral pattern, complete with a lid that fits snugly on top and once belonged to Great Aunt Sarah. The memories held me in a warm embrace. I conjured the aroma of fresh-cut grass and the air laden with the summer's humidity mingling with Aunt Sarah's motel's distinctive scent, the used bars of soap from the guest's vacated rooms we collected to wash the linens. Holding the bowl was like being given back a tiny piece of my childhood.

My mother took my hands in hers and said, "I want you to know, Sam, before your grandfather died, I made him get out of bed, as weak as he was, and kneel and pray to God for forgiveness for what he did to you. I told him it was the only way the Lord was going to let him into heaven."

Hearing Mom confronted Pap about what he did to me, caught me off guard. But it left me void of emotion envisioning JD Deemer beg for forgiveness from God for admission to heaven. It did nothing to comfort me. It only made me want to ask Mom why she felt he deserved God's forgiveness for destroying my childhood and nearly killing me. I knew my mother didn't have a clue what life, since I ran away, was like—she didn't realize how many nights I cried myself to sleep, just wanting to hear her voice. Did she understand that the damage inflicted on me as a child sent me careening toward adulthood without any life skills and little self-esteem? I wondered if she ever felt remorseful about all of the lost time between us. I waited a long time for this moment—but now that it was here, I felt underwhelmed. If she could believe God would forgive a child rapist and unrepentant pedophile, it didn't matter what I thought. If it gave her peace to believe God forgave her father's sins, who was I to stand in judgment?

Clutching the relic that belonged to Aunt Sarah, I said, "Thanks, Mom. It is a beautiful bowl, and I will treasure it always."

A few days later, Tommy and my mom drove Vignette and me to the airport. As I hugged my mother goodbye, there was such a sense of normalcy between us; it was as though we were like most mothers and daughters who visit each other and say goodbye at airports.

Hirth was a no-show at court, so my divorce petition was granted. I waived rights to any child support but asked for sole custody of Vignette and to change our last names to Hart. Removing the last vestiges of my past by tossing off the name of my father's affair, and Vignette's now absentee father felt empowering. It was official. We were the Hart family. I typed up a company-wide memorandum that filtered through the Geffen Records' mailroom to everyone's inboxes, informing them of my name change. People assumed I'd chosen the name as one might pick a bloom from a patch of wildflowers at the side of the road, just because it's there and looking a little forlorn.

Word got back to Hirth's parents, and they felt insulted and hurt. They sent Hirth over to our apartment, demanding we return the old baby photo of Hirth's grandmother displayed in a custom frame on Vignette's dresser alongside a photo of my grandmother. Hirth ripped it out of the frame, and grabbed the baby picture Helen gave me of Hirth playing the saxophone in his diaper, before storming out. I understood their hurt over our changing our last names, but I couldn't understand why that meant Vignette was no longer entitled to baby photos of her great-grandmother and father. If there was anyone for the Martinez' to blame, it was their son. I wanted Vignette to be a part of their lives, but Hirth wasn't interested in seeing his daughter or taking her to visit his parents. Everyone was expecting me to behave the same way his first ex-wife did, dropping off his daughter in East LA at every opportunity for babysitting. I wanted to be with my daughter, and I didn't need anyone to assume responsibility for Vignette. I only needed people to love her.

A couple of years slipped by, and Vignette grew to look more and more like her father. Though they had little contact, she had his artistic spirit and natural talent. At five years old, she wrote a poem I thought he should hear;it sounded so similar to lyrics her dad wrote, even though she never read his poetry or song lyrics. I gave Hirth a call to share the poem, hoping it might spark his interest in seeing his daughter. I wanted him to know Vignette inherited more than his beautiful features. She inherited his genius as a writer. I wanted Hirth to bond with her and praise her as only a father can. I also wanted Hirth to hear Vignette sing. She had perfect pitch just as he did and could belt out sophisticated lyrics to jazz songs and show tunes.

Vignette and I frequented an upscale restaurant on Sunset Boulevard called "Cravings" who had a piano player, and Vignette would get up and entertain the crowded restaurant to big applause. Sometimes, she even sang for our supper as the restaurant comped our dinner. I wanted more than anything to share how beautiful our daughter had become inside and out. But my motives were also selfish. I wanted Vignette to have contact with Hirth because I knew the day would come when she might resent me for his not being part of her life. I knew firsthand how unbearable it could feel to grow up without a father's presence. You end up telling your darkest secrets to a seventy-foot-tall cardboard cowboy as I had been doing since he rode into town on his horse, taking up residence on the Sunset Strip.

When I read Hirth Vignette's poem, I could hear him breathing over the phone. When I finished, he said nothing, so I asked, "What do you think?"

"Is that it?"

"Well, she's been writing a lot. You know, at school. All of the teachers think she is talented."

"Great. I was right in the middle of writing myself, so I have to go now."

He hung up the phone.

I wasn't sure if he felt jealous of the words that flowed from a budding artist still so young and full of possibility, or was irritated to hear my voice. All I could hope for was the day when Hirth and Vignette would reunite as father and daughter. I reflected on how much it meant to me to have reconnected with Wild Bill. Even though he wasn't the hero I dreamt he'd be, he was still Dad.

Within several weeks of that conversation with Hirth, I received a phone call for which I was unprepared. The voice on the other end of the line sounded solemn.

"Your father passed away. He died of a heart attack. I thought you should know."

It was the myth of Wild Bill, the cowboy dressed in white, who I turned to time and time again throughout my life for strength and guidance, always asking myself, "What would Wild Bill do?" Wild Bill had become a symbol of my guardian angel. It was difficult to imagine I would never see him again. He was only fifty-six years old. The sadness and sorrow I felt, came from such a deep place of longing, wishing we could have had a closer and more meaningful relationship. I could count the number of rum and cokes I drank while leaning into his every word. I could overlook his stealing the poinsettias and even forgive him for making me believe Johnny Cash wrote a song inspired by me. Now that this larger-than-life character was gone, who would protect me?

It became imperative to me to forge a relationship between Vignette and her father so they would have a chance at building memories, even if they were "too thin to chew."

There was no changing course of the dusty trail I followed to find my father. But if my father's passing could lead to reuniting Hirth and Vignette, maybe his death would have meaning.

When I reached him at his parents' house, his standard comment was, "I have a gig," the same excuse he gave to his first ex-wife. But I didn't want his money—I wanted something more valuable. I wanted his time. I offered to pay Hirth to give Vignette guitar lessons thinking it might benefit them both, but he refused the offer.

My career was taking off, and I didn't want Vignette stuck in daycare after school every day, and sharing a nanny was becoming more challenging as the kids were getting older. It had been two years since Hirth last saw our daughter, and I was done hoping he'd become responsible. I hired a full-time nanny, but because she didn't drive, I had to race out of work to pick up Vignette at school, drop her off with the nanny, and then rush back to work. It broke my heart because I could tell Vignette resented that I couldn't spend more time with her.

Every so often, I brought her back to work with me, which was always entertaining. Though it wasn't ideal, how many kids can say they sat on Kurt Cobain's knee, conversed with Slash, and met Rob Zombie?

When the CFO of Geffen Records, Jim Walker, asked me to attend a WEA Manufacturing convention in Olyphant, Pennsylvania, I was thrilled to represent the company. I was equally ecstatic the trip would entail a stop in Manhattan, and it had been way too long since I had been to the city. I hired a friend named Missy, to pick Vignette up from school while I was away.

When I arrived in New York, it was as though nothing had changed except for me. When I looked out my hotel window on the city below, I realized how far I had come from the girl who once went howling through the streets with Party Marty.

The next day, a town car picked me up at my hotel to take me to the manufacturing plant where I would meet up with my colleagues from other labels, all men, to tour the facility. Having been to manufacturing plants many times with Windham Hill, I was bored on the guided tour and wandered off when I came upon a machine I'd never seen before. It was making a rhythmic sound that caught my attention.

I stood staring at it before asking a worker, "What is this contraption?"

He responded, "That's our automatic J-card folding machine. It folds the cards then stuffs them into the plastic cases before shooting the cassettes inside."

Suddenly, those boring ledger sheets Jim Walker tasked

me to review made sense. One of the line items was for "manual hand-folding." It cost five cents per unit to fold the cards by hand.

"So, how long has this been operational? Must be a big time-saver," I said, trying to sound more dumb blonde than super sleuth.

"A little over a year, I guess."

"Cool," I replied as I began to calculate what this meant.

When I got back to my hotel room before the dinner banquet, I rang Jim Walker.

"What's up, Sam, and make it quick because I'm meeting with Mr. Geffen in a few minutes."

"I think this might be important," I said, before laying out the details.

"If this is correct, we've been overcharged five cents a unit on every cassette they've manufactured for the past year. And if that's the case, you just wrote your own ticket. Well done, Sam."

On the entire plane ride home, I repeated Jim's words in my head, "Well done, Sam." Did this mean I had finally found my worth?

I was still on cloud nine when I got home to find Vignette already sleeping. Missy had stayed to fill me in on her homework, and we sat down to have a cup of tea.

"So, what's up with Vignette's dad, anyway? Shouldn't he be able to help you out with driving her around? I mean, I don't mind helping out when I can, and I appreciate making some pocket money, but it's weird she never sees him. She asked me why, and I didn't know what to say. She said she thinks it's because you don't like him."

"She knows that isn't true," I offered somewhat hopeful.

"Sorry to say this, Sam, but she will probably resent you one day, assuming you are the reason she never got to see him."

I knew Vignette might blame me for the lack of a relationship with her father, but hearing it from someone else made the veins on my forehead pop.

"There's no way I would ever tell Vignette Hirth doesn't want to see her. I don't know why he refuses. I've tried to make it easy for him. I'm still paying for his stupid car payment and insurance; it's been almost two years now."

"That's whack. Okay, you're not as smart as I thought you were," Missy chided. "I would just go get the damn car tonight, and give it to the nanny."

"She doesn't know how to drive."

"Then teach her to drive or get a new nanny. Or sell the stupid car. What kind of car is it? I have, like, three friends who need wheels. Why are you letting him take advantage of you?"

She was right. Why was I paying for Hirth's car? I realized the brown Nissan was the only thing connecting us, and I realized I was having a hard time letting go. I still cherished Hirth, the man I loved from the moment we met. But if our daughter weren't enough to keep us connected, a car wouldn't do it.

I decided on the spot that night, with Missy's help, to drive down to Hirth's parents' house and repossess the car. I knew Hirth's habits, and he never went out on a weekday night. If he were playing music somewhere, it would be on the weekend. Missy and I left Vignette with Therese, the nanny, and headed for East LA in my Honda. The fact it could be dangerous driving to that part of town at night being blonde women never occurred to either of us. We were on a mission.

When we arrived, it was just after 9:30 p.m. The small house at 324 North Townsend appeared locked up for the night, but a light was still visible in the living room. There were two houses on their property, and the family lived in the one in back. I hopped the fence to the front house and sprinted across the lawn. When I opened the garden gate, the bells rang out to signal an intruder, and I could hear the family assembled around the television reacting. I walked up the front steps and knocked on the door with confidence. The sound of slippers shuffling across the linoleum could be heard, and I could feel eyes peering at me through slits in the sheer curtains before Hirth, at last, opened the door.

"Hi, Hirth. I'm here to get the Nissan. Over a year has passed—going on two years—and you've made no effort to see our daughter, which means you haven't kept up your part of the bargain in keeping the car to pick up Vignette. So, I'm taking back the car for the nanny to help me drive Vignette to and from school."

I could hear Hirth's mother whispering to her husband in an angry tone. Our divorce upset her, and she blamed me for everything that happened. She didn't know the truth because Hirth was never honest with her. He never told her I paid for the child support payments for his older daughter to keep him out of jail. He lied about everything, even telling them he was making child support payments to me for Vignette.

"Please, Hirth, I don't want to make a scene; just give me the keys, and I'll be on my way."

Blood was rushing to my head, and the adrenaline was surging through my veins. There wasn't much Hirth could say or do. He disappeared into the back bedroom, came out, and handed me the keys. I didn't want a fight, but deep down, I hoped Hirth would ask to talk it over. I thought he might step outside the safety of his parents' house and ask for another chance, telling me he would try harder and accept the responsibility. I wanted it for our daughter. And if I were, to be honest, at that moment, I still wanted it for myself. But it was Hirth's lack of reciprocal emotion that made me want nothing more than to get those goddamn keys and get the hell out of East LA before I changed my mind.

Hirth stepped away from the door and retreated into the house in silence. He wasn't willing to risk exposing all the lies he told his parents. It was Papa who came out into the crisp Los

Angeles night air to unlock the old wooden gate on rollers so that I could back the car out of the driveway into the alley. He turned his face away from me, and we never locked eyes. It broke my heart, knowing this might be the last time I would see Vignette's beloved grandfather. I wanted to hug him and say, "Papa, it's not my fault! I need to take care of your granddaughter. If only Hirth could be to his daughter one-tenth the father you have been to your son, everything would be fine." But there were no words. I couldn't speak, I couldn't penetrate the wall Papa had put up to protect his emotions. His love for Hirth transcended any feelings he could share with me, as my passion for Vignette exceeded any sense of remorse that I might have about leaving Hirth.

Once Missy caught sight of me backing the brown Nissan into the dark alleyway, she took off in my Honda. My hands trembled as they grasped the unfamiliar steering wheel of a car I had never driven. It was Hirth's car. The inside smelled like Hirth, bringing up memories I had long forgotten or swept aside. I kept the windows rolled up as though that would contain the memories and prevent them from escaping.

To say we had happy times together was too trite—the music, the songs, and poetry, our long walks going nowhere. I loved every curl on his head, every whisker of his beard. As I sped along the 101 freeway, my mind was racing at full horsepower. Snapshots of my life began flashing before me like signposts. I remembered how tall my shadow seemed as I ran across the street in the afternoon sun when I was four, and my parents fought. I remembered the first time we played Tiger and the years of sadness that followed. I remembered telling Stuart my name was Pam, not Angie, and wanting to die rather than celebrate my sixteenth birthday as it felt anything but sweet. I could hear Bernie telling me I had to find my worth. I could picture Eugene's angry face lashing out at me, losing my baby, and being seduced by heroin to escape the pain.

Somewhere in the distance, a burning fire was lighting up the horizon. The rising smoke created a bouquet of black roses in the sky against the full moon's light—a swollen face of sorrow.

As a girl, being abused put me on a path of self-destruction, fear, and self-loathing to numb the pain. I identified with the innocent sheep slaughtered by the wolves, believing it was my destiny to be found, desecrated, and abandoned. Or not found at all but to evaporate like morning fog. My quest to find love almost killed me.

A driver flashed his headlights at me and honked to signal I hadn't turned on the lights. I panicked because having never driven Hirth's car, I didn't know how to turn them on. While fumbling around on the dashboard trying to figure it out, I noticed the Nissan was almost out of gas. "Typical," I mumbled to myself as I pulled off the freeway and began driving down Sunset to find the nearest station. Pushing the emotional memories aside, I dealt with the practical matter of taking over for Papa in "gassing up" Hirth's car.

Holding the nozzle, I looked up, and there in front of me was the Marlboro man, standing vigilant, watching over the city. When I ran away, I thought I lost my mother's protection, when, in reality, I ran away to protect myself. When my father passed away, it felt as though I lost my guardian angel, making me look up to the urban monument as though he were real. But now, standing alone, I realized no one had ever watched over me. I had always been on my own. The Marlboro man's only practical usefulness was to glamorize a nasty habit—a dying symbol of a by-gone era, counting down the days until his last puff.

Breathing in deeply, I turned the key in the ignition when it occurred to me, the brown Nissan wasn't Hirth's car. It was my car because I bought it with my money, and it was in my name.

I found the headlights, and when I switched them on, my soul began swelling up inside. Turning on the radio, I spun the dial and stopped on Guns 'N Roses' "Sweet Child of Mine." Cranking up the volume, I peeled out of the gas station and roared down Sunset. The crack in my heart burst open, and I could feel the light of love shining into the hollow cavern. I rolled down the windows, allowing the memories to be free to stay or float away into the smoke-filled night. The sound of my blind pony, Princess, galloping up Gobbler's Knob rang out over the city before me.

When I was twelve, I wrote in my journal that I would one day pen a story about me, nobody special. But now, no longer blinded by fear, my life's journey helped me see who I had become, and how far I had yet to travel. I was a woman—a woman named Sam. And I was me, somebody special.

ABOUT THE AUTHOR

Samantha Hart found her calling in the entertainment industry in Los Angeles, holding numerous high profile positions in music, film, and advertising, as a senior creative executive. She has won awards for creative direction, copywriting, and design.

She continues to live in Los Angeles with her husband, James, and their sons Davis and Denham. Sam's daughter, Vignette, lives near Boston with her husband and two daughters.

CPSIA information can be obtained
at www.ICGtesting.com
Printed in the USA
BVHW071922231120
594038BV00010B/80/J